Learning Nagios

Third Edition

Learn and monitor your entire IT infrastructure to ensure your systems, applications, services, and business function effectively

Wojciech Kocjan

Piotr Beltowski

BIRMINGHAM - MUMBAI

Learning Nagios

Third Edition

First published: October 2008

Second edition: March 2014

Third edition: August 2016

Production reference: 1260816

Published by Packt Publishing Ltd.
Livery Place
35 Livery Street
Birmingham
B3 2PB, UK.
ISBN 978-1-78588-595-2

www.packtpub.com

Credits

Authors

Wojciech Kocjan

Piotr Beltowski

Reviewer

Jørgen van der Meulen

Commissioning Editor

Pratik Shah

Acquisition Editor

Prachi Bisht

Content Development Editor

Mehvash Fatima

Technical Editor

Pratik Tated

Copy Editors

Tom Jacob

Safis Editing

Project Coordinator

Shweta H. Birwatkar

Proofreader

Safis Editing

Indexer

Hemangini Bari

Graphics

Kirk D'Penha

Production Coordinator

Shantanu N. Zagade

About the Authors

Wojciech Kocjan is a system administrator and programmer with 10 years of experience. His work experience includes several years of using Nagios for enterprise IT infrastructure monitoring. He also has experience with wide variety of devices and servers, routers, Linux, Solaris, AIX servers and i5/OS mainframes. His programming experience includes multiple languages (such as Java, Ruby, Python, and Perl) and focuses on web applications as well as client-server solutions.

Piotr Beltowski is an IT and software engineer, and co-author of several US patents and publications. A Master of Science in telecommunications, his technical experience includes various aspects of telecommunication, such as designing IP networks or implementing support for network protocols. Piotr's experience as Level 3 customer support lead makes him focused on finding simple solutions to complex technical issues.

His professional career includes working in international corporations such as IBM and Ericsson.

About the Reviewer

Jørgen van der Meulen is a Nagios Certified Administrator with over eleven years of experience deploying Nagios monitoring for customers. He works for Conclusion Xforce as Solutions Consultant and his main focus is helping customers implement Nagios XI, Nagios Log Server, or Nagios Network Analyzer.

Besides monitoring his main areas of expertise are Linux, Unix, virtualization and networking. Jørgen started his professional career as HP-UX System Administrator in 1995 after becoming enthusiastic about the power of Unix commands. He started to write scripts to automate his recurring tasks on the HP-UX platform and also developed skills in networking, databases, and the Microsoft Windows platform as well. Over the years he had different roles including Systems Administrator, Network Administrator, Database Administrator, Middleware Specialist, Manager Systems Support, Product Manager and Project Manager.

The knowledge he gained from being a sysadmin who likes to automate his work has proven to be very useful for a consultant in the field of monitoring operating systems, networks, applications, and even business processes. Monitoring the proper parts of a business critical ICT environment can be quite a challenge, especially with regards to keeping monitoring configurations manageable and easy to maintain.

His advice to people who would like to become a monitoring professional would be: first, become a sysadmin or application admin. Struggle with the implementing, deploying, tuning, and administration aspects and learn to enjoy it. Then use your sysadmin/application admin knowledge for setting up monitoring, dealing with best practices with regards to tuning and availability. In the end, the answer to the question "What should I monitor?" will be an easy one.

In his spare time, Jørgen contributes to various open source projects, enjoys art and culture and spending time with his family (wife and two kids).

You can find him on LinkedIn at `https://www.linkedin.com/in/jivdmeulen`.

www.PacktPub.com

eBooks, discount offers, and more

Did you know that Packt offers eBook versions of every book published, with PDF and ePub files available? You can upgrade to the eBook version at www.PacktPub.com and as a print book customer, you are entitled to a discount on the eBook copy. Get in touch with us at customercare@packtpub.com for more details.

At www.PacktPub.com, you can also read a collection of free technical articles, sign up for a range of free newsletters and receive exclusive discounts and offers on Packt books and eBooks.

https://www2.packtpub.com/books/subscription/packtlib

Do you need instant solutions to your IT questions? PacktLib is Packt's online digital book library. Here, you can search, access, and read Packt's entire library of books.

Why subscribe?

- Fully searchable across every book published by Packt
- Copy and paste, print, and bookmark content
- On demand and accessible via a web browser

Table of Contents

Preface

This book is a practical guide to setting up Nagios, an open source network-monitoring tool. It is a system that checks whether hosts and services are working properly and notifies users when problems occur. The book covers the installation and configuring of Nagios 4 on various operating systems, with a focus on the Ubuntu Linux operating system. The book takes you through all the steps of compiling Nagios from source and installing and configuring advanced features such as redundant monitoring. It also mentions how to monitor various services, such as e-mail, WWW, databases, and file sharing. The book describes what SNMP is and how it can be used to monitor various devices. It also provides details of monitoring Windows computers. The book contains troubleshooting sections that aid you in case any problems arise while setting up Nagios functionalities. No previous experience with network monitoring is required, although it is assumed that you have a basic understanding of Unix systems. It also mentions examples to extend Nagios in JavaScript. The book also covers Nagios XI, a commercial offering built on top of the open source Nagios monitoring engine. It covers the basics of using Nagios XI as well as outlining the main differences between the open source version and the commercial product. When you finish this book, you'll be able to set up Nagios to monitor your network and will have a good understanding of what can be monitored.

What this book covers

Chapter 1, *Introducing Nagios*, talks about Nagios and system monitoring in general. It shows the benefits of using system-monitoring software and the advantages of Nagios in particular. It also introduces the basic concepts of Nagios.

Chapter 2, *Installing Nagios 4*, covers the installation of Nagios, from source code and using system packages such as rpm and deb. Installation from source code uses a fully automated script to set up Nagios that works on most Linux distributions; the process is explained in detail.

Chapter 3, *Configuring Nagios*, describes the process of configuring Nagios. Details on how to configure users, hosts, and services as well as information on how Nagios sends notifications to users are given in this chapter.

Chapter 4, *Using the Built-in Web Interface*, talks about how to use the Nagios web interface. It describes the basic views for hosts and services and provides detailed information about each item. It also introduces some features such as adding comments, scheduled downtimes, viewing detailed information, and generating reports.

Chapter 5, *Using Additional Interfaces*, mentions additional web interfaces that can be used to check the status of Nagios. The chapter mentions dashboards showing status, complete replacements for Nagios UI, as well as mobile applications that allow checking host and service status.

Chapter 6, *Using the Nagios Plugins*, goes through the standard set of Nagios plugins that allow you to perform checks of various services. It shows how you can check for standard services such as e-mail, Web, file, and database servers. It also describes how to monitor resources such as CPU usage, storage, and memory usage.

Chapter 7, *Advanced Configuration*, focuses on the efficient management of large configurations and the use of templates. It shows how dependencies between hosts and services can be defined and discusses custom variables and adaptive monitoring. It also introduces the concept of flapping and how it detects services that start and stop frequently.

Chapter 8, *Notifications and Events*, describes the notification system in more detail. It focuses on effective ways of communicating problems to users and how to set up problem escalations. It also describes how events work in Nagios and how they can be used to perform the automatic recovery of services.

Chapter 9, *Passive Checks and NRDP*, focuses on cases where external processes send results to Nagios. It introduces the concept of the passive check, which is not scheduled and run by Nagios, and gives practical examples of when and how it can be used. It also shows how to use the Nagios Remote Data Processor (NRDP) protocol to send notifications.

Chapter 10, *Monitoring Remote Hosts*, covers how Nagios checks can be run on remote machines. It walks through the details of deploying checks remotely over SSH using public key authentication. It also shows how Nagios Remote Plugin Executor (NRPE) can be used for deploying plugins remotely.

Chapter 11, *Monitoring Using SNMP*, describes how the Simple Network Management Protocol (SNMP) can be used from Nagios. It provides an overview of SNMP and its versions. It explains reading SNMP values from SNMP-aware devices and covers how that can then be used to perform checks from Nagios.

`Chapter 12`, *Advanced Monitoring*, focuses on how Nagios can be set up on multiple hosts and how that information could be gathered on a central server. It also covers how to monitor computers that run Windows.

`Chapter 13`, *Programming Nagios*, shows how to extend Nagios. It explains how to write custom check commands, how to create custom ways of notifying users, and how passive checks and NRDP can be used to integrate your solutions with Nagios. The chapter uses on JavaScript the programming language, but because of how Nagios works, the example can be implemented in any programming language.

What you need for this book

This book requires a Linux server to run Nagios on. As all of the examples are created using Ubuntu Linux, it is recommended that you use this distribution. However, the installation process should work on most Linux distributions. The book goes through the process of setting up Nagios and its web interface in `Chapter 2`, Installing Nagios 4, so installing it is not a prerequisite.

Who this book is for

This book is targeted at system administrators, both those who have no prior knowledge of Nagios and those experienced with it. It not only covers the basics of Nagios, but also the advanced features.

Conventions

In this book, you will find a number of text styles that distinguish between different kinds of information. Here are some examples of these styles and an explanation of their meaning.

Code words in text, database table names, folder names, filenames, file extensions, pathnames, dummy URLs, user input, and Twitter handles are shown as follows:Code words in text are shown as follows: "The `service-http` service will define a check using `check_http` and optionally additional options for the check itself."

A block of code is set as follows:

```
define service
{
use generic-service
host_name mainrouter
service_description OpenVPN
check_command check_openvpn_remote
check_interval 15
max_check_attempts 3
notification_interval 30
notification_period 24x7
}
```

Any command-line input or output is written as follows:

```
CHANGE_SVC_CHECK_COMMAND;linux1;PING;check_ping!500.0,50%
```

New terms and **important words** are shown in bold. Words that you see on the screen, for example, in menus or dialog boxes, appear in the text like this: "The shortcuts in this book are based on the `Mac OS X 10.5+` scheme."

Warnings or important notes appear in a box like this.

Tips and tricks appear like this.

Reader feedback

Feedback from our readers is always welcome. Let us know what you think about this book—what you liked or disliked. Reader feedback is important for us as it helps us develop titles that you will really get the most out of. To send us general feedback, simply e-mail feedback@packtpub.com, and mention the book's title in the subject of your message. If there is a topic that you have expertise in and you are interested in either writing or contributing to a book, see our author guide at www.packtpub.com/authors.

Customer support

Now that you are the proud owner of a Packt book, we have a number of things to help you to get the most from your purchase.

Downloading the example code

You can download the example code files for this book from your account at `http://www.packtpub.com`. If you purchased this book elsewhere, you can visit `http://www.packtpub.com/support` and register to have the files e-mailed directly to you.

You can download the code files by following these steps:

1. Log in or register to our website using your e-mail address and password.
2. Hover the mouse pointer on the **SUPPORT** tab at the top.
3. Click on **Code Downloads & Errata**.
4. Enter the name of the book in the **Search** box.
5. Select the book for which you're looking to download the code files.
6. Choose from the drop-down menu where you purchased this book from.
7. Click on **Code Download**.

Once the file is downloaded, please make sure that you unzip or extract the folder using the latest version of:

- WinRAR / 7-Zip for Windows
- Zipeg / iZip / UnRarX for Mac
- 7-Zip / PeaZip for Linux

The code bundle for the book is also hosted on GitHub at `https://github.com/PacktPublishing/Learning-Nagios-Third-Edition`. We also have other code bundles from our rich catalog of books and videos available at `https://github.com/PacktPublishing/`. Check them out!

Downloading the color images of this book

We also provide you with a PDF file that has color images of the screenshots/diagrams used in this book. The color images will help you better understand the changes in the output. You can download this file from `https://www.packtpub.com/sites/default/files/downloads/LearningNagiosThirdEdition_ColorImages.pdf`.

Errata

Although we have taken every care to ensure the accuracy of our content, mistakes do happen. If you find a mistake in one of our books-maybe a mistake in the text or the code-we would be grateful if you could report this to us. By doing so, you can save other readers from frustration and help us improve subsequent versions of this book. If you find any errata, please report them by visiting `http://www.packtpub.com/submit-errata`, selecting your book, clicking on the **Errata Submission Form** link, and entering the details of your errata. Once your errata are verified, your submission will be accepted and the errata will be uploaded to our website or added to any list of existing errata under the Errata section of that title.

To view the previously submitted errata, go to `https://www.packtpub.com/books/content/support` and enter the name of the book in the search field. The required information will appear under the **Errata** section.

Piracy

Piracy of copyrighted material on the Internet is an ongoing problem across all media. At Packt, we take the protection of our copyright and licenses very seriously. If you come across any illegal copies of our works in any form on the Internet, please provide us with the location address or website name immediately so that we can pursue a remedy.

Please contact us at `copyright@packtpub.com` with a link to the suspected pirated material.

We appreciate your help in protecting our authors and our ability to bring you valuable content.

Questions

If you have a problem with any aspect of this book, you can contact us at `questions@packtpub.com`, and we will do our best to address the problem.

1
Introducing Nagios

Imagine you're an administrator of a large IT infrastructure. You have just started receiving e-mails that a web application has suddenly stopped working. When you try to access the same page, it just does not load. What are the possibilities? Is it the router? Maybe the firewall? Perhaps the machine hosting the page is down? The server process has crashed? Before you even start thinking rationally about what to do, your boss calls about the critical situation and demands explanations. In all this panic, you'll probably start plugging everything in and out of the network, rebooting the machine… and it still doesn't help.

After hours of nervous digging into the issue, you've finally found the root cause: although the web server was working properly, it continuously timed out during communication with the database server. This is because the machine with the database did not get an IP address assigned. Your organization requires all IP addresses to be configured using the DHCP protocol and the local DHCP server ran out of memory and killed several processes, including the dhcpd process responsible for assigning IP addresses. Imagine how much time it would take to determine all this manually! To make things worse, the database server could be located in another branch of the company or in a different time zone, and it could be the middle of the night over there.

But what if you had Nagios up and running across your entire company? You would just go to the web interface and see that there are no problems with the web server and the machine on which it is running. There would also be a list of issues—the machine serving IP addresses to the entire company does not do its job and the database is down. If the setup also monitored the DHCP server, you'd get a warning e-mail that little swap memory is available or too many processes are running. Maybe it would even have an event handler for such cases to just kill or restart non-critical processes. Also, Nagios would try to restart the dhcpd process over the network in case it is down.

In the worst case, Nagios would reduce hours of investigation to ten minutes. Ideally, you would just get an e-mail that there was such a problem and another e-mail that it's already fixed. You would just disable a few services and increase the swap size for the DHCP machine and solve the problem permanently. Hopefully, it would be solved fast enough so that nobody would notice that there was a problem in the first place!

Understanding the basics of Nagios

Nagios is an open source tool for **system monitoring**. It means that it watches servers and other devices on your network and makes sure that they are working properly. Nagios constantly checks if other machines are working properly. It also verifies that various services on those machines are working properly. In addition, Nagios can accept information from other processes or machines regarding their status; for example, a web server can send information to Nagios if it is overloaded.

The main purpose of system monitoring is to detect if any system is not working properly as soon as possible and notify the appropriate staff, and if possible, try to resolve the error—such as by restarting system services if needed.

System monitoring in Nagios is split into two categories of objects, **hosts** and **services**:

- Hosts represent a physical or virtual device on your network (servers, routers, workstations, printers, and so on)
- Services are particular functionalities, for example, a **SecureShell** (**SSH**) server (*sshd* process on the machine) can be defined as a service to be monitored

Each service is associated with a host on which it is running. In addition, machines can be grouped into host groups, as shown here:

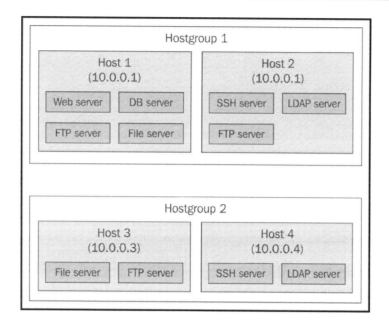

A major benefit of Nagios' performance checks is that it only uses four distinct states—**Ok**, **Warning**, **Critical**, and **Unknown**. Another advantage is that it is based on the framework of plugins, allowing you to develop your own plugin; this means if you want to check something that's not yet possible to do, you just need to write a simple piece of code and that's it! Writing your own plugins is described in more details in Chapter 13, *Programming Nagios*.

The approach to offer only three states (excluding Unknown as it informs about not being able to determine the current state) allows administrators to ignore monitoring values themselves and just decide on what the warning/critical limits are. This is a proven concept, and is far more efficient than monitoring graphs and analyzing trends. This is similar to traffic lights, where green indicates Ok and means a service is working correctly, a Warning state is same as the yellow light, and a Critical state is same as the red traffic light.

For example, system administrators tend to ignore things such as gradually declining storage space. People often simply ignore early warnings until a critical process runs out of disk space. Having a strict limit to watch is much better, because you always catch a problem regardless of whether it turns from warning to critical in fifteen minutes or in a week. This approach is exactly what Nagios does. Each check performed by Nagios is turned from numerical values (such as the amount of disk space or CPU usage) to one of the three possible states.

Another benefit is a clear report stating that X services are up and running, Y are in the warning state, and Z are currently critical, which is much more readable than a matrix of values. It saves you the time of analyzing what's working and what's failing. It can also help prioritize what needs to be handled first and which problems can be handled later.

Introducing plugins

Nagios performs all of its checks using plugins. These are external components for which Nagios passes information on what should be checked and what the warning and critical limits are. Plugins are responsible for performing the checks and analyzing the results. The output from such a check is the status (Ok, Warning, Critical, or Unknown) and additional text describing information on the service in detail. This text is mainly intended for system administrators to be able to read the detailed status of a service.

Nagios comes with a set of standard plugins that allow performance checks for almost all the services your company might use or offer. See Chapter 6, *Using the Nagios Plugins*, for detailed information on plugins that are developed along with Nagios. Moreover, if you need to perform a specific check (for example, connect to a web service and invoke methods), it is very easy to write your own plugins. And that's not all—they can be written in any language and it takes less than 15 minutes to write a complete check command! Chapter 13, *Programming Nagios*, talks about this ability in more detail.

Benefits of monitoring

There are many reasons for you to ensure that all your resources are working as expected. If you're still not convinced after reading the introduction to this chapter, here are a few important points why it is important to monitor your infrastructure.

The main reason is quality improvement. If your IT staff can notice failures quicker by using a monitoring tool, they will also be able to respond to them much faster. Sometimes it takes hours or days to get the first report of a failure, even if many users bump into errors. Nagios ensures that if something is not working, you'll know about it. In some cases, event handling can even be done so that Nagios can switch to the backup solution until the primary process is fixed. A typical case would be to start a dial-up connection and use it as a primary connection in cases when the company VPN is down.

Another reason is much better problem determination. Very often what the users report as a failure is far from the root cause of the problem, such as when an e-mail system is down due to the LDAP service not working correctly. If you define dependencies between hosts correctly, then Nagios will point out that the IMAP or POP3 e-mail server is assumed to be not working because the LDAP service that it depends upon has a problem. Nagios will start checking the e-mail server as soon as the problem with LDAP has been resolved.

Nagios is also very flexible when it comes to notifying people of what isn't functioning correctly. In most cases, your company has a large IT team or multiple teams. Usually, you want some people to handle servers and others to handle network switches/routers/modems. There might also be a team responsible for network printers, or a division is made based on geographical location. You can instruct Nagios about who is responsible for particular machines or groups of machines, so that when something is wrong, the right people will get to know about it. You can also use Nagios' web interface to manage who is working on which issue.

Monitoring resources is not only useful for identifying problems, but it also saves you from having them, as Nagios handles warnings and critical situations differently. This means that it's possible to be aware of situations that may become problems really soon. For example, if your disk storage on an e-mail server is running out, it's better to be aware of this situation before it becomes a critical issue.

Monitoring can also be set up on multiple machines across various locations. These machines will then communicate all their results to a central Nagios server so that information on all hosts and services in your system can be accessed from a single machine. This gives you a more accurate picture of your IT infrastructure as well as allows testing more complex systems such as firewalls. For example, it is vital that a testing environment is accessible from a production environment, but not the other way around.

It is also possible to set up a Nagios server outside the company's intranet (for example, over a dedicated DSL) to make sure that traffic from the Internet is properly blocked. It can be used to check if only certain services are available, for example, to verify that only SSH and **HypertextTransferProtocol** (**HTTP**) are accessible from external IP addresses, and that services such as databases are inaccessible to users.

Main features

Nagios' main strength is flexibility—it can be configured to monitor your IT infrastructure in the way you want it. It also has a mechanism to react automatically to problems and has a powerful notification system. All of this is based on a clear object definition system, which in turn is based on a few types of object, as follows:

- **Commands**: These are definitions of how Nagios should perform particular types of check. They are an abstraction layer on top of actual plugins that allow you to group similar types of operation.
- **Time periods**: Date and time spans during which an operation should or should not be performed. For example, Monday-Friday, 09:00 A.M. – 5:00 P.M.
- **Hosts and host groups**: These are devices along with the possibility of group hosts. A single host might be a member of more than one group.
- **Services**: Various functionalities or resources to monitor on a specific host, for example, CPU usage, storage space, or web server.
- **Contacts and contact groups**: People that should be notified, with information about how and when they should be contacted; contacts can be grouped, and a single contact might be a member of more than one group.
- **Notifications**: These define who should be notified of what; for example, all errors related to the linux-servers host group should go to the linux-admins contact group during working hours and to the critsit-team (critical situations handling team) contact group outside of working hours. Notifications are not strictly an object, but a combination of all the preceding objects and are an essential part of Nagios.
- **Escalations**: Extension to notifications; escalations define these after an object is in the same state for a specific period of time, other people should get notified of certain events. For example, a critical server being down for more than four hours should alert IT management so that they track the issue.

A beneficial feature of using Nagios is that it is a mature dependency system. For any administrator, it is obvious that if your router is down then all machines accessed via it will fail. Some systems don't take that into account, and in such cases, you get a list of several failing machines and services. Nagios allows you to define dependencies between hosts to reflect actual network topology. For example, if a router that connects you to the rest of your network is down, Nagios will not perform checks for the subsequent parts and machines that are dependent on the router. This is illustrated in the following image:

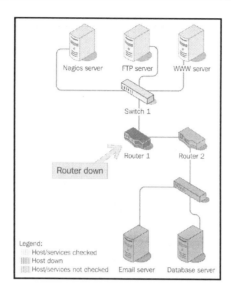

You can also define that a particular service depends on another service, either on the same host or a different host. If one of the dependent services is down, a check for a service is not even performed.

For example, in order for your company's intranet application to function properly, both the underlying web and database servers must be running properly. So, if a database service is not working properly, Nagios will not perform checks and/or not send notifications that your application is not working, because the root cause of the problem is that the database is not working properly. The database server might be on the same or on a different host. If the database is not working properly or the dependent machine is down or not accessible, all services dependent on the database service will not be checked as well.

Nagios offers a consistent system of macro definitions. These are variables that can be put into all object definitions and depend on the context. They can be put inside commands, and depending on the host, service, and many other parameters, macro definitions are substituted accordingly. For example, a command definition might use an IP address of the host it is currently checking in all remote tests. It also makes it possible to put information such as the previous and current status of a service in a notification e-mail. Nagios also offers various extensions to macro definitions, which makes it an even more powerful mechanism.

Additionally, there is a built-in mechanism for scheduling planned downtime. This is mainly used when maintenance of the IT infrastructure is to be carried out, and servers and/or services they provide are out of order for a period of time. You can let Nagios know that such an event will occur, and it will not send notifications about problems with hosts and/or services that have a scheduled downtime. In such cases, dependencies are also taken into consideration—if a database has a scheduled downtime, notifications for the services that depend on it will not be sent out. Nagios can also notify people of planned downtime automatically. This allows creating an integrated process of scheduling downtime that will also handle informing users.

Soft and hard states

Nagios works by checking if a particular host or service is working correctly and storing its status. Because the status is only one of four possible values, it is crucial that it precisely reflects the actual situation. In order to avoid detecting random and temporary failures, Nagios uses soft and hard states to describe what the current status is for a host or service.

Imagine that an administrator is restarting a web server, which in turn makes web pages inaccessible for around five seconds. Since such restarts are usually done at night to lower the number of users affected, this is an acceptable period of time. However, a problem might be that Nagios will try to connect to the server and notice that it is actually down. If it only relies on a single result, Nagios could trigger an alert that a web server is down. It would actually be up and running again in a few seconds, but Nagios would require another couple of minutes to find that out.

To handle situations where a service is down for a very short time, or the test has temporarily failed, soft states were introduced. When a previous status of a check is unknown or is different from the previous one, Nagios will retest the host or service a couple of times to make sure the change is permanent. Nagios assumes that the new result is a soft state. After additional tests have verified that the new state is permanent, it is considered a hard one.

Each host and service check defines the number of retries to perform before assuming a change to be permanent. This allows more flexibility over how many failures should be treated as an actual problem instead of a temporary one. Setting the number of checks to 1 will cause all changes to be treated as hard instantly. The following figure is an illustration of soft and hard state changes, assuming that number of checks to be performed is set to 3:

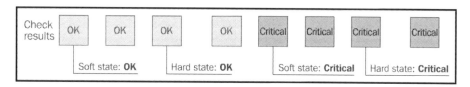

This feature is very useful for checks that should skip short outages of a service or use a protocol that might fail in case of extensive traffic, such as ICMP or UDP. Monitoring devices over SNMP is also an example of a check that can fail in cases where a single check fails; nevertheless, the check will eventually succeed during the second or third check.

Summary

In this chapter, you learned the basics of Nagios as a tool for performing system monitoring. It can be used to ensure that services are working correctly, problems are detected earlier, and appropriate people are aware when something's wrong.

You learned the basic types of objects in Nagios—commands, hosts, services, time periods, contacts, as well as object grouping. You also found out about notifications and escalations, which can be used to notify administrators about problems.

The chapter also introduced the concept of dependencies that helps in understanding the root cause of complex problems.

The next chapter will guide you through the process of installing Nagios and the standard Nagios plugins.

2
Installing Nagios 4

The previous chapter described what Nagios is, the basic concepts of monitoring, and types of objects in Nagios. This chapter describes how to install Nagios and the standard Nagios plugins.

We will cover multiple ways in which Nagios can be installed and how it can be run—using binary packages from various Linux distributions and building Nagios from source code. We will also discuss how to run Nagios in your machine, using Docker containers as well as run it inside a virtual machine.

We have provided an easy-to-run script that works on most popular Linux distributions including Debian, Ubuntu, CentOS, and Red Hat Enterprise Linux. For consistency, we recommend that you use this script for Nagios installation as it will also use the same paths for configuration files, binaries, and statuses that further chapters will refer to.

Also, this script will download and install the latest version of Nagios. Many Linux distributions do not ship latest versions of Nagios; instead, they ship the same versions of Nagios as when the distribution was originally created.

In this chapter, we will cover the following items:

- Installing Nagios
- Compiling and installing Nagios from source code
- Running Nagios using virtualization

Installing Nagios

Nagios itself as well as the standard plugins are written in C and need to be compiled into a native Linux binary. Both Nagios and Nagios plugins use the standard `configure`, `make`, `make install` approach that is common for most Unix applications written in C.

This section will guide you through either using an automated script for performing the installation, which we recommend, or performing the installation manually.

Upgrading from previous versions

If you already have a previous version of Nagios installed, it is always a good idea to upgrade to the latest Nagios and Nagios plugins. It is especially true if upgrading from Nagios 3 or 2 as Nagios 4 includes performance improvements when monitoring large number of hosts and/or services.

When upgrading, it is recommended that you use the manual steps described later in this chapter, and use same usernames, groups, and paths as when the original installation took place. If you have performed the Nagios installation based on steps from the previous revisions of this book, the paths, system user, and group are the same and do not need any changes.

Let's start with the installation:

1. It is required to stop all Nagios processes before performing an upgrade. This can usually be done by invoking the following command:

    ```
    service nagios stop
    ```

    The preceding command works on all modern Linux distributions and supports services installed such as SysVinit (in `/etc/init.d` or `/etc/rc.d/init.d`) and Upstart services (added in `/etc/init` and using a different format of the service file definition).

    If the preceding command did not work properly, running the `init.d` script directly should work:

    ```
    service nagios stop
    ```

2. It is recommended that you stop Nagios while compiling and installing a new version. You should then proceed with the installation steps described in the next sections. Almost all of Nagios 4 configuration parameters are backward compatible, so your current configuration will work fine after upgrading.

3. Once the new version of Nagios is installed, it is recommended that you check the Nagios configuration with the new version to ensure that there are no incompatibilities:

```
/opt/nagios/bin/nagios -v /etc/nagios/nagios.cfg
```

4. We can now simply run the following command:

```
service nagios start
```

If the preceding command did not work properly, run the following init.d script, and the upgrade process should be complete:

```
/etc/init.d/nagios start
```

Another option is to remove the previous installation completely and install a fresh copy of Nagios, only preserving the configuration files. The downside of this is that you will lose all the historical data of Nagios results.

Performing installation with automated script

To perform a fresh, automated installation of Nagios and Nagios standard plugins, simply run the following as the root user:

```
curl -sSL https://raw.github.com/learning-nagios/nagios-install/master/install.sh | sh
```

This will download the automated install script from GitHub and run it.

Please note that this requires the curl command to be available. The installation can also be done using the wget command if curl is not available:

```
wget -qO-
https://raw.github.com/learning-nagios/nagiosinstall/master/install.sh | sh
```

The script installs prerequisite packages, including Apache web server. Next, the script will create appropriate system accounts and compile Nagios and Nagios plugins from the source code. It will also install Nagios as a system service using the built-in init.d script. Finally, the script will also add a configuration for Apache to allow accessing the Nagios web interface, as http://(ip-address)/nagios

 Please note that the username when using the automated script is set to nagiosadmin and the password is nagiosadmin. The Nagios web interface is described in more detail in Chapter 4, *Using the Built-in Web interface.*

All that is needed is to restart the web server, which varies depending on the Linux distribution, but it should be one of the following commands:

```
apachectl restart
service apache2 restart
service httpd restart
```

The script works on all major Linux distributions that use the yum/rpm or apt-get/dpkg package managers. For Linux distributions that do not support these package managers, as well as in this case and in the rare case of errors, the script will exit and an error will be shown rather than the actual output. In this case, it is recommended that you manually follow the steps from the further sections of this chapter and perform the troubleshooting.

After a successful finish, you should see the following message:

Congratulations! Nagios and standard plugins are now installed.

If this is the case, then you are done with the installation and may continue to the next chapter or read more about using Nagios in virtualized environments and containers or learn more about the exact steps the automated script is performing.

When the automated installation is used, the paths to key Nagios directories and files are as follows:

Path	Description
/etc/nagios	Configuration directory
/etc/nagios/nagios.cfg	Main Nagios configuration file
/var/nagios	Nagios local state directory
/var/nagios/archives	Historical information regarding Nagios; this directory can grow over time and may be put on a separate partition
/var/nagios/status.dat	Nagios current state file
/var/nagios/rw/nagios.cmd	Pipe for writing commands to Nagios
/opt/nagios/share	Web UI files that should be served via web server, such as http://(ip-address)/nagios
/opt/nagios/sbin	CGI scripts that should be served via web browser, such as http://(ip-address)/nagios/cgi-bin
/opt/nagios/plugins	Path to Nagios plugins used for performing checks

These paths are used in the next chapters in this book and their meanings will be referred to later in this book, but it is worth noting all the key paths.

Please note that the script is not fully setting contexts for **Security-Enhanced Linux** (**SELinux**). If you are using SELinux, you may need to set appropriate contexts for all Nagios related files and directories to enable the web interface to work properly or disable the SELinux forcing of security contexts.

On CentOS/RedHat Linux distribution, disabling SELinux enforcement can be done by editing /etc/sysconfig/selinux and set SELINUX to permissive, such as:
SELINUX=permissive

After that, a reboot of the machine is required to change the SELinux policy enforcing mode.

Installing Nagios using package managers

Nagios can also be installed using prebuilt packages. Nagios packages are available for most Linux distributions. In many cases, the exact paths for things such as configuration files, local state directory, and web interface-related files may differ. If you choose to install Nagios using packages, keep in mind that some examples in the remaining chapters can require slight modifications.

In this section, we will focus on installing Nagios and the plugins on top of popular Linux distributions—using apt-get for Debian and Ubuntu as well as yum for RHEL, CentOS, and Oracle Linux.

Installation with apt-get/dpkg

Both the latest Ubuntu **Long-Term Support** (**LTS**) (which currently is 14.04) and Debian 8 provide only Nagios version 3. To install it, simply run the following command:

```
apt-get -y install nagios3 nagios-plugins
```

The installation will prompt for the password for the web interface. Similar to the automated installation script, the username will be nagiosadmin. To access the website, you should navigate to http://(ip-address)/nagios3/

When installing Nagios 3 from the deb packages, the paths to key Nagios directories and files are as follows:

Path	Description
`/etc/nagios3`	Configuration directory
`/etc/nagios3/nagios.cfg`	Main Nagios configuration file
`/var/cache/nagios3`	Nagios local state directory
`/var/lib/nagios3/rw/nagios.cmd`	Pipe for writing commands to Nagios
`/var/cache/nagios3/status.dat`	Nagios current state file
`/usr/share/nagios3/htdocs`	Web UI files that should be served via a web server, such as `http://(ip-address)/nagios`
`/opt/nagios/sbin`	CGI scripts that should be served via a web browser, such as `http://(ip-address)/nagios/cgi-bin`
`/usr/lib/nagios/plugins`	Path to Nagios plugins used for performing checks

These paths differ from the paths used by the automated installation script, which we strongly recommend, as it makes following the book easier and uses the same paths for all Linux distributions. Since the paths to the preceding key items differ, some examples shown thorough this book may use slightly different paths and need adjustments if you use the Nagios installed from binary packages.

Installation with yum/rpm

Nagios is not provided in The Red Hat Enterprise Linux distribution and all distributions that originate from it, such as CentOS, Fedora, and Oracle Linux. It is, however, provided as part of **Extra Packages for Enterprise Linux** (**EPEL**), documented in more detail at the following link: `https://fedoraproject.org/wiki/EPEL`

The only way to install Nagios from RPM packages on those systems is to use the EPEL. Its installation varies depending on the exact version of the distribution and is described in more details in the EPEL documentation.

For example, we can use the following command to install EPEL on CentOS 7:

```
rpm -Uvh
https://dl.fedoraproject.org/pub/epel/epel-release-latest-7.noarch.rpm
```

This will set up EPEL and allow the installation of additional packages via YUM, including the Nagios and Nagios plugins.

The next step is to make sure the packages are up to date and install Nagios along with Nagios plugins:

```
yum update -y ; yum install -y nagios nagios-plugins-all
```

The last step is to set the password for the `nagiosadmin` web user by running the following command:

```
htpasswd -c /etc/nagios/passwd nagiosadmin
```

This will prompt for the password for the user. Using `nagiosadmin` as the username is described in more detail in `Chapter 4`, *Using the Built-in Web interface*.

After that, Nagios should be installed. For CentOS 7, Nagios is version 4 and the key Nagios directories and files are as follows:

Path	Description
`/etc/nagios`	Configuration directory
`/etc/nagios/nagios.cfg`	Main Nagios configuration file
`/var/log/Nagios`	Nagios local state directory
`/var/spool/nagios/cmd/nagios.cmd`	Pipe for writing commands to Nagios
`/var/log/nagios/status.dat`	Nagios current state file
`/usr/share/nagios/html`	Web UI files that should be served via web server, such as `http://(ip-address)/nagios`
`/usr/lib64/nagios/cgi-bin`	CGI scripts that should be served via web browser, such as `http://(ip-address)/nagios/cgi-bin` NOTE: For 32-bit systems, the path will be `/usr/lib/nagios/cgi-bin`
`/usr/lib64/nagios/plugins`	Path to the Nagios plugins used for performing checks NOTE: For 32-bit systems, the path will be `/usr/lib/nagios/plugins`

These paths differ from the paths used by the automated installation script, which we strongly recommend, as it makes following the book easier and uses the same paths for all Linux distributions. Since the paths to the preceding key items differ, some examples shown thorough the book may use slightly different paths and need adjustments if you use Nagios installed from binary packages.

Compiling Nagios from source code manually

This section describes the steps that the automated script performs and looks into the compilation process in more details.

This section is also meant to help troubleshooting errors with the automated script and explains more about how Nagios and Nagios plugins can be compiled and various options that can be used to change how and where they are compiled.

If you already have a setup running and are not interested in the details of how Nagios is installed, you may continue to the *Running Nagios using virtualizations* section, which describes how Nagios can be run inside a container or virtual machine.

Installing prerequisites

Building Nagios from sources requires a C compiler, standard C library development files, and the make/imake command. Additionally, development files for OpenSSL should be installed so that network-based plugins will be able to communicate over an SSL layer. MySQL and PostgreSQL development packages should also be installed so that database checks can be run.

First of all, if we're planning to build the Nagios system, a compiler along with several build tools will be required. These are gcc, make, cpp, and binutils. It also needs standard C library development files. All these packages are often already installed, but make sure that they are present as they are needed before compilation.

Nagios by itself does not have a large number of packages that need to be installed on your system in order for it to offer basic functionality. However, if we want to use all the functionalities that Nagios can offer, it is necessary to install additional software.

If we want to use the Nagios web interface, a web server capable of serving CGI scripts is required. Apache web is the recommended and also the most popular web server on a Linux installation. This section, as well as automated scripts describe setting up Apache as the web server, but Nagios should work with any web server supporting CGI and PHP-such as NGINX.

Several of the standard Nagios plugins are written in Perl and will not work if Perl is not installed. Some plugins also need Perl's Net::Snmp package to communicate with devices over the SNMP protocol.

The GD graphics library is also needed for the Nagios web interface to create status map and trends images. We will also install libraries for JPEG and PNG images so that GD can create images in these formats.

All of the packages mentioned earlier are usually installed with many operating systems and most of them are already available for almost any Unix-based platform.

A majority of popular Linux distributions use package managers. There are two popular package formats and package managers:

- the deb format and dpkg/apt-get command line tools—this is the package system used by Debian and Ubuntu Linux distributions
- the rpm format and rpm/yum command line tools—used by the **RedHat Enterprise Linux** (**RHEL**) and derivatives, such as CentOS, Oracle Linux, and Fedora

Fortunately, the list of dependencies is the same for all deb format based distributions. So, to install all of the prerequisites on any recent Ubuntu (such as 12.04, 14.04, or 16.04 LTS editions) or Debian (7 or 8), all that is needed is to run the following commands:

```
apt-get -y install wget gcc make binutils cpp \
    libpq-dev libmysqlclient-dev \
    libssl1.0.0 libssl-dev pkg-config \
    libgd2-xpm-dev libgd-tools \
    perl libperl-dev libnet-snmp-perl snmp \
    apache2 apache2-utils libapache2-mod-php5 \
    unzip tar gzip
```

This will download all of the tools needed to compile Nagios as well as the Apache 2 web server and the PHP module for serving PHP files, which Nagios requires.
Similarly, the package list is also same for all distributions that use the rpm package format. To install all the prerequisites, we need to run the following commands:

```
yum -y install wget gcc make imake binutils cpp \
    postgresql-devel mysql-libs mysql-devel \
    openssl openssl-devel pkgconfig \
    gd gd-devel gd-progs libpng libpng-devel \
    libjpeg libjpeg-devel perl perl-devel \
    net-snmp net-snmp-devel net-snmp-perl net-snmp-utils \
    httpd php unzip tar gzip
```

This will install prerequisites as well as the Apache 2 web server and PHP module for serving PHP files.

Setting up users, groups, and directories

The first thing that needs to be done is to decide where to install Nagios. For the purpose of this book, we are installing Nagios binaries into the /opt/nagios directory. This is a location for all Nagios binaries, plugins, and additional files.

The Nagios local state data will be stored in the /var/nagios directory. This is where the all statuses and historical data are kept. It can be a part of the Nagios binaries installation directory or a separate directory, as in our case. The Nagios configuration will be put into /etc/nagios. These directories will be created as part of the Nagios installation process.

After we have decided on our directory structure, we need to set up the users and groups for Nagios data. We'll also create a system user and a group named nagios, which will be used by the daemon. We'll also set up the nagioscmd group that can communicate with the daemon. The nagios user will be a member of the nagios and nagioscmd groups. The following commands will create the groups and users:

```
groupadd nagios
groupadd nagioscmd
useradd -g nagios -G nagioscmd -d /opt/nagios nagios
```

The Nagios daemon will use a dedicated user and group. This increases security and allows a more flexible setup. Nagios also communicates with external components over a Unix socket. This is a socket that works similar to a file on your filesystem. All commands are passed to Nagios via the pipe; therefore, if you want your processes to be able to send reports or changes to Nagios, you need to make sure that they have access to the socket. One of typical uses for this is that the Nagios web interface needs to be able to send commands to the monitoring process.

In order to properly set up Nagios to use the web interface, it is necessary to determine the user that the web server is running as and add the user that your web server runs as to the nagioscmd group. This will allow the web interface to send commands to Nagios.

The user that the web server is working as is usually www-data, apache, httpd, or daemon. It can be checked with a simple grep command:

```
root@ubuntu:~# grep -r ^User /etc/apache* /etc/httpd*
/etc/apache2/apache2.conf:User www-data
```

For our preceding example, we now know that the username is www-data. Sometimes on Ubuntu, the setting is slightly different, as shown in the following command:

```
root@ubuntu:~# grep -r ^User /etc/apache* /etc/httpd*
/etc/apache2/apache2.conf:User ${APACHE_RUN_USER}
```

In that case, the value is defined in the /etc/apache2/envvars file:

```
# grep APACHE_RUN_USER /etc/apache2/envvars
/etc/apache2/envvars:export APACHE_RUN_USER=www-data
```

In this case as well, the username is www-data.

Now let's add this user to the nagioscmd group using the following command:

```
usermod -G nagioscmd www-data
```

The next step is to set up the Nagios destination directories and change their owners accordingly. The following commands will create the directories and change their owner user and group to nagios:

```
mkdir -p /opt/nagios /etc/nagios /var/nagios
chown nagios:nagios /opt/nagios /etc/nagios /var/nagios
```

Obtaining Nagios and Nagios plugins

Nagios is an open source application, which means that the source code of all Nagios components is freely available from the Nagios home page: `https://www.nagios.org/projects/nagios-core/`.

Nagios is distributed under the **GNU General Public License (GPL)** Version 2 (refer to `http://www.gnu.org/licenses/old-licenses/gpl-2.0.html` for more details), which means that the Nagios source code can be redistributed and modified almost freely under the condition that all changes are also distributed as source code.

Nagios plugins is a project that provides over fifty Nagios plugins that allow monitoring many types of services and devices. They are developed independently of the Nagios service itself and are an open source project using the GNU GPL Version 3 (refer to `http://www.gnu.org/licenses/gpl-3..html` for more details).

Nagios can be downloaded from the following
URL: `https://www.nagios.org/downloads/nagios-core/`
At the time of writing , the latest version of Nagios was 4.1.1.
Nagios plugins can be downloaded from the following URL: `https://www.nagios.org/downloads/nagios-plugins/`
At the time of writing , the latest version of Nagios plugins was 2.1.1.

We will now create a source directory for compilation. This is where all of our compilation will take place. For the purpose of this book, it will be `/usr/src/nagios`.

We need to extract our Nagios and standard plugins tarball into this directory using the following commands:

```
mkdir /usr/src/nagios
tar -xzf /path/to/nagios-4.1.1.tar.gz
tar -xzf /path/to/nagios-plugins-2.1.1.tar.gz
```

The extraction will create the `nagios-4.1.1` and `nagios-plugins-2.1.1` sub-directories (or similar ones, depending on your source versions). The `/path/to/` path should be replaced with the actual path to where both tarball with source code have been downloaded.

Compiling and installing Nagios

Now let's go to the directory where the Nagios sources are located; in our case it is `/usr/src/nagios/nagios-4.1.1`. We'll configure Nagios parameters for the directories, we plan to install it by running the `configure` script. Some of the options that the script accepts are described in the following table:

Option	Description
`--prefix=<dir>`	**Specifies the main directory in which all Nagios binaries are installed; this defaults to** `/usr/local/nagios`
`--sysconfdir=<dir>`	Specifies the directory where all Nagios configurations will be stored; this defaults to `[PREFIX]/etc`
`--localstatedir=<dir>`	Specifies the directory where all Nagios statuses and other information will be kept; this defaults to `[PREFIX]/var`
`--with-nagios-user=<user>`	Specifies the Unix user to be used by the Nagios daemon; this defaults to `nagios`
`--with-nagios-group=<grp>`	Specifies the Unix group to use for the Nagios daemon; this defaults to `nagios`
`--with-mail=<path>`	Specifies the path to the `mail` program used for sending e-mails
`--with-httpd-conf=<path>`	Specifies the path to the Apache configuration directory; this can be used to generate Apache configuration files
`--with-init-dir=<path>`	Specifies the directory where all scripts required for setting up a system service should be installed; this defaults to `/etc/rc.d/init.d`

For the directory structure that was described earlier in this section, the following configure script should be used:

```
sh configure \
        --prefix=/opt/nagios \
        --sysconfdir=/etc/nagios \
        --localstatedir=/var/nagios \
        --libexecdir=/opt/nagios/plugins \
        --with-command-group=nagioscmd
```

The script might take time to complete as it will try to guess the configuration of your machine and verify how to build Nagios. If the `configure` script fails, the most probable reason is that one or more prerequisites are missing. At this point, you will need to analyze which test failed and install or configure additional packages. Most of the times, the output is quite clear, and it is easy to understand what went wrong.

Assuming the configure command worked, we now need to build Nagios. The build process uses the `make` command, similar to almost all Unix programs. The following commands can be used to build or install Nagios:

Command	Description
make all	Compiles Nagios; this is the first thing you should be doing
make install	Installs the main program, CGI, and HTML files
make install-commandmode	Installs and configures the external command file
make install-config	Installs the sample Nagios configuration; this target should only be used for fresh installations
make install-init	Installs scripts to set up Nagios as a system service

First, we'll need to build every module within Nagios. To do this, simply run the following command:

```
make all
```

If an error occurs, it is probably due to some header files missing or a development package not being installed. The following is a sample output from a successful Nagios build. It finishes with a friendly message saying that compiling has completed successfully.

```
cd ./base && make
make[1]: Entering directory '/usr/src/nagios/base'
[...]
*** Compile finished ***
[...]
**************************************************************
Enjoy.
```

If an error occurs during the build, the information about it is also shown. For example, the following is a sample output from the build:

```
[...]
In file included from checks.c:40:
../include/config.h:163:18: error: ssl.h: No such file or
directory
[...]
make[1]: *** [checks.o] Error 1
make[1]: Leaving directory '/usr/src/nagios/base'
make: *** [all] Error 2
```

If this or a similar error occurs, please make sure that you have all the prerequisites mentioned earlier installed. Also, please make sure that you have enough memory and storage space during compilation as this might also cause unexpected crashes during builds.

On Ubuntu systems, it is possible to look for development packages using the `apt-cache search` command; for example, `apt-cache search ssl` will find all packages related to OpenSSL. Development packages always have the `-dev` suffix in their package name; in this case, it would be the `libssl-dev` package. Combined with the `grep` command to filter only development packages, for SSL the command would be as follows:

```
apt-cache search ssl | grep -- -dev
```

On RedHat Enterprise Linux, CentOS, and Fedora Core, it is possible to look for development packages using the `yumsearch` command:

```
yum search ssl | grep -- -devel
```

Now, we need to install Nagios by running the following commands:

```
make install
make install-commandmode
```

For a fresh install, it is recommended that you also install sample configuration files that will be used later for configuring Nagios:

```
make install-config
```

At this point, Nagios is installed. It is recommended that you keep all of your Nagios sources as well as prepare dedicated scripts that install Nagios. This is just in case you decide to enable/disable specific options and don't want to guess how exactly Nagios was configured to build the last time it was installed.

The next step is to make sure that Nagios is working properly after being set up. To do this, we can simply run Nagios with the sample configuration that was created by `install-config`.

We should run it as a `nagios` user, since the process will be run as normally only as a `nagios` user. We will use the `su` command to switch the user and run the Nagios binary with the `-v` option, which validates the correctness of the configuration file:

```
# su -c '/opt/nagios/bin/nagios -v /etc/nagios/nagios.cfg'
nagios
Nagios Core 4.1.1
Copyright (c) 2009-present Nagios Core Development Team and
Community Contributors
Copyright (c) 1999-2009 Ethan Galstad
Last Modified: 08-19-2015
License: GPL
Website: https://www.nagios.org
Reading configuration data...
   Read main config file okay...
   Read object config files okay...
Running pre-flight check on configuration data...
Checking objects...
        Checked 8 services.
        Checked 1 hosts.
        Checked 1 host groups.
        Checked 0 service groups.
        Checked 1 contacts.
        Checked 1 contact groups.
        Checked 24 commands.
        Checked 5 time periods.
        Checked 0 host escalations.
        Checked 0 service escalations.
```

```
Checking for circular paths...
        Checked 1 hosts
        Checked 0 service dependencies
        Checked 0 host dependencies
        Checked 5 timeperiods
Checking global event handlers...
Checking obsessive compulsive processor commands...
Checking misc settings...
Total Warnings: 0
Total Errors:   0
Things look okay - No serious problems were detected during the
pre-flight check
```

Compiling and installing Nagios plugins

In order to compile Nagios plugins manually, first change the working directory to the directory where Nagios plugins source code is located. In our case, it is `/usr/src/nagios/nagios-plugins-2.1.1`.

We'll configure Nagios plugin parameters for the directories we plan to install it by running the configure script. Some of the options that the script accepts are described in the following table:

Option	Description
`--prefix=<dir>`	Specifies the main directory in which all Nagios binaries are installed; defaults to `/usr/local/nagios`
`--sysconfdir=<dir>`	Specifies the directory where all Nagios configurations will be stored; defaults to `[PREFIX]/etc`
`--libexecdir=<dir>`	Specifies the directory where all Nagios plugins will be installed; defaults to `[PREFIX]/libexec`
`--localstatedir=<dir>`	Specifies the directory where all Nagios statuses and other information will be kept; defaults to `[PREFIX]/var`
`--enable-perl-modules`	Installs the `Nagios::Plugin` package along with all dependent packages
`--with-nagios-user=<user>`	Specifies the Unix user used by the Nagios daemon; defaults to `nagios`
`--with-nagios-group=<grp>`	Specifies the Unix group to use for the Nagios daemon; defaults to `nagios`

`--with-pgsql=<path>`	Specifies the path to PostgreSQL installation; required for building PostgreSQL testing plugins
`--with-mysql=<path>`	Specifies the path to the MySQL installation; required for building MySQL testing plugins
`--with-openssl=<path>`	Specifies the path to the OpenSSL installation; can be specified if OpenSSL is installed in a non-standard location (such as `/opt/nagios/openssl`)
`--with-perl=<path>`	Specifies the path to Perl installation; can be specified if Perl is installed in a non-standard location (such as `/opt/nagios/perl`)

The `--enable-perl-modules` option enables installing additional Perl modules (`Nagios::Plugin` and its dependencies) that aid in developing your own Nagios plugins in Perl. It is useful to enable this option if you are familiar with Perl.

The `--with-pgsql` and `--with-mysql` options allow us to specify locations for the installations of the PostgreSQL and/or MySQL databases. It is used to create plugins for monitoring PostgreSQL and/or MySQL. If not specified, the build process will look for the development files for these databases in their default locations. Installing development files for these databases is described in the *Installing prerequisites* section. For the directory structure that was described earlier in this section, the following `configure` script should be used:

```
sh configure \
        --prefix=/opt/nagios \
        --sysconfdir=/etc/nagios \
        --localstatedir=/var/nagios \
        --libexecdir=/opt/nagios/plugins
```

The script should run for some time and succeed, assuming that all prerequisites are installed. If not, the script should indicate what the missing component is. The build process also uses the make command similar to how Nagios is compiled. In this case, only all and install targets will be used. Therefore, the next step is to run the make commands shown here:

```
make all
make install
```

If any of these steps fail, an investigation into what exactly has failed is needed, and if it is due to a missing library or a development package, install these and try again. If all of the preceding commands succeeded, then you now have a fully installed Nagios and Nagios plugins setup. Congratulations!

Setting up a web server

The final step is to add the Nagios configuration to the web server. For Debian and Ubuntu, run the following commands to enable CGI and the basic authentication:

```
a2enmod cgi
a2enmod auth_basic
```

This will enable the required modules for Apache 2. For other distributions, the CGI and authentication are enabled already, but these are not needed.

First, we need to determine where the configuration should be placed. The Apache configuration directory should be either /etc/apache2 (which is the case for Debian and Ubuntu) or /etc/httpd (for all rpm based distributions).

If the conf-available and conf-enabled sub-directories exist (that is, /etc/apache2/conf-available is a directory), then our configuration file should be placed as /etc/apache2/conf-available/nagios.conf.

If the conf.d directory exists inside the Apache configuration directory (that is, /etc/httpd/conf.d), we can simply place the file as /etc/apache2/conf.d/nagios.conf.

The contents of the file should be as follows:

```
ScriptAlias /nagios/cgi-bin /opt/nagios/sbin
Alias /nagios /opt/nagios/share
<Location "/nagios">
AuthName "Nagios Access"
AuthType Basic
AuthUserFile /etc/nagios/htpasswd.users
require valid-user
</Location>
<Directory "/opt/nagios/share">
AllowOverride None
Options +ExecCGI -MultiViews +SymLinksIfOwnerMatch
Require all granted
Order allow,deny
Allow from all
```

```
</Directory>
<Directory "/opt/nagios/sbin">
AllowOverride None
Options +ExecCGI -MultiViews +SymLinksIfOwnerMatch
Require all granted
Order allow,deny
Allow from all
</Directory>
```

This will make alias to the /nagios URL that will serve the Nagios website. It will also add the /nagios/cgi-bin URL prefix that will be used for CGI scripts. The additional options also ensure that both directories can be accessed as many Linux distributions prevent access to pages outside of the /var/www directory structure completely by default.

If the file was put in the conf-available directory (such as on Debian and Ubuntu Linux distributions), we'll also need to explicitly enable the configuration by running the following command:

```
a2enconf nagios
```

This will create a proper symbolic link and ensure that Apache reads the configuration file on next restart.

Finally, we need to create the htpasswd.users file, which should contain the username and hash of the password for the user that will be able to access the UI console.

The username should be nagiosadmin, and the password can be anything. The file can be created by running the following command:

```
htpasswd -c /etc/nagios/htpasswd.users nagiosadmin
```

This will prompt for the password for the user. Using nagiosadmin as username is described in more details in Chapter 4, *Using the Built-in Web interface*.

After that we can restart the Apache web server. Restarting the web server itself varies by Linux distributions, but it should be one of the following commands:

```
apachectl restart
service apache2 restart
service httpd restart
```

We can now check that the web interface is available at `http://(ip-address)/nagios/`, where `(ip-address)` should be the actual IP address of the machine where Nagios was set up. The page should look similar to the following image:

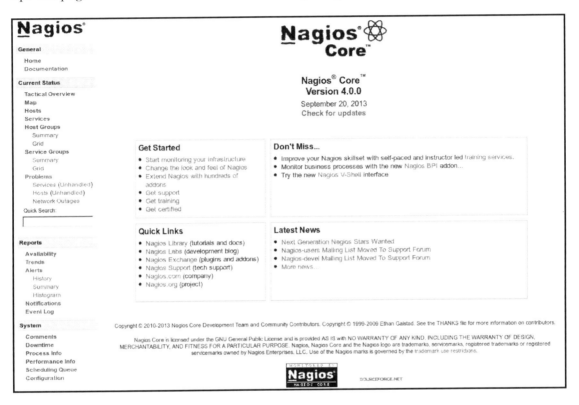

Troubleshooting the web server

There might be cases where accessing the Nagios URL shows an error instead of the welcome screen. If this happens it can be due to many things—web server not started, Nagios-related configuration set up incorrectly, or incorrect permissions on directories.

The first thing that we should check is whether Apache is working properly. We can manually run the check_http plugin from Nagios. If the web server is up and running we should see something similar to the following example:

```
# /opt/nagios/plugins/check_http -H 127.0.0.1
HTTP OK HTTP/1.1 200 OK - 296 bytes in 0.006 seconds
```

If Apache is not currently running, the plugin will report an error similar to the following one:

```
# /opt/nagios/plugins/check_http -H 127.0.0.1
HTTP CRITICAL - Unable to open TCP socket
```

If it was stopped, start it by running one of the following commands, depending on the Linux distribution:

```
apachectl restart
service apache2 restart
service httpd restart
```

The next step is to check whether the http://127.0.0.1/nagios/ URL is working properly. We can also use the same plugin for this. The -u argument can specify the exact link to access and -a allows specifying the username and password to authorize. It is passed in the form of <username>:<password>.

```
# /opt/nagios/plugins/check_http -H 127.0.0.1 \
  -u /nagios/ -a nagiosadmin:<yourpassword>
HTTP OK HTTP/1.1 200 OK - 979 bytes in 0.019 seconds
```

We can also check actual CGI scripts by passing a URL to one of the scripts:

```
# /opt/nagios/plugins/check_http -H 127.0.0.1 \
  -u /nagios/cgi-bin/tac.cgi -a nagiosadmin:<yourpassword>
HTTP OK HTTP/1.1 200 OK - 979 bytes in 0.019 seconds
```

If any of these checks returned any HTTP code other than 200, it means that this is the problem.

If the code is `500`, then it means that Apache is not correctly configured. In such cases, the Apache error log contains useful information about any potential problem. On most systems, including Ubuntu Linux, the filename is `/var/log/apache2/error.log`. An example error log could be:

```
[error] [client 127.0.0.1] need AuthName:
/nagios/cgibin/tac.cgi
```

In this particular case, the problem is missing the `AuthName` directive for CGI scripts.

Internal errors can usually be resolved by making sure that the Nagios-related Apache configuration is correct. If you followed the installation steps from this and the previous chapters, Apache configuration should be exactly the same as in the preceding examples.

If this does not help, it is worth checking other parts of the configuration, especially those related to virtual hosts and CGI configuration. Commenting out parts of the configuration can help to determine which parts of the configuration are causing problems.

Another possibility is that either check whether the `/nagios/` or `/nagios/cgi-bin/tac.cgi` URL returned code 404. This code means that the page was not found. In this case, make sure that Apache is configured according to the previous steps.

Another option for troubleshooting the issue is to enable more verbose debugging to a custom file. The following Apache 2 directives can be added to the `nagios.conf` configuration file created earlier in the appropriate directories of either `/etc/apache2` or `/etc/httpd`:

```
LogFormat "%h %l %u "%r" %>s %b %{Host}e %f" debuglog
CustomLog /var/log/apache2/access-debug.log debuglog
```

The `/var/log/apache2` path may also be different depending on the Linux distribution. It is recommended that you check if that directory exists and change it appropriately or use the `/var/log` directory.

The first entry defines the custom logging format that also logs exact paths to files. The second one enables logging with this format to a dedicated file. An example entry in such a log would be as follows:

```
127.0.0.1 - - "GET /nagios/ HTTP/1.1" 404 481 127.0.0.1
/var/www/nagios
```

This log entry tells us that `http://127.0.0.1/nagios/` was incorrectly expanded to the `/var/www/nagios` directory. In this case, the `Alias` directive describing the `/nagios/` prefix is missing. Making sure that the actual configuration matches the one provided in the previous section will also resolve this issue.

Another error that you can get is 403, which indicates that Apache was unable to access either CGI scripts in `/opt/nagios/sbin` or Nagios static pages in `/opt/nagios/share`. In this case, you need to make sure that these directories are readable by the user that Apache is running as.

It might also be related to directories above `/opt/nagios` or `/opt`. One of these might also be inaccessible to the user that Apache is running as, which will also cause the same error to occur.

If you run into any other problems, then it is best to start by making sure that the Nagios-related configuration matches the examples from the previous section. It is also a good idea to reduce number of enabled features and virtual hosts in your Apache configuration.

Running Nagios using virtualizations

Apart from running Nagios on a physical machine, it can also be run inside virtualizations, like almost all other applications. This section is mainly intended for users already familiar with different types of virtualization and willing to run Nagios in such an environment.

Nagios works well both using hardware virtualization such as provided by VMware, Virtual Box, or Hyper-V applications as well as in Linux containers such as Docker.

Containers allow Nagios to run in a shared, single instance of the Linux kernel, which allows better sharing of memory and other resources and is much easier to set up in general—all that is needed is installing Docker, which will take care of provisioning everything else.

Hardware virtualization has the benefit of not sharing the Linux kernel and having dedicated resources such as configuring the amount of available RAM memory—so it is possible to limit the resources that Nagios can use.

Running Nagios inside containers

Containers are an operating system-level virtualization technology. It can be used to run multiple isolated Linux systems on a single Linux machine.

 Introduction to containers and Docker as the technology in particular can be found at `https://docs.docker.com/engine/`.

The best way to work with Nagios inside Docker is to first create a Docker image using a `Dockerfile` and then simply run one or more containers using the newly created image.

 The Dockerfile's syntax is described in more details at `https://docs.docker.com/engine/reference/builder/`.

The basic `Dockerfile` to create a Nagios image is very trivial:

```
FROM ubuntu:14.04
RUN apt-get update && \
  apt-get -y install curl && \
  curl
https://raw.github.com/learning-nagios/nagios-install/master/install.sh |
sh
```

This will create an image based on Ubuntu version 14.04; install the curl package, then download and run the install script.

To test it, create an empty directory, write the preceding text as a new file called `Dockerfile`, and then run the following command inside that directory:

```
docker build --tag automated_nagios_image .
```

This will create an image using the preceding command.

The next step is to create a script to start both Apache and Nagios. Create a file called entrypoint.sh in the same directory as Dockerfile with the following contents:

```sh
#!/bin/sh
# capture stop signals from Docker
trap stop_all 1 2 3 4 5 6 15
stop_all() {
    echo "Stopping services..."
    /etc/init.d/nagios stop
    apachectl stop
}
start_all() {
    echo "Starting services..."
    apachectl start
    /etc/init.d/nagios start
}
# start services and wait indefinitely
start_all
sleep 10000d
```

This script will start Apache and Nagios and then terminate them once a terminate signal (such as Ctrl–C) is received.

Then add the following lines to Dockerfile:

```
EXPOSE 80
ADD entrypoint.sh /entrypoint.sh
CMD ["sh", "/entrypoint.sh"]
```

The first line specifies that TCP port 80 (the port that is used by the http protocol) should be exposed. The next line adds the newly created entrypoint.sh file to the image. Finally, the last line specifies when the image is started; it should run the entrypoint.sh script.

Now let's rebuild the image:

```
docker build --tag automated_nagios_image .
```

As the next step, we can simply start it:

```
docker run -P automated_nagios_image
```

This will start a new container using the newly created image. The -P flag specifies that the exposed ports should be redirected. This will basically make the Apache available at a random port on all IP addresses of the Docker host machine.

 Port redirection in Docker is described in more details at https://docs.d ocker.com/engine/reference/run/#expose-incoming-ports.

We can also force providing port 80 as any port on the docker host machine with the following command:

```
docker run -p 8080:80 automated_nagios_image
```

This will export the Nagios web server as port 8080 on the local machine. This way it can be accessed with: http://(ip-address):8080/nagios.

At this point, we can run one or multiple Docker containers based on the image that already includes a precompiled version of Nagios and a web server, with a predefined password.

Installing Nagios inside virtual machines

Nagios can also be easily run as a separate virtual machine using hardware virtualizations such as those provided by VMware, Virtual Box, or Hyper-V solutions.

 Virtualization and its types are described in more details at https://en.w ikipedia.org/wiki/Virtualization#Hardware_virtualization.

The process of setting up Nagios inside a virtual machine is very similar to setting it up natively or inside a container. All that is needed is to run a Linux virtual machine. Using the latest Ubuntu LTS, such as 16.04, is a safe choice for a distribution.

All that is needed is to set it up or download a ready to use image, such as from https://cl oud-images.ubuntu.com/.

The next step is to ensure that the curl command is available:

```
apt-get update ; apt-get -y install curl
```

Next, simply run the same script to download and run the automated setup script:

```
curl -sSL https://raw.github.com/learning-nagios/nagios-
install/master/install.sh | sh
```

Please note that setting up Nagios requires the machine to be able to access the Internet for downloading the required packages as well as the Nagios sources.

At this point, the compilation should succeed and the machine will have Apache and Nagios already set up.

After this step, it is possible to clone or create a template of the machine to be able to start new instances with Nagios already installed. The procedure for creating a clone or template may vary depending on the virtualization technology that you are using.

Another option is to use the official Nagios virtual machines. They are available as a commercial offering and can be purchased from the following link: `https://www.nagios.org/downloads/nagios-core/`

It is also possible to use the Nagios XI virtual machine image, which can be downloaded from the following link: `https://www.nagios.com/downloads/nagios-xi/`

Summary

Our Nagios setup is now complete and ready to be configured! We have covered various ways to get Nagios up and running—both from source code and using prebuilt binary packages. In this chapter, you also learned how to run Nagios in virtualizations such as containers and virtual machines.

If you have used the automated script for setting up Nagios, which we strongly recommend, the key system paths to keep in mind are as follows :

- `/opt/nagios`: This is where Nagios binaries and HTML files were installed
- `/opt/nagios/plugins`: This is where Nagios plugins are installed
- `/etc/nagios`: All configuration files should be placed here
- `/var/nagios`: This is where Nagios will keep its local state

If you have used a different method for setting up Nagios, such as using the prebuilt packages, please keep in mind that these are the paths that are used throughout the rest of this book and may need adjusting for your particular installation.

The next chapter will guide you through the Nagios configuration and help you set up a basic monitoring configuration that will check various resource types.

3
Configuring Nagios

The previous chapter described how to set up and configure Nagios. Now that our Nagios system is up and running, we can move on to add hosts and services that should be monitored.

In this chapter, we will cover the following points:

- Configuring Nagios
- Understanding macro definitions
- Configuring hosts and host groups
- Configuring services and service groups
- Configuring commands and time periods
- Configuring contacts and contact groups
- Verifying configuration
- Understanding notifications
- Templates and object inheritance

Configuring Nagios

In this chapter, you will learn about other ways in which the Nagios status can be checked as well as how Nagios itself can be managed.

Nagios configuration is stored in a separate directory. Usually it's either in `/etc/nagios` or `/usr/local/etc/nagios`. If you have followed the steps for manual installation, it will be in the `/etc/nagios` directory.

The default installation creates a sample host called localhost and a few services. We will now create additional hosts and services, and create a more robust directory structure to manage all of the objects.

The main Nagios configuration file is called `nagios.cfg`, and it's the main file that is loaded during Nagios startup.

Its syntax is simple, a line beginning with # is a comment, and all lines in the form of `<parameter>=<value>` set a value. In some cases, a value might be repeated (such as specifying additional files/directories to read).

The following is a sample of the Nagios main configuration file:

```
# log file to use
log_file=/var/nagios/nagios.log
# object configuration directory
cfg_dir=/etc/nagios/objects
# storage information
resource_file=/etc/nagios/resource.cfg
status_file=/var/nagios/status.dat
status_update_interval=10
(...)
```

The main configuration file needs to define a log file to use and that has to be passed as the first option in the file. It also configures various Nagios parameters that allow tuning its behavior and performance. The following are some of the commonly used options:

Option	Description
`log_file`	Specifies the log file to use; defaults to `[localstatedir]/nagios.log`
`cfg_file`	Specifies the configuration file to read for object definitions; might be specified multiple times
`cfg_dir`	Specifies the configuration directory where all files in it should be read for object definitions; might be specified multiple times
`resource_file`	File that stores additional macro definitions; `[sysconfdir]/resource.cfg`
`temp_file`	Path to a temporary file that is used for temporary data; defaults to `[localstatedir]/nagios.tmp`
`lock_file`	Path to a file that is used for synchronization; defaults to `[localstatedir]/nagios.lock`

`temp_path`	Path to where Nagios can create temporary files; defaults to `/tmp`
`status_file`	Path to a file that stores the current status of all hosts and services; defaults to `[localstatedir]/status.dat`
`status_update_interval`	Specifies how often (in seconds) the `status` file should be updated; defaults to `10` (seconds)
`nagios_user`	User to run the daemon
`nagios_group`	Group to run the daemon
`command_file`	It specifies the path to the external command line that is used by other processes to control the Nagios daemon; defaults to `[localstatedir]/rw/nagios.cmd`
`use_syslog`	Whether Nagios should log messages to syslog as well as to the Nagios log file; defaults to `1` (enabled)
`state_retention_file`	Path to a file that stores state information across shutdowns; defaults to `[localstatedir]/retention.dat`
`retention_update_interval`	How often (in seconds) the retention file should be updated; defaults to `60` (seconds)
`service_check_timeout`	After how many seconds should a service check be assumed that it has failed; defaults to `60` (seconds)
`host_check_timeout`	After how many seconds should a host check be assumed that it has failed; defaults to `30` (seconds)
`event_handler_timeout`	After how many seconds should an event handler be terminated; defaults to `30` (seconds)
`notification_timeout`	After how many seconds should a notification attempt be assumed that it has failed; defaults to `30` (seconds)
`enable_environment_macros`	Whether Nagios should pass all macros to plugins as environment variables; defaults to `1` (enabled)
`interval_length`	Specifies the number of seconds a "unit interval" is; this defaults to `60`, which means that an interval is one minute; it is not recommended to change the option in any way, as it might end up with undesirable behavior

For a complete list of accepted parameters, refer to the Nagios documentation available at `h` `ttp://library.nagios.com/library/products/nagioscore/manuals/`.

The Nagios `resource_file` option defines a file to store user variables. This file can be used to store additional information that can be accessed in all object definitions. These usually contain sensitive data as they can only be used in object definitions and it is not possible to read their values from the web interface. This makes it possible to hide passwords of various sensitive services from Nagios administrators without proper privileges. There can be up to 256 macros, named `$USER1$`, `$USER2$` ... `$USER256$`. The `$USER1$` macro defines the path to Nagios plugins and is commonly used in check command definitions.

The `cfg_file` and `cfg_dir` options are used to specify files that should be read for object definitions. The first option specifies a single file to read and the second one specifies the directory to read all files with the `.cfg` extension in the directory and all child directories. Each file may contain different types of objects. The next section describes each type of definition that Nagios uses.

One of the first things that needs to be planned is how your Nagios configuration should be stored. In order to create a configuration that will be maintainable as your IT infrastructure changes, it is worth investing some time to plan out how you want your host definitions set up and how that could be easily placed in a configuration file structure. Throughout this book, various approaches to make your configuration maintainable are discussed. It's also recommended to set up a small Nagios system to get a better understanding of the Nagios configuration before proceeding to larger setups.

Sometimes, it is best to have the configuration grouped into directories by the locations in which hosts and/or services are. In other cases, it might be best to keep the definitions of all servers with a similar functionality in one directory.

A good directory layout makes it much easier to control the Nagios configuration; for example, massively disable all objects related to a particular part of the IT infrastructure. Even though it is recommended to use downtimes, it is sometimes useful to just remove all entries from the Nagios configuration.

Throughout all the configuration examples in this book, we will use the directory structure. A separate directory is used for each object type, and similar objects are grouped within a single file. For example, all command definitions are to be stored in the `commands/` subdirectory. All host definitions are stored in the `hosts/<hostname>.cfg` file.

For Nagios to read the configuration from these directories, edit your main Nagios configuration file (`/etc/nagios/nagios.cfg`), remove all the `cfg_file` and `cfg_dir` entries, and add the following ones:

```
cfg_dir=/etc/nagios/commands
cfg_dir=/etc/nagios/timeperiods
cfg_dir=/etc/nagios/contacts
cfg_dir=/etc/nagios/contactgroups
cfg_dir=/etc/nagios/hosts
cfg_dir=/etc/nagios/hostgroups
cfg_dir=/etc/nagios/services
cfg_dir=/etc/nagios/servicegroups
```

The next step is to create the directories by executing the following commands:

```
root@ubuntu:~# cd /etc/nagios
root@ubuntu:/etc/nagios# mkdir commands timeperiods \ contacts
contactgroups hosts hostgroups services  servicegroups
```

In order to use default Nagios plugins, copy the default Nagios command definition file `/etc/nagios/objects/commands.cfg` to `/etc/nagios/commands/default.cfg`. Also, make sure that the following options are set as follows in your `nagios.cfg` file:

```
check_external_commands=1
interval_length=60
accept_passive_service_checks=1
accept_passive_host_checks=1
```

If any of the options is set to a different value, change them and add them to the end of the file if they are not currently present. After making such changes in the Nagios setup, you can now move on to the next sections and prepare a working configuration for your Nagios installation.

Understanding macro definitions

The ability to use macro definitions is one of the key features of Nagios. They offer a lot of flexibility in object and command definitions. Nagios also provides custom macro definitions, which give you greater possibility to use object templates for specifying parameters common to a group of similar objects.

All command definitions can use macros. Macro definitions allow parameters from other objects, such as hosts, services, and contacts, to be referenced so that a command does not need to have everything passed as an argument. Each macro invocation begins and ends with a $ sign.

A typical example is a HOSTADDRESS macro, which references the address field from the host object. All host definitions provide the value of the address parameter.

The following is a sample host and command definition:

```
define host{
  host_name        somemachine
  address          10.0.0.1
  check_command    check-host-alive
  }

define command{
  command_name     check-host-ssh
  command_line     $USER1$/check_ssh -H $HOSTADDRESS$
  }
```

For this example, the following command will be invoked by Nagios to perform the check:

```
/opt/nagios/plugins/check_ssh -H 10.0.0.1
```

This check will validate whether it is possible to connect to the SSH service on the said machine. This is a simple and effective way to check machines that have SSH service present, as it is often blocked by any firewalls. Other ways to test connectivity for hosts and services are described in more detail in Chapter 6, *Using the Nagios Plugins*.

Both $USER1$ and $HOSTADDRESS$ will be substituted appropriately. The USER1 macro was also used and expanded as a path to the Nagios plugins directory. This is a macro definition that references the data contained in a file that is passed as the resource_file configuration directive.

Even though it is not required for the USER1 macro to point to the plugins directory, all standard command definitions that come with Nagios use this macro, so it is not recommended that you change it.

Some of the macro definitions are listed in the following table:

Macro	Description
HOSTNAME	The short, unique name of the host; maps to the `host_name` directive in the host object
HOSTADDRESS	The IP or hostname of the host; maps to the `address` directive in the host object
HOSTDISPLAYNAME	Description of the host; maps to the `alias` directive in the host object
HOSTSTATE	The current state of the host (one of UP, DOWN, UNREACHABLE)
HOSTGROUPNAMES	Short names of all host groups a host belongs, separated by a comma
LASTHOSTCHECK	The date and time of last check of the host, in Unix timestamp (number of seconds since 1970-01-01)
LASTHOSTSTATE	The last known state of the host (one of UP, DOWN, UNREACHABLE)
SERVICEDESC	Description of the service; maps to the `description` directive in the service object
SERVICESTATE	The current state of the service (one of OK, WARNING, UNKNOWN, CRITICAL)
SERVICEGROUPNAMES	Short names of all service groups a service belongs, separated by a comma
CONTACTNAME	Short, unique name of the contact; maps to the `contact_name` directive in the contact object
CONTACTALIAS	Description of the contact; maps to the `alias` directive in the contact object
CONTACTEMAIL	The e-mail address of the contact; maps to the `email` directive in the contact object
CONTACTGROUPNAMES	Short names of all contact groups a contact belongs to, separated by a comma

This table is not complete and only covers commonly used macro definitions. A complete list of available macros can be found in the Nagios documentation available at `http://library.nagios.com/library/products/nagioscore/manuals/`

All macro definitions need to be prefixed and suffixed with a $ sign, for example $HOSTADDRESS$ to refer to the HOSTADDRESS macro definition.

Another interesting functionality is **on-demand macro definitions**. These are macros that allow the referencing of any other object and if found in a command definition, will be parsed and substituted accordingly.

These macros accept one or more arguments inside the macro definition name, each passed after a colon. This is mainly used to read specific values, not related to the current object. In order to read the contact e-mail for the user jdoe, regardless of who the current contact person is, the macro would be $CONTACTEMAIL:jdoe$, which means getting a CONTACTEMAIL macro definition in the context of the jdoe contact.

Nagios also offers custom macro definitions. These work in a way that administrators can define additional attributes in each type of an object, and that macro can then be used inside a command.

This is used to store additional parameters related to an object; for example, you can store a MAC address in a host definition and use it in certain types of host checks.

Simply start a directive inside an object with an underscore and write its name in uppercase. It can then be referenced in one of the following ways, based on the object type it is defined

```
$_HOST<variable>$ - for directives defined within a host object
$_SERVICE<variable>$ - for directives defined within a service object
$_CONTACT<variable>$ - for directives defined within a contact object
```

This can be used for any type of command to refer to a custom attribute of an object such as the following:

```
define host{
    host_name        somemachine
    address          10.0.0.1
    _MAC             12:12:12:12:12:12
    check_command    check-host-by-mac
    }
```

This defines a MAC address for a host that can be used inside commands.

A corresponding check command that uses this attribute inside a check is as follows:

```
define command{
    command_name      check-host-by-mac
    command_line      $USER1$/check_hostmac -H $HOSTADDRESS$ -m
       $_HOSTMAC$
    }
```

`$_HOSTMAC$` will be replaced with an `_MAC` custom directive from the host the check is running for.

It is also a good idea to prefix the custom variables with two underscores so that the actual reference also includes an underscore as shown here:

```
define host{
    host_name        somemachine
    address          10.0.0.1
    __MAC            12:12:12:12:12:12
    check_command    check-host-by-mac
    }
```

Then the MAC address can be referenced as `$_HOST_MAC$` (rather than `$_HOSTMAC$` from the earlier example) and is more readable when reading the configuration files.

A majority of standard macro definitions are exported to check commands as environment variables so that the plugins can access them as any other variable. Environment variable names are the same as macros, but are prefixed with `NAGIOS_`; for example, `HOSTADDRESS` is passed as the `NAGIOS_HOSTADDRESS` environment variable. For security reasons, the `$USERn$` variables are also not passed to commands as environment variables. It is also not possible to query on-demand or custom macro definitions.

Configuring hosts

Hosts are objects that describe machines that should be monitored—either physical hardware or virtual machines. A host consists of a short name, a descriptive name, and an IP address or host name.

Host definition also specifies when and how the system should be monitored, as well as who will be contacted regarding any problem related to this host. It also describes how often the host should be checked, how retrying the checks should be handled, and details regarding how the notifications about problems should be sent out.

A sample definition of a host is as follows:

```
define host{
    host_name                linuxbox01
    hostgroups               linuxservers
    alias                    Linux Server 01
    address                  10.0.2.15
    check_command            check-host-alive
    check_interval           10
    retry_interval           1
    max_check_attempts       5
    check_period             24x7
    contact_groups           linux-admins
    notification_interval    30
    notification_period      24x7
    notification_options     d,u,r
    }
```

The preceding example defines a Linux box that will use the `check-host-alive` command to make sure it is up and running. The test will be performed every 10 minutes and after 5 failed tests it will assume that the host is down. If it is down, a notification will be sent out every 30 minutes.

The following is a table of common directives that can be used to describe hosts, items in bold are required when specifying a host:

Option	Description
host_name	The short, unique name of the host
alias	The descriptive name of the host
address	An IP address or a fully qualified domain name of the host; it is recommended to use an IP address as all tests will fail if DNS servers are down
parents	The list of all parent hosts on which this host depends, separated by a comma; this is usually one or more switch and router to which this host is directly connected
hostgroups	The list of all host groups this host should be a member of; separated by a comma
check_command	The short name of the command that should be used to test if the host is alive; if a command returns an OK state, the host is assumed to be up; it is assumed to be down otherwise

`check_interval`	Specifies how often a check should be performed; the value is in minutes
`retry_interval`	Specifies how many minutes to wait before retesting if the host is up
`max_check_attempts`	Specifies how many times a test needs to report that a host is down before it is assumed to be down by Nagios
`check_period`	Specifies the name of the time period that should be used to determine time during which tests if the host is up should be performed
`contacts`	The list of all contacts that should receive notifications related to host state changes sent; separated by a comma; at least one contact or contact group needs to be specified for each host
`contact_groups`	List of all contact groups that should receive notifications related to host state changes sent; separated by a comma; at least one contact or contact group needs to be specified for each host
`first_notification_delay`	Specifies the number of minutes before the first notification related to a host being down is sent out
`notification_interval`	Specifies the number of minutes before each next notification related to a host being down is sent out
`notification_period`	Specifies time periods during which notifications related to host states should be sent out
`notification_options`	Specifies which notification types for host states should be sent, separated by a comma; should be one or more of the following: d: the host DOWN state u: the host UNREACHABLE state r: host recovery (UP state) f: the host starts and stops flapping s: notify when scheduled downtime starts or ends

For a complete list of accepted parameters, refer to the Nagios documentation available at:

`http://library.nagios.com/library/products/nagioscore/manuals/`

By default, Nagios assumes all host states to be UP. If the `check_command` option is not specified for a host, then its state will always be set to UP. When the command to perform host checks is specified, then scheduled checks will take place regularly and the host state will be monitored using the `check_interval` value as the number of minutes between checks.

Nagios uses a soft and hard state logic to handle host states. Therefore, if a host state has changed from UP to DOWN since the last hard state, then Nagios assumes that the host is in the soft DOWN state and performs retries of the test, waiting for the `retry_interval` minutes between each test. Once the result is the same after the `max_check_attempts` number of times, Nagios assumes that the DOWN state is a hard state. The same mechanisms apply for DOWN to UP transitions. Notifications are also only sent if a host is in a hard state. This means that a temporary failure that only occurred for a single test will not cause a notification to be sent if `max_check_attempts` was set to a number higher than 1.

The host object `parents` directive is used to define the topology of the network. Usually, this directive points to a switch, router, or any other device that is responsible for forwarding network packets. The host is assumed to be unreachable if the parent host is currently in the hard DOWN state. For example, if a router is down, then all machines accessed via it are considered unreachable and no tests will be performed on these hosts.

If your network consists of servers connected via switches and routers to a different network, then the router will be the parent for all servers in the local network and the router would also be the switch. The parent of the router on the other side of the link would be the local router.

The following diagram shows the actual network infrastructure and how Nagios hosts should be configured in terms of parents for each element of the network:

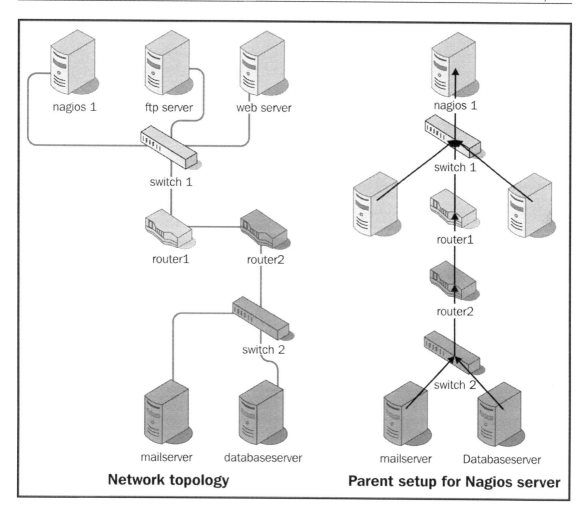

Network topology   **Parent setup for Nagios server**

In the preceding diagram, the actual network topology is shown on the left and parent hosts setup for each of the machine is shown on the right. Each arrow represents mapping from a host to a parent host.

There is no need to define a parent for hosts that are directly on the network with your Nagios server. So, in this case, `switch 1` should not have a parent host set.

Some devices such as switches cannot be easily checked if they are down. However, it is still a good idea to describe them as part of your topology. In that case, you might use functionality such as scheduled downtime to keep track of when the device is going to be offline or mark it as down manually. This helps in determining other problems because Nagios will not scan any hosts that have the router somewhere along the path that is currently scheduled for downtime. This way, you will not receive multiple notifications that are reported due to the scheduled downtime.

Checks and notification periods specify the time periods during which checks for host state and notifications are to be performed. These can be specified so that different hosts can be monitored at different times.

It is also possible to set up where information that a host is down is kept, without notifying anyone about it. This can be done by specifying `notification_period` that will tell Nagios when a notification should be sent out. No notifications will be sent out outside this time period.

A typical example is a server that is only required during business hours and has a daily maintenance window between 10 P.M. and 4 A.M. You can set up Nagios so as not to monitor host availability outside business hours, or you can make Nagios monitor it, but without notifying that it is actually down. If monitoring is not done at all, then Nagios will perform fewer operations during this period. In the second case, it is possible to gather statistics on how much of the maintenance window is used, which can be used if changes to the window need to be made.

Configuring host groups

Nagios offers the `hostgroup` objects that are a group of one or more machines. This allows managing hosts or adding services to groups or hosts more efficiently.

A host might be a member of more than one host group. Usually, grouping is done by the type of machines, the location they are in, or the role of the machine. Each host group has a unique short name used to identify it, a descriptive name, and one or more hosts that are members of this group.

The following are the examples of host group definitions that define groups of hosts and a group that combines both groups:

```
define hostgroup{
    hostgroup_name                    linux-servers
    alias                             Linux servers
    members                           linuxbox01,linuxbox02
    }

define hostgroup{
    hostgroup_name                    aix-servers
    alias                             AIX servers
    members                           aixbox1,aixbox2
    }

define hostgroup{
    hostgroup_name                    unix-servers
    alias                             UNIX servers servers
    hostgroup_members                 linux-servers,aix-servers
    }
```

The following table contains directives that can be used to describe host groups; items in bold are required when specifying a host group:

Option	Description
hostgroup_name	**The short, unique name of the host group**
alias	The descriptive name of the host group
members	The list of all hosts that should be a member of this group; separated by a comma
hostgroup_members	The list of all other host groups whose members should also be members of this group; separated by a comma

Host groups can also be used when defining services or dependencies.

For example, it is possible to tell Nagios that all Linux servers should have their SSH services monitored and all AIX servers should have telnet accepting connections.

It is also possible to define dependencies between hosts. They are, in a way, similar to the parent-host relationship, but dependencies offer more complex configuration options. Nagios will only issue host and service checks if all dependent hosts are currently up. More details on dependencies can be found in Chapter 7, *Advanced Configuration*.

For the purpose of this book, we will define at least one host in our Nagios configuration directory structure. To be able to monitor a local server that the Nagios installation is running, we will need to add its definition into the `/etc/nagios/hosts/localhost.cfg` file:

```
define host{
  host_name                   localhost
  alias                       Localhost
  address                     127.0.0.1
  check_command               check-host-alive
  check_interval              5
  retry_interval              1
  max_check_attempts          5
  check_period                24x7
  contact_groups              admins
  notification_interval       60
  notification_period         24x7
  notification_options        d,u,r
  }
```

Although Nagios does not require a naming convention, it is a good practice to use the hostname as the name of the file. To make sure that Nagios monitoring works, it is also a good idea to set the `address` to a valid IP address of a local machine, such as `127.0.0.1`, as stated in the preceding code, or the IP address in your network if it is static.

If you are planning on monitoring other servers as well, you will want to add them—the recommended approach is to define a single object definition in a single file.

Configuring services

Services are objects that describe a functionality that a particular host provides. This can be virtually anything—network servers such as NFS or FTP, resources such as storage space, or CPU load.

A service is always tied to a host that it is running. It is also identified by its description, which needs to be unique within a particular host. A service also defines when and how Nagios should check if it is running properly and how to notify the people responsible for this service. A short example of a web server that is defined on the `localhost` machine created earlier is as follows:

```
define service{
    host_name                   localhost
    service_description         www
    check_command               check_http
    check_interval              10
    check_period                24x7
    retry_interval              3
    max_check_attempts          3
    notification_interval       30
    notification_period         24x7
    notification_options        w,c,u,r
    contact_groups              admins
    }
```

This definition tells Nagios to monitor that the web server is working correctly every `10` minutes. The recommended file for this definition is `/etc/nagios/services/localhost-www.cfg`. With services, a good approach is to use `<host>-<servicename>` as the name of the file if a single host or host group is being set up for monitoring.

The following table is about the common directives that can be used to describe a service; items in bold are required when specifying a service:

Option	Description
host_name	The short name of the hosts on which the service is running; when specifying multiple objects, the list names of hosts should be separated by a comma
hostgroup_name	The short name of the host groups that the service is running on; when specifying multiple objects, the list names of hosts should be separated by a comma
service_description	The description of the service that is used to uniquely identify services running on a host
servicegroups	The list of all service groups of which this service should be a member; separated by a comma

`check_command`	The short name of the command that should be used to test if the service is running
`check_interval`	Specifies how often a check should be performed; the value is in minutes
`retry_interval`	Specifies how many minutes to wait before retesting whether the service is working
`max_check_attempts`	Specifies how many times a test needs to report that a service is down before it is assumed to be down by Nagios
`check_period`	Specifies the name of the time period that should be used to determine the time during which tests should be performed if the service is working
`contacts`	The list of all contacts that should receive notifications related to service state changes; separated by a comma; at least one contact or contact group needs to be specified for each service
`contact_groups`	The list of all contacts groups that should receive notifications related to service state changes, separated by a comma; at least one contact or contact group needs to be specified for each service
`first_notification_delay`	Specifies the number of minutes before the first notification related to a service state change sent out
`notification_interval`	Specifies the number of minutes before each next notification related to a service not working correctly is sent out
`notification_period`	Specifies time periods during which notifications related to service states should be sent out
`notification_options`	Specifies which notification types for service states should be sent, separated by a comma; should be one or more of the following: `w`: the service WARNING state `u`: the service UNKNOWN state `c`: the service CRITICAL state `r`: the service recovery (back to OK) state `f`: the host starts and stops flapping `s`: notify when the scheduled downtime starts or ends

For a complete list of accepted parameters, refer to the Nagios documentation available at `h` `ttp://library.nagios.com/library/products/nagioscore/manuals/`.

Nagios requires that at least one service should be defined for every host and one service for it to run. That is why we will now create a sample service in our configuration directory structure. For this purpose, we'll monitor the SSH protocol.

In order to monitor whether the SSH server is running on the Nagios installation, we will need to add its definition into the `/etc/nagios/services/localhost-ssh.cfg` file:

```
define service{
  host_name                 localhost
  service_description       ssh
  check_command             check_ssh
  check_interval            5
  retry_interval            1
  max_check_attempts        3
  check_period              24x7
  contact_groups            admins
  notification_interval     60
  notification_period       24x7
  notification_options      w,c,u,r
  }
```

If you are planning on monitoring other services as well, you will want to add a definition as well.

In many cases the same services (such as SSH) should be monitored on multiple hosts. It is possible to define a service once and add it to multiple hosts or even specify host groups. The items should be separated using a comma, as shown here:

```
define service{
  hostgroup_name            linux-servers
  host_name                 localhost,aix01
  service_description       SSH
  (...)
  }
```

It is also possible to specify hosts for which checks will not be performed by prefixing the host or host group with an exclamation mark (!), such as if a service is present on all hosts in a group except for a specific box. To specify that SSH should be checked on an `aix01` machine, all Linux servers except for `linux01`—the `aix01` machine, a `service` definition similar to the following has to be created:

```
define service{
    hostgroup_name            linux-servers
    host_name                 !linuxbox01,aix01
    service_description       SSH
    (...)
    }
```

Services may be configured to be dependent on one another, similar to hosts. In this case, Nagios will only perform checks on a service if all dependent services are working correctly. More details on dependencies can be found in `Chapter 7`, *Advanced Configuration*.

Configuring service groups

Service objects can be grouped similar to hosts. This can be used to manage services more conveniently. It also helps when checking service reports on the Nagios web interface. Service groups are also used to configure dependencies in a more convenient way.

The following table describes attributes that can be used to define a group, items in bold are required when specifying a service group:

Option	Description
`servicegroup_name`	**The short, unique name of the service group**
`alias`	The descriptive name of the service group
`members`	The list of all hosts and services that should be a member of this group, separated by a comma
`servicegroup_members`	The list of all other service groups whose all members should also be members of this group; separated by a comma

The format of the `members` directive of service group object is one or more
`<host>,<service>` pair.

An example of a service group is shown here:

```
define servicegroup{
    servicegroup_name      databaseservices
    alias                  All services related to databases
    members                linuxbox01,mysql,linuxbox01,
                               pgsql,aix01,db2

    }
```

This service group consists of the `mysql` and `pgsql` services on a `linuxbox01` host and `db2`
on the `aix01` machine. It is uniquely identified by its name `databaseservices`.

It is possible to specify groups that a service should be member of inside the service
definition itself. To do this, add groups so that it will be a member of in the
`servicegroups` directive in the service definition. It is also possible to define an empty
service group and have the service definitions specify to which service groups they belong.
Observe the following example:

```
define servicegroup{
    servicegroup_name      databaseservices
    alias                  All services related to databases
    }

define service{
    host_name              linuxbox01
    service_description    mysql
    check_command          check_ssh
    servicegroups          databaseservices
    }
```

In most cases, this approach is easier to maintain. Having a list of service groups that each
service is a member of inside its definition and a definition of the service group without
services explicitly listed makes it easier to manage, especially when creating services on
multiple hosts, such as by using host groups, as explained earlier in this chapter.

Configuring commands

Command definitions describe how host/service checks should be done. They are also used to specify how notifications about problems or event handlers should work.

Commands defined in Nagios tell how it can perform checks, such as what commands to run to check if a database is working properly, how to check if SSH, SMTP, or FTP servers are properly working, or if the DHCP server is assigning IP addresses correctly.

Commands are also used in notifications to let users know of issues, or try to recover a problem automatically.

Nagios makes no distinction between commands provided by the Nagios plugins project and custom commands either created by a third party or written by you. Since its interface is very straightforward, it is very easy to create your own checks.

> Chapter 13, *Programming Nagios*, talks about writing custom commands to perform tasks such as monitoring custom protocols and communicating with installed applications.

Commands are defined in a manner similar to other objects in Nagios. A command definition has two parameters, namely, name and command line. The first parameter is a name that is then used for defining checks and notifications. The second parameter is an actual command that will be run along with all parameters.

Commands are used by hosts and services. They define what to run when making sure a host or service is working properly. A check command is identified by its unique name.

When used with other object definitions, it can also have additional arguments and use exclamation mark as a delimiter. Commands with parameters have the syntax as, `command_name[!arg1][!arg2][!arg3][...]`.

A command name is often the same as the plugin that it runs, but it can be different. The command line includes macro definitions (such as $HOSTADDRESS$). Check commands also use $ARG1$, $ARG2$ ... $ARG32$ macros if a check command for a host or service passed additional arguments. The following is an example that defines a command to ping a host to make sure that it is working properly; it does not use any arguments:

```
define command{
    command_name    check-host-alive
    command_line    $USER1$/check_ping -H $HOSTADDRESS$
                    -w 3000.0,80% -c 5000.0,100% -p 5
}
```

A very short host definition that would use this check command could be similar to the one shown here:

```
define host{
   host_name        somemachine
   address          10.0.0.1
   check_command    check-host-alive
   }
```

Such a check is usually done as part of the host checks. This allows Nagios to make sure that a machine is working properly if it responds to ICMP requests. Commands allow to pass arguments as this offers a more flexible way of defining checks. So, a definition accepting parameters could be as follows:

```
define command{
   command_name     check-host-alive-limits
   command_line     $USER1$/check_ping -H $HOSTADDRESS$
                    -w $ARG1$ -c $ARG2$ -p 5
   }
```

The corresponding host definition is as follows:

```
define host{
   host_name        othermachine
   address          10.0.0.2
   check_command    check-host-alive-limits!3000.0,80%!5000.0,100%
   }
```

The following is another example that sets up a check command for a previously defined service:

```
define command{
   command_name     check_http
   command_line     $USER1$/check_http -H $HOSTADDRESS$
   }
```

This check can be used when defining a service to be monitored by Nagios. Our Nagios configuration includes the default Nagios plugin definitions that we have previously copied into /etc/nagios/commands/default.cfg.

Chapter 6, *Using the Nagios Plugins,* covers the standard Nagios plugins along with sample command definitions.

Configuring time periods

Time periods are definitions of dates and times during which an action should be performed or specific people should be notified. These describe ranges of days and times and can be reused across various operations. A time period definition consists of a name that uniquely identifies it in Nagios as well as a description. It also contains one or more days or dates along with time spans that define when a time period is valid.

A typical example of a time period would be working hours, which define that a valid time to perform an action is from Monday to Friday during business hours. Another definition of a time period can be weekends which mean Saturday and Sunday, all day long. The following is a sample time period for working hours:

```
define timeperiod{
  timeperiod_name  workinghours
  alias            Working Hours, from Monday to Friday
  monday           09:00-17:00
  tuesday          09:00-17:00
  wednesday        09:00-17:00
  thursday         09:00-17:00
  friday           09:00-17:00
  }
```

This particular example tells Nagios that a valid time to perform an action is from every Monday to Friday between 9 A.M. and 5 P.M. Each entry in a time period contains information on the date or weekday. It also contains a range of hours. Nagios first checks if the current date matches any of the dates specified. If it does, then it compares whether the current time matches the time ranges specified for that particular date.

There are multiple ways that a date can be specified. Depending on what type of date it is, one definition might take precedence over another. For example, a definition for December 24 is more important than a generic definition that on every weekday an action should be performed between 9 A.M. and 5 P.M.

Possible date types are mentioned here:

- **Calendar date**: For example, 2015-11-01, which means November 1, 2015; Nagios accepts dates in the YYYY-MM-DD format
- **Date recurring every year**: Such as July 4, which means 4th of July
- **Specific day within a month**: For example, day 14, which means the 14th day of every month

- **Specific weekday along with offset in a month**: For example, Monday 1 September, which means the first Monday in September; Monday -1 May would mean the last Monday in May
- **Specific weekday in all months**: Such as Monday 1, which means every the first Monday in a month
- **Weekday**: For example, Monday, which means all Mondays

It lists all the types in the order in which Nagios uses different date types. This means that a date recurring every year will always be used prior to an entry describing what should be done every Monday.

In order to be able to correctly configure all objects, we will now create some standard time periods that will be used in the configuration. The following example periods will be used in the remaining sections of this chapter, and it is recommended that you put them in the /etc/nagios/timeperiods/default.cfg file:

```
define timeperiod{
   timeperiod_name      workinghours
   alias                Working Hours, from Monday to Friday
   monday               09:00-17:00
   tuesday              09:00-17:00
   wednesday            09:00-17:00
   thursday             09:00-17:00
   friday               09:00-17:00
   }

define timeperiod{
   timeperiod_name      weekends
   alias                Weekends all day long
   saturday             00:00-24:00
   sunday               00:00-24:00
   }

define timeperiod{
   timeperiod_name      24x7
   alias                24 hours a day 7 days a week
   monday               00:00-24:00
   tuesday              00:00-24:00
   wednesday            00:00-24:00
   thursday             00:00-24:00
   friday               00:00-24:00
   saturday             00:00-24:00
   sunday               00:00-24:00
   }
```

The last time period is also used by the SSH service defined earlier. This way, monitoring the SSH server will be done all the time.

It is also possible to define multiple periods of time by separating them with a comma, as shown here:

```
define timeperiod{
  timeperiod_name       workinghours
  alias                 Working Hours, excluding lunch break
  monday                09:00-13:00,14:00-17:00
  tuesday               09:00-13:00,14:00-17:00
  wednesday             09:00-13:00,14:00-17:00
  thursday              09:00-13:00,14:00-17:00
  friday                09:00-13:00,14:00-17:00
  }
```

It is also possible to have one time period excluded whenever another period is active, as shown here:

```
define timeperiod{
  timeperiod_name       first-mondays
  alias                 First Mondays of each month
  monday 1 january      00:00-24:00
  monday 1 february     00:00-24:00
  monday 1 march        00:00-24:00
  monday 1 april        00:00-24:00
  monday 1 may          00:00-24:00
  monday 1 june         00:00-24:00
  monday 1 july         00:00-24:00
  monday 1 august       00:00-24:00
  monday 1 september    00:00-24:00
  monday 1 october      00:00-24:00
  monday 1 november     00:00-24:00
  monday 1 december     00:00-24:00
define timeperiod{
  timeperiod_name       workinghours-without-first-monday
  alias                 Working Hours, without first Monday of
                        each month
  monday                09:00-17:00
  tuesday               09:00-17:00
  wednesday             09:00-17:00
  thursday              09:00-17:00
  friday                09:00-17:00
  exclude               first-mondays
  }
```

The second time period will include all working days except for the first Monday of each month.

Configuring contacts

Contacts define people who can either be owners of specific machines or people who should be contacted in case of problems. Depending on how your organization might contact people in case of problems, a definition of a contact may vary a lot. A contact consists of a unique name, a descriptive name, one or more e-mail addresses, and pager numbers. Contact definitions can also contain additional data specific to how a person can be contacted.

A basic contact definition is shown here, and specifies the unique contact name, an alias, and the contact information. It also specifies event types that the person should receive and time periods during which notifications should be sent:

```
define contact{
  contact_name                 jdoe
  alias                        John Doe
  email                        john.doe@yourcompany.com
  contactgroups                admins,nagiosadmin
  host_notification_period     workinghours
  service_notification_period  workinghours
  host_notification_options    d,u,r
  service_notification_options w,u,c,r
  host_notification_commands   notify-host-by-email
  service_notification_commands notify-service-by-email
}
```

The `contactgroups` line defines that this user is a member of the `admins` group, which we'll define later in this chapter. Contact groups work similar to host and service groups, either a contact defines groups it belongs to or a contact group definition specifies users that belong to this group.

We will now create a similar file in `/etc/nagios/contacts`, setting values for `contact_name`, `alias`, and `email` based on your username, full name, and e-mail address. The recommended name for the file is based on `contact_name`.

The following table describes all available directives when defining a contact; items in bold are required when specifying a contact:

Option	Description
contact_name	The short, unique name of the contact
alias	The descriptive name of the contact; usually, this is the full name of the person
contactgroups	The list of all contact groups of which this user should be a member, separated by a comma
host_notifications_enabled	This specifies whether this person should receive notifications regarding host state
host_notification_period	This specifies the name of the time period that should be used to determine the time during which a person should receive notifications regarding the host state
host_notification_commands	Specifies one or more commands that should be used to notify the person of a host state, separated by a comma
host_notification_options	Specifies host states about which the user should be notified, separated by a comma; should be one or more of the following: d: the host DOWN state u: the host UNREACHABLE state r: the host recovery (UP state) f: the host starts and stops flapping s: notify when scheduled downtime starts or ends n: the person will not receive any service notifications
service_notifications_enabled	Specifies whether this person should receive notifications regarding the service state
service_notification_period	Specifies the name of the time period that should be used to determine the time during which a person should receive notifications regarding the service state
service_notification_commands	Specifies one or more commands that should be used to notify the person of a service state; separated by a comma

`service_notification_options`	Specifies service states about which the user should be notified, separated by a comma; should be one or more of the following: `w`: the service WARNING state `u`: the service UNKNOWN state `c`: the service CRITICAL state `r`: the service recovery (OK state) `f`: the service starts and stops flapping `n`: the person will not receive any service notifications
`email`	Specifies the e-mail address of the contact
`pager`	Specifies the pager number of the contact; it can also be an e-mail to the pager gateway
`address1 ... address6`	Additional six addresses that can be specified for the contact; these can be anything, based on how the notification commands will use these fields
`can_submit_commands`	Specifies whether the user is allowed to execute commands from the Nagios web interface
`retain_status_information`	Specifies whether the status-related information about this person is retained across restarts
`retain_nonstatus_information`	Specifies whether the non-status information about this person should be retained across restarts

For a complete list of accepted parameters, refer to the Nagios documentation available at `http://library.nagios.com/library/products/nagioscore/manuals/`

Contacts are also mapped to the users that log into the Nagios web interface. This means that all operations done via the interface will be logged as that particular user, and that the web interface will use the access granted to particular contact objects when evaluating if an operation should be allowed. The `contact_name` field from a contact object maps to usernames in the Nagios web interface.

Configuring contact groups

Similar to other object types, contacts can also be grouped. Usually, grouping is used to keep a list of which users are responsible for which tasks and maps to job responsibilities for particular people. It also makes it possible to define people that should be responsible for handling problems at specific time periods, and Nagios will automatically contact the right people for a particular time a problem has occurred.

A sample definition of a contact group is as follows:

```
define contactgroup{
   contactgroup_name            linux-admins
   alias                        Linux Administrators
   members                      jdoe,asmith
   }
```

This group is also used when defining the linuxbox01 and WWW service contacts. This means that both the jdoe and asmith contacts will receive information on the status of this host and service.

The following table is a complete list of directives that can be used to describe contact groups, items in bold are required when specifying a contact group:

Option	Description
contactgroup_name	**The short, unique name of the contact group**
alias	The descriptive name of the contact group
members	The list of all contacts that should be a member of this group; separated by a comma
contactgroup_members	The list of all other contact groups whose all members should also be members of this group; separated by a comma

The members of a contact group can either be specified in the contact group definition or using the contactgroups directive in a contact definition. It is also possible to combine both the methods—some of the members can be specified in the contact group definition and others can be specified in their contact object definition.

Contacts are used to specify who will be contacted if a status changes for one or more hosts or services. Nagios accepts both contacts and contact groups in their object definitions. This allows to make either specific people or entire groups responsible for particular machines or services.

It is also possible to specify different people or groups for handling host-related problems and service related problems—for example, hardware administrators for handling host problems and system administrators for handling service issues.

In order for our previously created user `jdoe` to work properly, we need to define the `admins` and `nagiosadmin` groups in the `/etc/nagios/contactgroups/admins.cfg` file:

```
define contactgroup{
  contactgroup_name              admins
  alias                          System administrators
}

define contactgroup{
  contactgroup_name              nagiosadmin
  alias                          Nagios administrators
  }
```

Verifying the configuration

At this point, our configuration file should be ready for use. We can now verify that all of the configuration statements are correct and that Nagios would start correctly with our configuration. We can do this by running the `nagios` command with the `-v` option.

The `-v` option will try to load the configuration and all of the objects into Nagios and validate that they are defined properly. This is meant to detect any configuration errors or other issues that would prevent Nagios from starting with the configuration file; this is especially useful in order to test configuration before restarting Nagios, as restarting Nagios with an invalid configuration will cause it to stop working in most cases.

For example, the following is an output of checking a valid configuration file:

```
root@ubuntu:~# /opt/nagios/bin/nagios -v /etc/nagios/nagios.cfg
Nagios Core 4.1.1
Copyright (c) 2009-present Nagios Core Development Team and Community
Contributors
Copyright (c) 1999-2009 Ethan Galstad
Last Modified: 08-19-2015
License: GPL
Website: http://www.nagios.org
Reading configuration data...
    Read main config file okay...
    Read object config files okay...
Running pre-flight check on configuration data...
Checking services...
        Checked 1 services.
Checking hosts...
        Checked 1 hosts.
Checking host groups...
        Checked 1 host groups.
Checking service groups...
        Checked 1 service groups.
Checking contacts...
        Checked 1 contacts.
Checking contact groups...
        Checked 1 contact groups.
Checking commands...
        Checked 24 commands.
Checking time periods...
        Checked 3 time periods.
Checking for circular paths...
        Checked 1 hosts
        Checked 0 service dependencies
        Checked 0 host dependencies
        Checked 3 timeperiods
Checking global event handlers...
Checking obsessive compulsive processor commands...
Checking misc settings...
Total Warnings: 0
Total Errors:   0
Things look okay - No serious problems were detected during the pre-
flight check
```

The preceding command indicates a correct configuration file.

If there are errors, the message will indicate the problem, as shown in the following command:

```
root@ubuntu:~# /opt/nagios/bin/nagios -v /etc/nagios/nagios.cfg
Nagios Core 4.1.1
Copyright (c) 2009-present Nagios Core Development Team and Community
Contributors
Copyright (c) 1999-2009 Ethan Galstad
Last Modified: 08-19-2015
License: GPL
Website: http://www.nagios.org
Reading configuration data...
    Read main config file okay...
Error: Contactgroup 'admin' is not defined anywhere
Error: Could not add contactgroup 'admin' to service (config file
'/etc/nagios/services/localhost-www.cfg', starting on line 1)
    Error processing object config files!
***> One or more problems was encountered while processing the config
files...
        Check your configuration file(s) to ensure that they contain valid
        directives and data defintions.  If you are upgrading from a
previous
        version of Nagios, you should be aware that some
variables/definitions
        may have been removed or modified in this version.  Make sure to
read
        the HTML documentation regarding the config files, as well as the
        'Whats New' section to find out what has changed.
```

The preceding example indicates that the contactgroup value admin is not valid for a service defined in the /etc/nagios/services/localhost-www.cfg file.

 It is always recommended that you verify the Nagios configuration file after making changes to ensure that it does not prevent Nagios from functioning properly.
Even if the /etc/init.d/nagios script prevents restarting when the configuration is incorrect, this would cause Nagios not to start after a system restart.

Understanding notifications

Notifications are meant to let people know that something is either wrong or has returned to the normal way of functioning. This is a very important functionality in Nagios, and configuring notifications correctly might seem a bit tricky in the beginning.

When and how notifications are sent out is configured as part of the contact configuration. Each contact has configuration directives for when notifications can be sent out and how they want to be contacted. Contacts also contain information about contact details, such as telephone number, e-mail address, and Jabber/MSN address. Each host and service is configured with when information about it should be sent and who should be contacted. Nagios then combines all this information in order to notify people of changes in the status.

Notifications may be sent out in any of the following situations:

- Host has changed its state to the DOWN or UNREACHABLE state; a notification is sent out after the `first_notification_delay` number of minutes specified in the corresponding host object
- Host remains in the DOWN or UNREACHABLE state; a notification is sent out every `notification_interval` number of minutes specified in the corresponding host object
- Host recovers to an UP state; a notification is sent out immediately and only once
- Host starts or stops flapping; a notification is sent out immediately
- Host remains flapping; a notification is sent out every `notification_interval` number of minutes specified in the corresponding host object
- Service has changed its state to the WARNING, CRITICAL, or UNKNOWN states; a notification is sent out after the `first_notification_delay` number of minutes specified in the corresponding service object
- Service remains in the WARNING, CRITICAL, or UNKNOWN states; a notification is sent out every `notification_interval` number of minutes specified in the corresponding service object
- Service recovers to an OK state; a notification is sent out immediately and only once
- Service starts or stops flapping; a notification is sent out immediately
- Service remains flapping; a notification is sent out every `notification_interval` number of minutes specified in the corresponding service object

If one of these conditions occurs, Nagios starts evaluating whether information about it should be sent out and to whom.

The first check is to compare the current date and time against the notification time period, which is taken from the `notification_timeperiod` field from the current host or the service definition. A notification will be sent out only if the time period includes the current date and time.

Next, a list of users based on the `contacts` and `contact_groups` fields is created. Based on all members of all groups and included groups, as well as all contacts directly bound with the current host or service, a complete list of users is made.

Each of matched users is checked whether they should be notified about the current event. In this case, each user's time period is also checked whether it includes the current date and time. The `host_notification_period` or `service_notification_period` directive is used, depending on whether the notification is for the host or the service.

For host notifications, the `host_notification_options` directive for each contact is also used to determine whether that particular person should be contacted; for example, different users might be contacted about an unreachable host if the host is actually down. For service notifications, the `service_notification_options` parameter is used to check every user if they should be notified about this issue.

If all of these criteria have been met, then Nagios will send a notification to this user. It will now use commands specified in the `host_notification_commands` and `service_notification_commands` directives.

It is possible to specify multiple commands that will be used for notifications, so it is possible to set up Nagios so that it sends both e-mail as well as a message on an instant messaging or chat system such as XMPP or Slack.

Nagios also offers escalations that allow sending e-mails to other people when a problem has not been resolved for too long. This can be used to propagate problems to the higher management or teams that might be affected by unresolved problems. It is a very powerful mechanism and is split between the host and service-based escalations. This functionality is described in more detail in `Chapter 8`, *Notifications and Events*.

Using inheritance and templates

In order to allow flexible configuration of machines, Nagios offers a powerful inheritance functionality. The main concept is that administrators can set up templates that define common parameters and reuse them in actual host or service definitions. The mechanism even offers the possibility to create templates that inherit parameters from other templates.

Templates are regular Nagios objects that have the `register` directive and set it to . This means that they will not be registered as an actual host or service that needs to be monitored. Objects that inherit parameters from a template or another host should have a `use` directive pointing to the short name of the template object they are using.

When defining a template, its name is always specified using the `name` directive. This is slightly different from how typical hosts and services are registered, as they require the `host_name` and/or `service_description` parameters.

Inheritance can be used to define a template for basic host checks with basic parameters such as IP address being defined for each particular host. The following code is an example of this:

```
define host{
    name                    generic-server
    check_command           check-host-alive
    check_interval          5
    retry_interval          1
    max_check_attempts      5
    check_period            24x7
    notification_interval   30
    notification_period     24x7
    notification_options    d,u,r
    register                0
}

define host{
    use                     generic-server
    host_name               linuxbox01
    alias                   Linux Server 01
    address                 10.0.2.1
    contact_groups          linux-admins
    }
```

It is possible to inherit from multiple templates. To do this, simply put multiple names in the use directive, separated by a comma. This allows an object to use several templates that define a part or all directives that it will use. If multiple templates specify the same parameters, the value from the first template specifying it will be used. The following is an example code:

```
define service{
    name                        generic-service
    check_interval              10
    retry_interval              2
    max_check_attempts          3
    check_period                24x7
    register                    0
}

define service{
    host_name                   workinghours-service
    check_period                workinghours
    notification_interval       30
    notification_period         workinghours
    notification_options        w,c,u,r
    register                    0
}

define service{
    use                         workinghours-service,generic-   service
    contact_groups              linux-admins
    host_name                   linuxbox01
    service_description         SSH
    check_command               check_ssh
}
```

In this case, values from both templates will be used. The value of workinghours will be used for the check_period directive as it was first specified in the workinghours-service template. Changing the order in the use directive to generic-service, workinghours-service would cause the value of the check_period parameter to be 24x7.

Nagios also accepts creating multiple levels of templates. For example, you can set up a generic service template and inherit it to create templates for various types of checks, such as local services, resource-sensitive checks, and templates for passive-only checks.

Let's consider the following object and template structure:

```
define host{
      host_name       linuxserver1
      use             generic-linux,template-chicago
      .....
      }
define host{
      register        0
      name            generic-linux
      use             generic-server
      .....
      }
define host{
      register        0
      name            generic-server
      use             generic-host
      .....
      }
define host{
      register        0
      name            template-chicago
      use             contacts-chicago,misc-chicago
      .....
      }
```

The following diagram shows how Nagios will look for values for all directives:

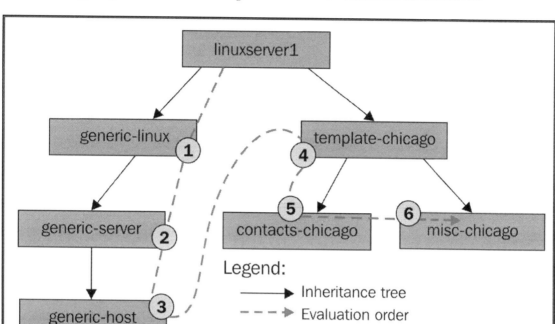

When looking for parameters, Nagios will first look for the value in the `linuxserver1` object definition. Next, it will use the following templates, in this order: `generic-linux`, `generic-server`, `generic-host`, `template-chicago`, `contacts-chicago`, and `misc-chicago` in the end.

It is also possible to set up host or service dependencies that will be inherited from a template. In that case, the dependent hosts or services can't be templates themselves and need to be registered as an object that will be monitored by the Nagios daemon.

Summary

This chapter introduced all types of objects in Nagios. You can now configure the actual hosts, services, contacts, and appropriate groups that match your infrastructure and resources that should be monitored.

We have covered the following types of objects and configuration items:

- Main Nagios configuration file
- Hosts and host groups
- Services and service groups
- Commands
- Time periods
- Contacts and contact groups

We have also covered how to validate the configuration and how the notification system works.

Chapter 4, *Using the Built-in Web interface* will cover how to use the Nagios standard web interface to view status of hosts and services. You will also learn how to schedule downtimes of hosts and services, add comments as well as generate reports.

4
Using the Built-in Web Interface

The previous chapter described how to set up and configure Nagios. Now, that our system is up and running, it will also send out notifications to people if something goes wrong. What we need now is a way to be able to view the current and historical information about the hosts and services that are failing. Nagios offers just that! It comes with a web interface that can be used to view the status of all hosts and services, read logs, and generate reports. Also, that's just a small part of its functionality.

Using any browser, you can access almost any information that Nagios keeps, namely status, performance data, history, and logs. You can easily check if all your hosts and services are working correctly with just a few clicks. The interface also offers the ability to change parts of configuration on the fly.

Having the possibility to check the status of all hosts and services is a very valuable functionality. Usually, a notification that something is wrong should just be a trigger to investigate the problem. Being able to see the big picture via various views of the web interface is very useful. You can use different detailed views and see both what is working properly and which hosts and/or services are in the warning or critical states.

In this chapter, we will cover the following items:

- Setting up and using the web interface
- Managing hosts and services
- Managing downtimes and adding comments
- Viewing Nagios information and generating reports
- Changing the look of the Nagios web interface

The Nagios web interface

`Chapter 3`, *Configuring Nagios*, described how to set up the Nagios web interface. In this section, we will briefly describe its structure and how to use it.

The Nagios web interface is a part of the main Nagios sources and binary distributions. Therefore, if you installed Nagios, you also have the web interface files. The only thing that you need is a web server with CGI and PHP support, which in our case will be Apache 2 (refer to `http://httpd.apache.org/` for more details).

The web interface uses **Common Gateway Interface** (**CGI**, a standard to generate dynamic websites; refer to `http://httpd.apache.org/docs/current/howto/cgi.html` for more details) to work as it is the most commonly offered way to run applications. It also allows a flexible set up in terms of security as CGI binaries can be run as a different user than the one web server is running as.

The web interface also uses additional files such as many static HTML pages, CSS style sheets, and images. Starting with Nagios 4, **PHP** (**PHP: Hypertext Preprocessor**, a scripting language for web development; refer to `http://php.net/` for more details) is used to ease configuring of the web interface HTML pages.

By default, all Nagios HTML and other static files that are used by the web interface are copied into the `share` subdirectory of Nagios installation and all CGI binaries go into the `sbin` subdirectory. Assuming that Nagios has been configured using the default directories used in `Chapter 2`, *Installing Nagios 4*, they will be `/opt/nagios/share` and `/opt/nagios/sbin`.

If you installed Nagios from a binary distribution it might have configured the web server so that it is accessible. In that case, the package management would have asked you for a password to access the Nagios web interface. You should start by trying to access `http://127.0.0.1/nagios/` from the machine that has Nagios installed. It will prompt you for a username and password. By default, the main Nagios administrator is called `nagiosadmin` and the password will be the one you supplied during package installation. For installation created using the automated script, the password is also `nagiosadmin`.

If you have followed all the steps mentioned in the previous chapter to install Nagios, then you will be able to use the web interface.

Accessing the web interface

We can now access the Nagios web interface by navigating to the `http://127.0.0.1/nagios/` URL from that machine. It will prompt for a username (`nagiosadmin`) and password configured at installation time. After a successful log in, you will see a welcome screen similar to the following one:

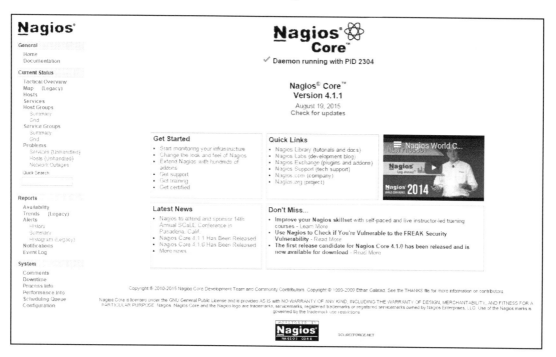

Using the web interface

The Nagios web interface always offers a menu on the left frame and the current information is shown in the remaining area. You can easily access all views from the menu on the left.

In case you want to replace the standard Nagios welcome screen with your own screen, all that is needed to be done is to change the `/opt/nagios/share/main.php` file. As this page is shown to everyone after they log in correctly, it can be used to provide the administrators with some guidelines on how Nagios monitoring is used within your company and what should be done in certain circumstances. It can also be used to define links to commonly checked hosts or commonly accessed services.

It is also possible to extend the menu on the left, which is defined in the `/opt/nagios/share/side.php` file. This way, quick links can be added to the menu and/or unused functionality can be removed from it.

Throughout the rest of this chapter, we will use the configuration that is different from the one we created in the previous chapter. This will allow to show more functionality in Nagios and its web interface. In the configuration used in this chapter, we have four hosts (two Linux-based, one Windows-based, and one network access point running OpenWrt software) with a total of 18 services being checked on those hosts, where two of these services are failing.

Checking the tactical overview

Nagios offers a panel that shows an overall status of all hosts, services, and other features. It can be accessed by clicking on the **Tactical Overview** link from the menu on the left. You can easily assess the scale of problems, such as number of hosts and services failing, flapping, and pending checks. It also shows how many hosts are unreachable due to other hosts being down.

The following is an example screenshot of the **Tactical Overview** page. All **4** hosts are up and running, **16** services are in the **OK** state, and **2** are **Critical**:

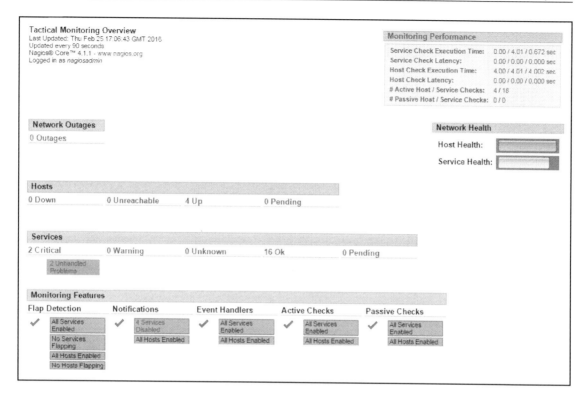

Tactical Overview presents the overall information on Nagios and monitoring. The page informs about the host and service conditions. It shows how many hosts and services are in which status. It also shows if any hosts and services have their checks, notifications, or event handlers disabled.

Performance information is shown in the top right-hand corner. It shows details on checks that have been performed. It also reports latency when performing checks and the time that it takes to perform checks, on average. These values are pretty important since if there are too many checks scheduled, then Nagios might not be able to perform some of them. Usually, you should tweak your Nagios installation in cases where latency is getting larger than a couple of seconds.

Below the performance information there is a status showing host and service health. It contains bars showing the number of hosts and services that are in an **OK** state. If all services are currently working properly then the bar spans to full width and is green. If some hosts or services are not working then the color of the bar will change to yellow or red accordingly.

Tactical Overview can also be used to view hosts or services list filtered to specific criteria. Clicking on any status count text in the **Network Outages**, **Hosts**, or **Services** section will show a list of hosts or services with specified status; if we would click on the **16 Ok** text in the **Services** section, it will show a list of all services with the **OK** status.

Viewing the status map

Nagios can show a graphical map of host parent-child relations along with the statuses. It can be accessed by clicking on the **Map** link in the menu on the left of the Nagios web interface. This can be used to keep track of hosts along with their statuses. So, you can see how a host being down causes other parts of your network to be unreachable.

The following is an example screenshot of a status page depicting our **Nagios Process** monitoring all four hosts:

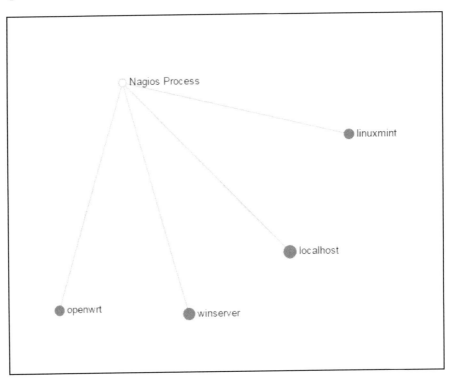

The status page can be shown in many ways. The preceding image shows a circular tree of all hosts; it is also possible to show a top-down tree of all hosts.

Managing hosts

Nagios offers several pages that can be used to view and modify host information. The Nagios web interface offers a view of all defined hosts, their status, and basic information. These can be used to determine the status of hosts. Host group-related views also show the status for services bound to hosts. Host Information pages can also modify several parameters related to the host configuration.

Checking status

Nagios offers a panel that shows all hosts along with their status. It can be accessed by clicking on the **Hosts** link in the menu on the left.

The following is a screenshot reporting four hosts, all of which are currently up:

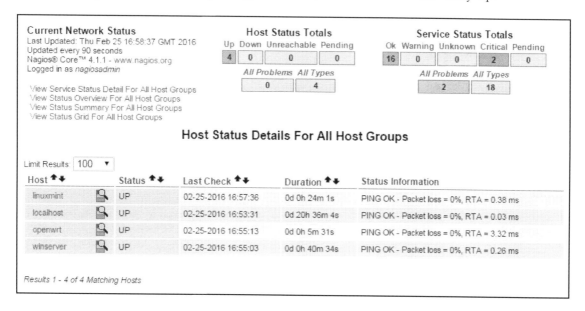

The page in the preceding image shows a list of all hosts, their status, and basic information such as when the host was last checked and when the status changed last. It also shows the information text response from the check. The order of how the table is shown can be changed by using the arrow buttons next to each column's header.

Similar to the **Tactical Overview** page, the Totals at the top of the page can be used to filter hosts or services to only the ones with a specific status. After clicking on any status type in the **Host Status Totals** table, the list of hosts is filtered by the ones that currently have that status. Clicking on any status type in **Service Status Totals** will show a list of services filtered by the ones that currently have the specified status.

There is also a quick jump menu on the left that allows moving to a list of all services and views related to the host groups.

Nagios also offers three views that show the status of all host groups. One such view is the status grid, which shows host groups along with the hosts in them, and each service for that host along with its status. It can be accessed by clicking on the **Grid** option under the **Host Groups** link in the menu on the left.

The following is a screenshot of such a status grid view:

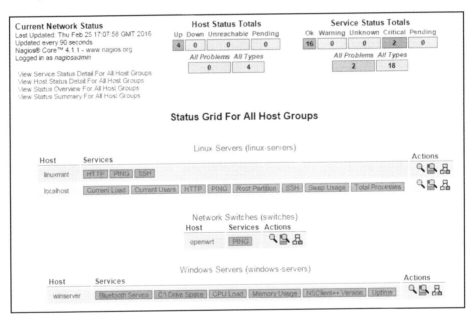

Similar to the previous view, clicking on **Host Status Totals** or **Service Status Totals** will cause Nagios to filter results according to the specified criteria. The page also contains a quick jump menu on the left that can be used to change the currently selected view.

Clicking on any host group description will show a list of all services on all hosts within that group.

Clicking on a host group name, which is specified in brackets, will show a host group menu that allows modifying attributes for all hosts or services related to that host group.

Clicking on a host name in any host or service-related view will cause Nagios to show detailed information about the chosen host.

Viewing host information

Clicking on a host in any view of the web interface will take you to the **Host Information** page. It contains details about the current host status, a list of comments, and a commands panel that allows modifying the host configuration, scheduling checks, and sending custom notifications.

The following is a screenshot of the Host (Windows machine) Information page:

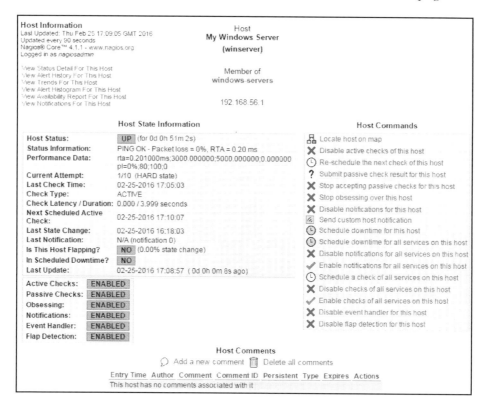

This page contains detailed information on the selected host. It shows the current status and host checks that have been or will be performed. It also contains information on what functionality is enabled or disabled for the specified host, whether the host is flapping along with the flapping threshold value.

The menu on the right can be used to perform operations related to this host. It allows toggling whether active checks should be performed, if Nagios should accept passive check results or if it should detect flapping. You can also configure if Nagios should obsess over a host or send notifications and events. It is also possible to view options or schedule checks for all services bound to this host. You can also submit passive check results over the web interface.

The **Host Information** page also allows reading and modifying all comments related to this host. All current comments are listed under the **Host Comments** section. Clicking on a trash icon under the **Actions** column will delete a comment. You can also delete all comments and add a new comment bound to this host.

Managing services

Similar to the host-related information and operations, Nagios has similar panels for working with services. It consists of several service and service group views along with being able to view, detailed information on each service and modify its parameters.

Checking status

The Nagios web interface offers a view of all the defined services, their statuses, and basic information. It can be accessed by clicking on the **Services** link in the menu on the left.

The following is a screenshot reporting **18** services where **2** are failing and the rest are currently working correctly. We can quickly see that one of the Linux hosts has no SSH access, and the free disk space on Windows machine is very low.

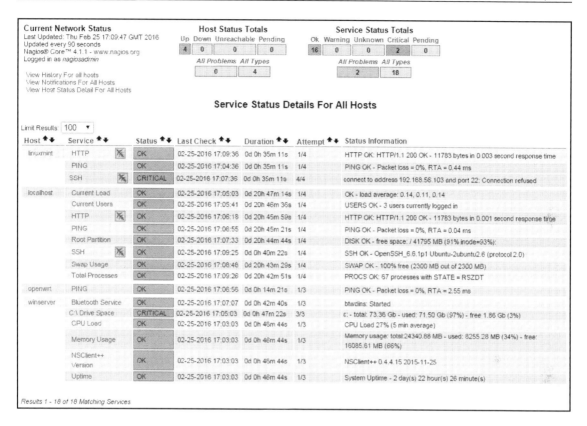

The main part of the page is the table showing all services along with their statuses and detailed information on the output from checks.

The default order by which the table is sorted is that all services are grouped by the host they are configured for and they are sorted by service description. It is possible to sort the table according to your needs by clicking on the arrows in any column in the header of the table.

Above the table, there are total values for each host and service statuses. They can also be used to filter the service table to show specific statuses or services for the host with a specific status.

The page also contains a quick menu that allows navigation to commonly used views. It allows jumping to the history and notification log as well as navigating to a list of all hosts along with their detailed statuses.

Clicking on any host will take you to a **Host Information** page for the selected object. Similarly, clicking on any service will show the detailed information page for that object.

Another interesting view is a summary of all services specified for each service group. It can be accessed by clicking on the **Grid** option under the **Service Groups** link from the menu on the left.

In our configuration, we defined two service groups (**Critical Services** and **Noncritical Services**) and added some of the services to them. Note that some services are not bound to any of the groups. The following is a screenshot of the page:

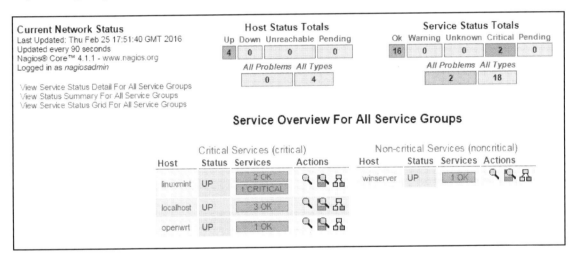

It shows each service group along with the count of all services for each status. The page contains the status summary for all services that are members of a specific service group. It also shows the status summary for all hosts that have at least one service configured.

Clicking on any status summary column will show a list of all services in that group along with detailed information. Clicking on a service group will show an overview of services split into individual hosts.

Viewing service information

Clicking on a service in any view of the web interface will take you to the **Service Information** page. It contains details on the current service status, list of comments, and a commands panel that allows modifying service configuration, scheduling checks, or sending custom notifications.

Let's check the status of the HTTP service running on one of the Linux hosts. The service is running correctly and is not added to any of the service groups, as shown here:

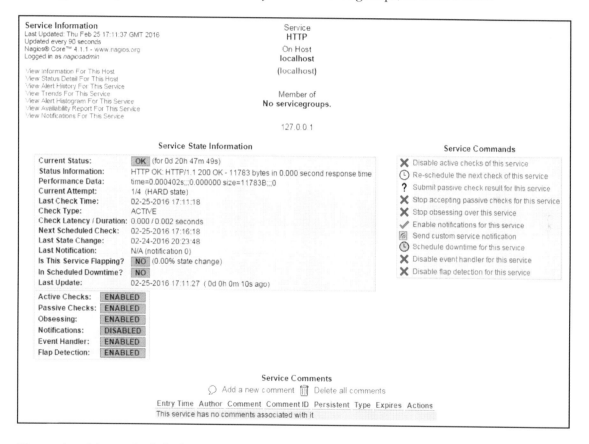

The main table on the left shows detailed information on the service, namely the current status, output from the check, and detailed information on the last and next planned checks. The page also shows whether the service is flapping along with the flapping threshold and when the last notification was sent out.

The menu on the right allows modifying whether checks should be performed, notifications and events should be done, and if Nagios should obsess over this service. There is also an option to schedule when the next check is to be performed.

At the bottom, there is a **Service Comments** section containing a table that shows all existing comments related to this service similar to the **Host Information** page. It is also possible to add a comment and delete a single or all comments related to this service.

Managing downtimes

Nagios allows the use of the web interface to manage scheduled downtimes for hosts and services. This includes listing, adding, and deleting downtimes for both hosts and services.

Checking downtimes statuses

The Nagios web interface lists of all the scheduled downtimes. This page can be accessed by clicking on the **Downtime** link from the menu on the left. The following is a screenshot of the page:

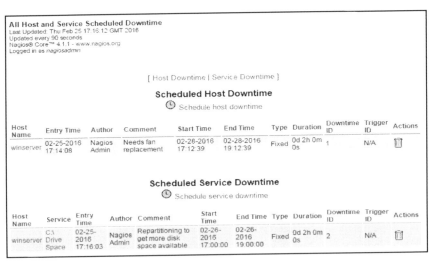

The page consists of two pages of all the scheduled downtimes, separately for hosts and services. You can delete a downtime by clicking the trash icon on the right in the row that describes this particular downtime entry.

Downtimes can be triggered by other downtimes. When a host downtime is scheduled, Nagios automatically adds downtimes for all child hosts.

Scheduling downtimes

In order to schedule a downtime, open a **Host Information** or **Service Information** page and use the **Schedule downtime for this host** or **Schedule downtime for this service** option. It is also possible to use the Downtime page to schedule downtimes directly. In that case, you will need to know the host name and service description of the service you want to disable as Nagios will not fill these in automatically.

The following is a screenshot of scheduling downtime for the HTTP service:

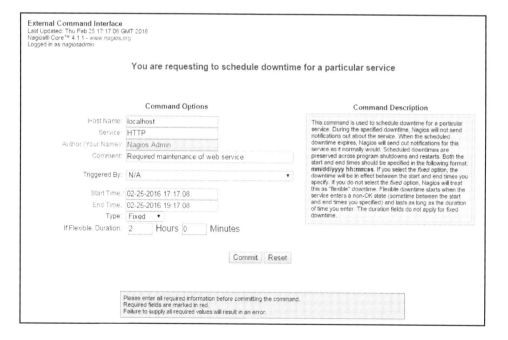

The form consists of the host and service name, a comment, and an optional option list to choose a downtime that triggered this host/service to also be down. When specifying time during which the downtime should be scheduled, it is possible to enter **Start Time** and **End Time** or use the **Duration** field. If you want to specify how long the offline will take, choose **Flexible** in the **Type** field. Otherwise choose **Fixed** to specify the start and end time.

Scheduling downtime for a host is very similar; the only differences are that the **Service** field is not available and the **Child Hosts** option list is added to specify how child hosts should be handled.

Nagios can automatically schedule downtimes for child hosts. When scheduling a host downtime, an additional option is present on whether child hosts should also be scheduled for downtime and set to be triggered by this downtime.

Managing comments

Nagios allows putting one or more comments associated with a host or a service. These can be anything from *Third machine from the top on the left shelf* to *Reset button not working*. Nagios also adds comments automatically in several cases, for example, when an object is scheduled for downtime a comment about it is placed.

Comments associated with a specific object are shown on the host and service detail information pages. They can also be added and removed from these pages.

Nagios also offers a page that allows managing comments for all hosts and services, similar to managing scheduled downtimes. It allows adding and deleting comments for all hosts. You can also navigate to the host or service detailed information page by clicking on an object name. The page can be accessed via the **Comments** link from the menu on the left.

The following is a screenshot of the comments page:

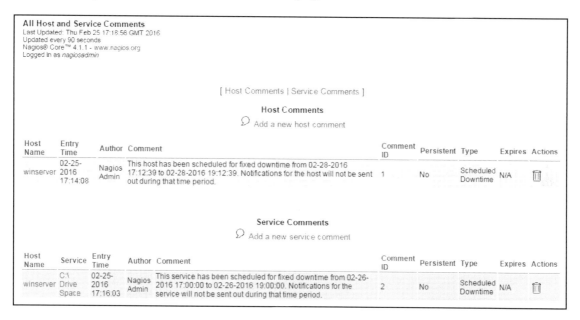

Clicking on the trash icon next to any comment will delete it. Adding a comment can be done by clicking on a host or service name and then doing so from the detailed information page or by clicking above the table with comments. In the latter case, you will need to specify the host name and service description in the add comment form.

Nagios information

The web interface allows us to check the Nagios daemon status along with general information on features enabled and disabled. It also allows to check the performance information related to Nagios. This can be used to make sure that your Nagios is not overloaded with checks to perform as well as see how much time checks take and how often they're performed.

Viewing process information

The **Nagios Process Information** page shows generic information about the Nagios process. It also allows performing several actions from the **Process Commands** panel. This page can be accessed via the **Process Info** link from the menu on the left.

The following is a screenshot of the page:

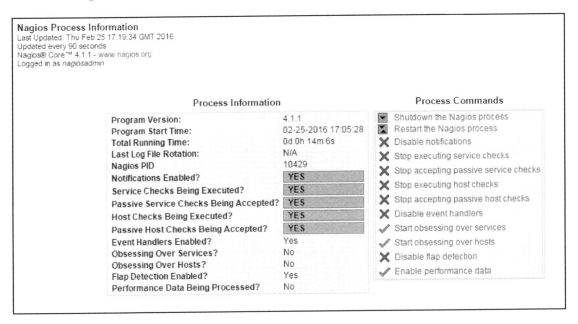

The page contains information on the Nagios version, process ID, status, and log rotation. It also shows whether checks, notifications, and many other functions are enabled.

The menu on the right also allows us to stop and restart the Nagios daemon. It also allows us to enable and disable performing checks by sending notifications. Flap detection and performance data processing can also be turned on or off from this page.

Checking performance information

The **Program-Wide Performance Information** page shows information about the performance and load of the Nagios process. This page can be accessed via the **Performance Info** link in the menu on the left.

The following is a screenshot of the page:

Performance Information
Last Updated: Thu Feb 25 17:20:06 GMT 2016
Updated every 90 seconds
Nagios® Core™ 4.1.1 - www.nagios.org
Logged in as *nagiosadmin*

Program-Wide Performance Information

Services Actively Checked:

Time Frame	Services Checked		Metric	Min.	Max.	Average
<= 1 minute:	4 (22.2%)		Check Execution Time:	0.00 sec	4.01 sec	0.672 sec
<= 5 minutes:	12 (66.7%)		Check Latency:	0.00 sec	0.00 sec	0.000 sec
<= 15 minutes:	18 (100.0%)		Percent State Change:	0.00%	11.05%	2.93%
<= 1 hour:	18 (100.0%)					
Since program start:	18 (100.0%)					

Services Passively Checked:

Time Frame	Services Checked		Metric	Min.	Max.	Average
<= 1 minute:	0 (0.0%)		Percent State Change:	0.00%	0.00%	0.00%
<= 5 minutes:	0 (0.0%)					
<= 15 minutes:	0 (0.0%)					
<= 1 hour:	0 (0.0%)					
Since program start:	0 (0.0%)					

Hosts Actively Checked:

Time Frame	Hosts Checked		Metric	Min.	Max.	Average
<= 1 minute:	0 (0.0%)		Check Execution Time:	4.00 sec	4.01 sec	4.003 sec
<= 5 minutes:	3 (75.0%)		Check Latency:	0.00 sec	0.00 sec	0.000 sec
<= 15 minutes:	4 (100.0%)		Percent State Change:	0.00%	4.80%	1.20%
<= 1 hour:	4 (100.0%)					
Since program start:	4 (100.0%)					

Hosts Passively Checked:

Time Frame	Hosts Checked		Metric	Min.	Max.	Average
<= 1 minute:	0 (0.0%)		Percent State Change:	0.00%	0.00%	0.00%
<= 5 minutes:	0 (0.0%)					
<= 15 minutes:	0 (0.0%)					
<= 1 hour:	0 (0.0%)					
Since program start:	0 (0.0%)					

Check Statistics:

Type	Last 1 Min	Last 5 Min	Last 15 Min
Active Scheduled Host Checks	0	3	10
Active On-Demand Host Checks	0	0	0
Parallel Host Checks	0	3	10
Serial Host Checks	0	0	0
Cached Host Checks	0	0	0
Passive Host Checks	0	0	0
Active Scheduled Service Checks	3	14	42
Active On-Demand Service Checks	0	0	0
Cached Service Checks	0	0	0
Passive Service Checks	0	0	0
External Commands	0	1	2

Buffer Usage:

Type	In Use	Max Used	Total Available
External Commands	0	0	0

The page contains information on the number of host and service checks performed within various periods of time as well as the number of reports received from external applications. It also contains a number of commands received from external applications; this usually means the web interface.

The page also contains information on average check execution times as well as latencies. This information is useful to determine if the Nagios process is not overloaded. If the average latency is above 60 seconds or is constantly growing then this means that Nagios is not able to perform all of the checks. In such cases, it is a good idea to increase the check or notification intervals so that the number of commands Nagios runs is lower.

Generating reports

One of the most important features of the web interface is the ability to create reports. Many large companies need these reports to make decisions at higher management levels; however, even smaller ones can benefit from it. The reporting functionality can also be used to browse historical notifications and alerts and see complete logs from a specified period.

Nagios offers the following types of reports:

- **Trend reporting for host or service:** This shows state history changes for a single object along with status information from performed checks
- **Availability report for hosts or services:** This shows reports on how much time an object has spent in a particular status; it can report all objects or a single object; it can also generate reports for host groups and service groups

- **Alert histogram:** This shows the number of alerts that have occurred over a period of time for a particular host or service

In addition, Nagios can report a history of alerts, notifications, or all events. This can be considered for reading Nagios logs in a more convenient way. It allows reading history either for all hosts and/or services as well as for a specific object. The logs are also formatted in a more readable way.

Generating most reports begins with choosing the report type, then the object type of the host, host group, service, or service group. Then either all or a specific object is chosen for which the report will be generated.

Next, a form for specifying the period for which a report should be generated along with many additional options, which can be dependent on the type of report that should be generated. Additionally, a time period can be specified so that the report only includes specific time periods such as working hours.

The following is a screenshot of a sample form for specifying parameters to a report, the actual fields might vary depending on the type of report you want to generate:

Hostgroup Availability Report
Last Updated: Thu Feb 25 17:22:58 GMT 2016
Nagios® Core™ 4.1.1 - www.nagios.org
Logged in as *nagiosadmin*

Step 3: Select Report Options

Report Period:	Last 7 Days ▼
If Custom Report Period...	
Start Date (Inclusive):	February ▼ 1 2016
End Date (Inclusive):	February ▼ 25 2016
Report time Period:	None ▼
Assume Initial States:	Yes ▼
Assume State Retention:	Yes ▼
Assume States During Program Downtime:	Yes ▼
Include Soft States:	No ▼
First Assumed Host State:	Unspecified ▼
First Assumed Service State:	Unspecified ▼
Backtracked Archives (To Scan For Initial States):	4
	Create Availability Report!

After specifying the parameters to the form and submitting it, the web interface will generate a report that matches your criteria. Some types of report also allow us to export the information into the CSV format for further analysis. For trend history report, it is also possible to zoom in or out in order to customize the period for which the report is generated.

The following is a screenshot of the availability report of all hosts. It shows how much time all hosts have been up, down, or unreachable due to parent machines not being up:

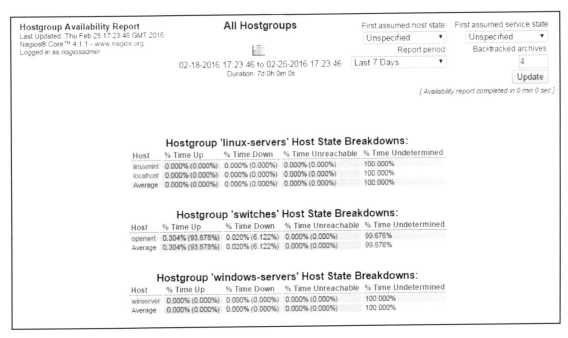

The report shows information for all hosts as a table along with the summary of overall availability.

It is possible to change the parameters of a report after it has been first generated to modify the reported period or information.

Changing the look of the Nagios web interface

Although the main focus of the web interface is its functionality and not its look, there is a possibility to change the way how it presents. The Nagios source code comes with two themes—**exfoliation** and **classical**. So far, all of the screenshots in this chapter have been prepared using the exfoliation theme, which is the default theme for Nagios since *version 3.3.1.*

The classical theme was the default for all Nagios versions up to *version 3.2.3*. To install the classical theme, we need to run the following command from the Nagios source code directory:

```
make install-classicui
```

This will install the classical theme and overwrite the theme currently installed for the Nagios web interface. After the command succeeds, the interface will look more familiar to people who use or have used Nagios *version 3.2.3* or older.

Depending on your preferences, you may choose to use the new default theme or use the classical one. Apart from a different look and feel, there is no difference in the Nagios UI features or behaviors. The GUI has the exact menu on the left as the theme installed by default, and all of the operations such as scheduling downtime, managing comments, and generating reports are performed in same way.

The **Tactical Monitoring Overview** page looks significantly different than the one from the exfoliation theme:

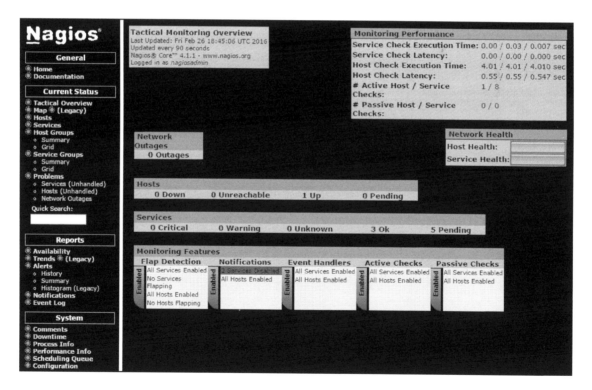

Also, the status pages for services and hosts look different than the ones shown before.

The following is a screenshot of the classic UI theme showing the services status:

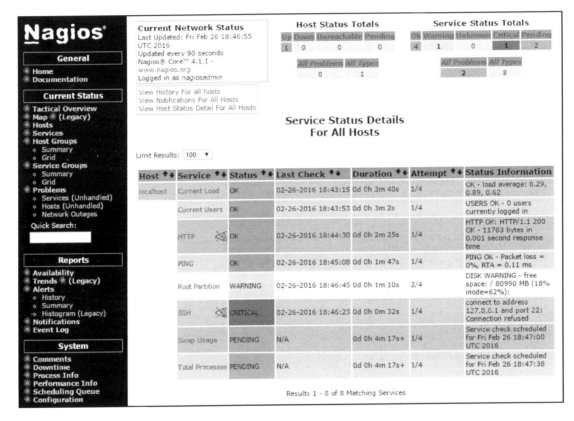

In order to install the exfoliation theme again, all that is needed is to run the following command from Nagios source code repository:

```
make install-exfoliation
```

This will restore the exfoliation theme that is installed by default with Nagios 4, and the GUI will now look same as before installing the classical theme.

 Here are also multiple additional themes available on Nagios Exchange at:
http://exchange.nagios.org/directory/Addons/Frontends-(GUIs-an
d-CLIs)/Web-Interfaces/Themes-and-Skins
When choosing a theme, be sure to verify that it is compatible with your version of Nagios.

One of the themes that work properly with Nagios 4 is the Arana theme. It is listed on Nagios Exchange and available directly from SourceForge at
http://sourceforge.net/projects/arana-nagios/

While the following instructions were written and tested against the latest Nagios version (4.1.1 at the time of writing), the steps should work for all Nagios versions. In case of any problems, it is recommended that you check the installation guide for the theme for any changes in the installation procedure.

1. The first thing we should do is to back up our Nagios web interface directory /opt/nagios/share, when installing Nagios according to the steps documented in Chapter 2, *Installing Nagios 4*

   This can be done using the following command:

   ```
   cp -pfR /opt/nagios/share /opt/nagios/share-backup
   ```

2. We need to download and unpack the theme. The link to download the theme can be found both on Nagios Exchange and on the SourceForge arana-nagios project. We'll need to download the archive and unpack it anywhere on the disk.

3. Next, copy the entire contents of the directory containing the unpacked Arana theme archive to /opt/nagios/share.

4. After this step, the theme should be properly installed and the Nagios page should look similar to the following screenshot:

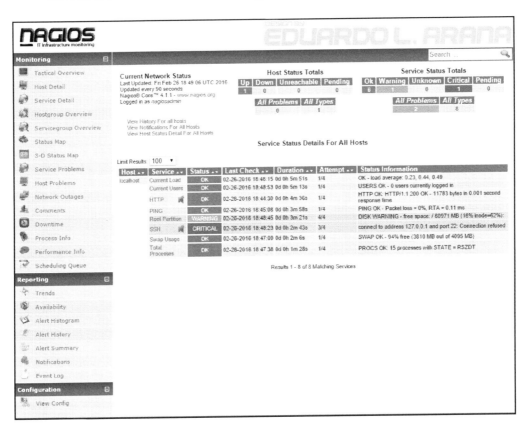

For most themes, the installation should be the same—extract it and copy its contents to the directory containing the Nagios web interface files.

Themes also usually come with readme or install text files that document the exact installation process; when installing a theme for the first time, it is recommended that you start by reading these files.

Not all Nagios themes and skins that were created for older versions of Nagios will work with Nagios 4. An improved web interface uses PHP for formatting of the templates while previous versions used static HTML pages and this may cause issues with themes not taking this into account.

Summary

The Nagios web interface is an easy and powerful tool for getting important information from our monitoring software. It allows us to drill down from the top-level overview to the detailed status of any host or service. We can access logs and generate reports, and thanks to the fact that it is web-based, all of it is within reach from virtually any place in the world. All that is required is a web browser and network connection toward our Nagios system.

You learned the following items:

- Checking the overall status with Tactical Overview
- Managing hosts and services
- Scheduling downtimes and adding comments
- Viewing Nagios information and generating reports

In this chapter, we used the built-in, available, and out-of-the-box Nagios Web interface. The Nagios ecosystem is far richer than this, so the next chapter will introduce other interfaces of various types (web, command line, and mobile) that are available for us to use.

5
Using Additional Interfaces

The previous chapter introduced the standard Nagios web interface and presented some insights on how it can be used to view the status and manage Nagios.

As with many popular projects, apart from the standard "official" web interface, there are many ways in which users can interact with Nagios—depending on their needs and connectivity options.

In this chapter, you will learn about other ways the Nagios status can be checked as well as how Nagios itself can be managed.

This chapter will cover the following items:

- Using third-party web interfaces
- Learning command line interfaces
- Using mobile applications to see the Nagios status

Introducing third-party web interfaces

In addition to the default web interface, Nagios can be managed using other web-based interfaces. A wide choice of additional web interfaces can be found on Nagios Exchange at:

```
http://exchange.nagios.org/directory/Addons/Frontends-(GUIs-and-CLIs)/Web-In
terfaces
```

Nagios Exchange, is a community website that lists various types of plugins and extensions for Nagios. It contains additional tools, web interfaces as well as plugins to perform checks.

In this section, we will cover some types of GUIs that can be used on top of Nagios—including dashboards that show the overall status of all Nagios hosts and services, visualization tools that show historical information gathered by Nagios as well as other web interfaces that are meant to replace or complement the built-in one.

Using Nagios dashboards

Many of the GUIs available on Nagios Exchange are dashboards. These show statuses for hosts, services, and errors. The dashboards are often supposed to be presented on a large display, such as a TV, so that the IT department can easily monitor the status of the infrastructure and identify problems that need to be fixed.

One example of a dashboard interface is called **Nagios Dashboard**. It is a small PHP script that shows the statuses of hosts and services. The dashboard first shows all hosts and services that have errors, such as with the Critical status.

The plugin can be found on Nagios Exchange at: `http://exchange.nagios.org/directory/Addons/Frontends-%28GUIs-and-CLIs%29/Web-Interfaces/Nagios-Dashboard--2D-PHP/details`

The entire interface is a single file. To install it, we simply need to unpack and copy the `nagios.php` file to any location, such as to `/opt/nagios/share`.

Next, if Nagios was installed according to the steps documented in `Chapter 2`, *Installing Nagios 4*, then we need to change the path to the `status.dat` file to point to our location, which is inside the `/var/nagios/` directory. To do this, we need to edit the file and change the third line to the following:

```
$file = fopen("/var/nagios/status.dat", "r") or exit("Unable  to open
file!"); //path to nagios file
```

We can then check the report by navigating to the appropriate URL; if the file was copied to `/opt/nagios/share`, it will be available at `http://localhost/nagios/nagios.php`.

Blue - Down		Yellow - Warning	Green - UP/OK	Grey - Disabled
Last Checked	**Host**	**Status Info**		**Service**
2013-10-06 19:42:00	windows7	CRITICAL - Socket timeout after 10 seconds		CPU Load
2013-10-06 19:42:05	windows7	PING CRITICAL - Packet loss = 100%		PING
2013-10-06 19:42:10	windows7	PING CRITICAL - Packet loss = 100%		HOST PING
2013-10-06 19:43:07	localhost	PING OK - Packet loss = 0%, RTA = 0.12 ms		HOST PING
2013-10-06 19:41:55	localserver	PING OK - Packet loss = 0%, RTA = 1.61 ms		HOST PING
2013-10-06 19:43:24	router	PING OK - Packet loss = 0%, RTA = 2.34 ms		HOST PING
2013-10-06 19:39:33	router-upc	PING WARNING - Packet loss = 93%, RTA = 13.09 ms		HOST PING
2013-10-06 19:42:01	localhost	APT OK: 0 packages available for upgrade (0 critical updates).		APT
2013-10-06 19:38:55	localhost	DISK OK - free space: / 21253 MB (92% inode=93%):		Disk
2013-10-06 19:40:30	localhost	SMTP OK - 0.003 sec. response time		SMTP
2013-10-06 19:42:55	localhost	SSH OK - OpenSSH_5.9p1 Debian-5ubuntu1.1 (protocol 2.0)		SSH
2013-10-06 19:36:33	localhost	HTTP OK: HTTP/1.1 200 OK - 453 bytes in 0.001 second response time		www
2013-10-06 19:38:25	localserver	SMTP OK - 5.009 sec. response time		SMTP
2013-10-06 19:43:50	localserver	SSH OK - OpenSSH_5.3p1 Debian-3ubuntu7 (protocol 2.0)		SSH
2013-10-06 19:37:23	router	PING OK - Packet loss = 0%, RTA = 2.20 ms		PING
2013-10-06 19:41:50	router-upc	PING OK - Packet loss = 0%, RTA = 12.45 ms		PING

There are many other dashboards for Nagios available at Nagios Exchange, such as **Nagios Dash**, which is a project based on Nagios Dashboard and they are quite similar.

Installing alternative Nagios web interfaces

There are also projects offering a more complete web interface, meant to complement or replace the Nagios web interface. A good example of such a project is **Nagios V-Shell**. It is a web interface that provides most of the features of the original Nagios GUI.

It is created in PHP, is designed to be lightweight, and does not use frames, which makes it more convenient to use on mobile devices. It is available for download on Nagios Exchange at http://exchange.nagios.org/directory/Addons/Frontends-%28GUIs-and-CLIs%29/Web-Interfaces/Nagios-V-2DShell/details

The project is also available at GitHub from `https://github.com/NagiosEnterprises/nagiosvshell/`

It requires Apache and PHP, which we have already set up for the Nagios web interface. It also requires **APC**, a caching mechanism for PHP. The `php-cli` command is also required to run the installation script for V-Shell.

To install the required dependencies, simply run the following command for Ubuntu:

```
# apt-get install php-apc php5-cli
```

Use the following command for RedHat/CentOS:

```
# yum install php-pecl-apc php-cli
```

The installation of V-Shell itself is very simple. After downloading and unpacking the archive, we need to edit the `config/vshell.conf` and `config/vshell_apache.conf` configuration files.

For Nagios installation, according to the steps documented in Chapter 2, *Installing Nagios 4*, the `config/vshell.conf` file should have the following values set for each of the variables in the file:

```
STATUSFILE = "/var/nagios/status.dat"
OBJECTSFILE = "/var/nagios/objects.cache"
CGICFG = "/etc/nagios/cgi.cfg"
NAGCMD = "/var/nagios/rw/nagios.cmd"
NAGLOCK = "/var/nagios/nagios.lock"
```

We also need to change the location of the `htpasswd.users` file in `config/vshell_apache.conf`. It should be as follows:

```
AuthUserFile /etc/nagios/htpasswd.users
```

For Debian and Ubuntu, we will also need to replace the `/etc/apache2/conf.d` path with `/etc/apache2/conf-available` in the `config.php` file as well as `/etc/nagios3/htpasswd.users` to `/etc/nagios/htpasswd.users`.

By default, the package will install itself to `/usr/local/vshell`. This can be changed by editing the `config.php` and `config/vshell_apache.conf` files by replacing all references to `/usr/local/vshell` with the installation directory such as `/opt/nagios/vshell`.

For the `config.php` file, there are multiple references. In the `config/vshell_apache.conf` file, change the first lines to:

```
Alias /vshell "/opt/nagios/vshell"

<Directory "/opt/nagios/vshell">
(...)
```

We can now install V-Shell by running the following command:

```
# php-cli install.php
```

This will run the installation script. It will automatically copy all the files and add the Apache configuration file to the appropriate directory.

For Debian and Ubuntu, we'll also need to explicitly enable the vshell configuration file by running:

```
# a2enconf vshell
```

After that, it is recommended that you restart Apache by running the following command:

```
# service apache2 restart
```

Now, V-Shell should be available at `http://127.0.0.1/vshell/`, as shown here:

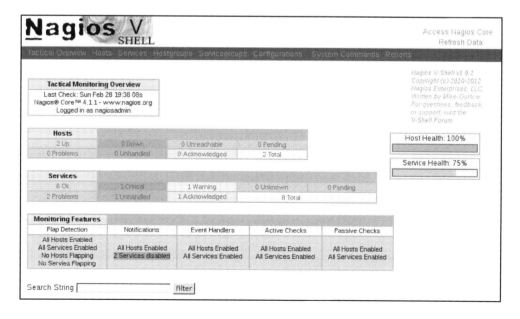

The V-Shell interface is very similar to the Nagios web interface; the main differences are that it does not use frames and the menu is shown on the top rather than on the left. The menu is also a drop-down menu, and hovering over one of the menu items shows a list of available elements.

V-Shell offers most of the views available in the standard web interface for Nagios, such as showing host details and all of the information related to host management.

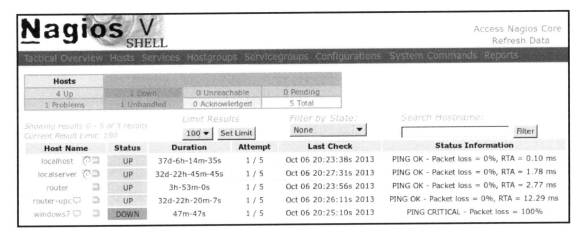

Similarly, the **Services** views also strongly resemble the original Nagios web interface.

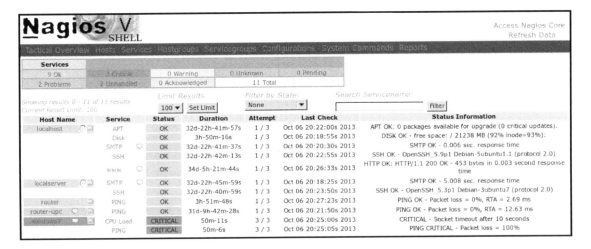

Nagios V-Shell provides views for most of the options available in the standard web interface. It also uses JavaScript for many operations, which makes it faster than the standard web interface. This is especially important for mobile devices that often have slower network connectivity.

Viewing performance data with nagiosgraph

Nagiosgraph is a very popular open source project that integrates with Nagios and generates graph data for all monitored hosts and services. The tool integrates with Nagios to store the history of the performance data and provides RRDtool-based graphs for visualizing the data. The project is written in Perl and can be found at:

```
http://nagiosgraph.sourceforge.net
```

Nagiosgraph works with any plugin that returns output including the performance data-this includes all of the standard Nagios plugins and many of the plugins available online. It also does not require any changes to the configuration of the objects themselves, and only small changes in the Nagios configuration are required.

To install Nagiosgraph we first need to install prerequisites, such as Perl, RRDtool, and Perl libraries for GD and RRD libraries. RRDtool is an open source data logging and graphing tool that is commonly used for creating graphs of time series data; more details can be found at:

```
http://www.rrdtool.org/
```

For Debian/Ubuntu distributions the command to install all the prerequisites is:

```
# apt-get -y install rrdtool perl libgd-perl librrds-perl
```

For RedHat/CentOS the command is:

```
# yum -y install rrdtool perl perl-GD perl-Digest-MD5 rrdtool-perl perl-CGI
```

Next, we'll need to download the tarball with Nagiosgraph sources from `https://sourcef orge.net/projects/nagiosgraph/files/` and unpack it using the following command:

```
# curl -sSL
https://sourceforge.net/projects/nagiosgraph/files/latest/download | tar -
xzv
```

Next, we'll need to go to the Nagiosgraph source directory and run the installer script. The following is an example for installing Nagiosgraph version 1.5.2 (the latest version at the time of writing this book):

```
# cd nagiosgraph-1.5.2
# perl install.pl
```

The installation will check for prerequisites, locate Nagios, and perform the installation. The installation script will work out-of-the-box for the Nagios installation and is performed according to instructions in Chapter 2, *Installing Nagios 4*.

Next, we'll need to add additional configuration options, such as a new command to send data to Nagiosgraph and additional options for Nagios to pass the data.

First, let's create the /etc/nagios/nagiosgraph.cfg file with the following contents:

```
define command {
  command_name process-service-perfdata-for-nagiosgraph
  command_line /usr/local/nagiosgraph/bin/insert.pl
}
```

This will create a command to pass data to Nagiosgraph.

The path in command_line should point to the bin/insert.pl script inside the directory where Nagiosgraph was installed-/usr/local/nagiosgraph-the default installation path.

Next let's add the following to the Nagios main configuration file-/etc/nagios/nagios.cfg:

```
cfg_file=/etc/nagios/nagiosgraph.cfg
process_performance_data=1
service_perfdata_file=/tmp/perfdata.log
service_perfdata_file_template=$LASTSERVICECHECK$||$HOSTNAME$||$SERVICEDESC$||$SERVICEOUTPUT$||$SERVICEPERFDATA$
service_perfdata_file_mode=a
service_perfdata_file_processing_interval=30
service_perfdata_file_processing_command=process-service-perfdata-for-nagiosgraph
```

The first line includes the newly created /etc/nagios/nagiosgraph.cfg file. The next options enable the processing of the performance data by Nagios and specify how to pass the information. This is the format that Nagiosgraph expects and is command defined in Nagios configuration that instructs Nagiosgraph to process the data.

After that, we should restart Nagios using one of the following commands:

```
service nagios restart
/etc/init.d/nagios restart
```

From now on, Nagios will pass the data to Nagiosgraph and periodically run the `insert.pl` script that stores the performance data.

Finally, we need to add the Apache 2 configuration to the alias `/nagiosgraph` URL prefix. This should be added to the same file where the Nagios Apache 2 configuration is stored, which can be `/etc/apache2/conf-available/nagios.conf` or `/etc/httpd/conf.d/nagios.conf` depending on the Linux distribution. The content to add is as follows:

```
# enable nagiosgraph CGI scripts
ScriptAlias /nagiosgraph/cgi-bin "/usr/local/nagiosgraph/cgi"
<Directory "/usr/local/nagiosgraph/cgi">
   Options ExecCGI
   AllowOverride None
   Require all granted
</Directory>
# enable nagiosgraph CSS and JavaScript
Alias /nagiosgraph "/usr/local/nagiosgraph/share"
<Directory "/usr/local/nagiosgraph/share">
   Options None
   AllowOverride None
   Require all granted
</Directory>
```

The `/usr/local/nagiosgraph` path should be changed if a nondefault installation directory was used.

Now, we need to restart Apache. Depending on the Linux distribution one of the following commands will restart Apache:

```
apachectl restart
service apache2 restart
service httpd restart
```

Now, Nagiosgraph should be available from `http://(ip-address)/nagiosgraph/cgi-bin/show.cgi`, where `(ip-address)` should be the IP address of the Nagios server.

We can now visit the page. It will provide us with a selector for host and service in the top-right corner and when host and service is selected, it will show the performance data graphs for the last day, week, month, and year.

The following is an example for a system load graph:

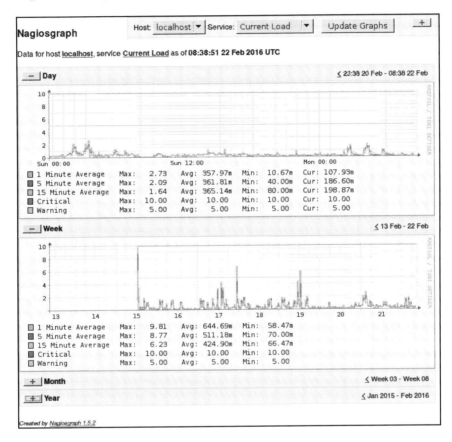

Graphs support zooming in and out using the mouse. To zoom in, simply select a range to zoom in using the left mouse button. The graph will zoom in to that data. To zoom out, simply click the right mouse button.

It is also possible to add a link to view the Nagiosgraph data for any service directly from the Nagios built-in web interface. To do this, simply add an `action_url` directive to a service definition in the Nagios configuration as shown here:

```
define service {
  name nagiosgraph
  action_url /nagiosgraph/cgi-bin/show.cgi?
  host=$HOSTNAME$&service=$SERVICEDESC$
  register 0
}
```

This will create a generic service template with the `action_url` directive that can be included in services.

Next, we can add the `nagiosgraph` template to services that should have the action link shown as:

```
define service {
  use generic-service,nagiosgraph
  (...)
}
```

This will show a link next to the service in the Nagios built-in web interface that will link to the Nagiosgraph view for that service.

For example, here is how a sample configuration looks with the `action_url` directive added; the link is shown as the graph icon to the right of the service name:

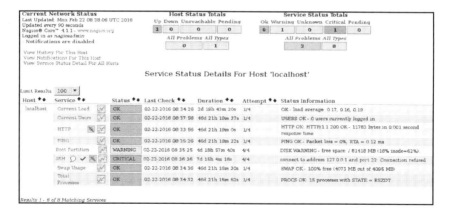

Learning command-line interfaces

So far, we have discussed using web-based applications to view the current status and manage things such as downtimes or comments.

There are also multiple tools that let us perform the same operations from the command line in a convenient way.

Using nagios_commander

One tool that provides an easy way to manage Nagios and view its data from command line is **nagios_commander**.

This is a shell script that communicates with Nagios using the web interface, using HTTP-based authentication. Since it is communicating over the network, the script can be run on any machine, not only on the machine where Nagios is running. It can also be used to manage multiple Nagios instances from a single machine.

All that is needed is to have the curl command available on your machine. For Ubuntu-based distributions, we'll need to run the following command:

```
root@ubuntu:~# apt-get -y install bsdmainutils curl
```

For CentOS, RHEL, and Oracle Linux, the command is:

```
[rootcentos ~]# yum install -y curl
```

Next, all that we have to do is download the nagios_commander script using the following commands:

```
root@ubuntu:~# curl -sSL
https://raw.github.com/brandoconnor/nagios_commander/master/nagios_commande
r.sh >/usr/local/bin/nagios_commander
root@ubuntu:~# chmod 0755 /usr/local/bin/nagios_commander
```

After that nagios_commander will work properly.

The command takes the URL to the Nagios web interface and the username and password from the command line using the -n, -u and -p arguments, respectively:

```
# nagios_commander -n 127.0.0.1/nagios -u nagiosadmin -p nagiosadmin \
-q list -h
Hostname        Status
linuxbox01      UP
localhost       UP
```

The preceding command will list all hosts on our Nagios instance and print their status. The `-q list -h` command indicates a list of hosts that will be printed, and will be described in more detail later in this section.

It is also a good idea to create an alias or a helper script that will not require passing the location, username, and password on each invocation.

```
# alias ncmd='nagios_commander -n 127.0.0.1/nagios -u nagiosadmin -p
nagiosadmin'
```

To be able to use it in all shells and not just the current one, the alias can be put in shell initialization scripts, such as `.bash_aliases`, in your home directory if you are using the bash shell.

This way we can simply call:

```
# ncmd -q list -h
```

Also, this should return the same result as the original command we invoked earlier.

The **nagios_commander** allows specifying a context for which a command is run. If not specified (or specified as an empty value for -h option), the context is global.

It is possible to run commands for specific hosts and hostgroups using the `-h` and `-H` options, respectively. The first one specifies that a specific host should be used. The `-H` option allows querying a specific hostgroup. For example, the `-q list -h localhost` command indicates that services for the host localhost should be shown.

```
# ncmd -q list -h localhost
Fetching services and health on localhost
---
Service            State
---
Current+Load       OK
Current+Users      OK
HTTP               OK
PING               OK
Root+Partition     OK
SSH                OK
Swap+Usage         OK
Total+Processes    OK
```

Similarly the `-H` option can be used to list the status of all hosts inside a hostgroup:

```
ncmd -q list -H linux-servers
Hostname        Status
localhost   UP
linuxbox01  UP
```

The `-s` option allow specifying services to run the query or command against. Similarly, the `-S` option can be used to run a command against a service group. These are only used when running commands to manage and/or acknowledge downtimes.

The `-q` option allows us to go information from Nagios. The following table shows the available query types:

Command	Contexts	Description
list	global, host	Lists all hosts or services, depending on the context
host_downtime	host	Lists host downtimes for all hosts or a specific host/hostgroup
service_downtime	service	Lists all service downtimes for all hosts, a specific host/hostgroup or for specific service/service group only
notifications	global	Shows whether notification sending is enabled
event_handlers	global	Shows whether running event handlers is enabled
active_svc_checks	global	Shows whether performing active service checks is enabled
active_host_checks	global	Shows whether performing active host checks is enabled
passive_svc_checks	global	Shows whether accepting passive service check results is enabled
passive_host_checks	global	Shows whether accepting passive host check results is enabled

Event handlers and notifications are described in more detail in Chapter 8, *Notifications and Events*. The concept of passive checks is explained in more detail in Chapter 9, *Passive Checks and NRDP*.

The -c option allows us to change Nagios settings and/or manage host and service downtimes from the command line. The first argument is the action to perform and the second argument is the scope. The flag also takes a third argument when the Nagios settings are to be changed.

To change any Nagios settings, the action has to be set and the scope should be notifications, event_handlers, active_svc_checks, active_host_checks, passive_svc_checks, or passive_host_checks. The third argument should either be enable or disable. For example, to disable or enable sending notifications we can run:

```
# ncmd -c set notifications disable
# ncmd -c set notifications enable
```

Another possibility is to manage downtimes. In this case, the action should either be set, del, or ack to add a downtime, delete it, or acknowledge a problem, respectively. The -h, -H, -s, and -S options can be used to specify the host, hostgroup, and service or service group the downtime is related to.

When adding downtime or acknowledging a problem, it is also required to specify a comment and planned downtime. The -C option is used to specify a comment, and the -t option specifies time in minutes.

For example, to add a downtime for two hours for the localhost host, we can use:

```
# ncmd -c add downtime -C "Planned downtime" -t 120 -h localhost
```

We can then check the downtime by running the following command:

```
# ncmd -q host_downtime
```

The output of the preceding command will be as follows:

```
Hostname   Downtime-id   End_date_and_time      Author        Comment
localhost      1         2-14-2016 20:49:46  Nagios Admin    Planned
                                                             downtime
```

The downtime id is the unique identifier of a downtime. In order to delete a downtime, we need to know its id and delete it using the del action:

```
# ncmd -c del downtime -d 1
```

This will delete a downtime with id 1.

The `ack` action can be invoked in order to acknowledge a problem. The command itself does not require any additional argument; the only required flag is `-C` to indicate the comment for acknowledgement, as shown here:

```
# ncmd -c ack -h localhost -s SSH -C "SSH upgrade in progress, will be up
soon"
```

This will add a new acknowledgement for service SSH on localhost.

Interacting with nagios-cli

Another command-line-based tool is **nagios-cli**, which provides a shell-like interface for Nagios. This is an open source project, whose homepage is `http://nagios-cli.maze.io/` and its source code is in GitHub at `https://github.com/tehmaze/nagios-cli`. This tool reads the Nagios status file and sends commands using the Nagios pipe. It has to be run on the same machine or container where the Nagios service is running.

To install nagios-cli, we first need to install the prerequisites, which include Python, pip tool for installing the Python package, `readline` library, and development packages for those as well as Git to be able to retrieve nagios-cli itself.

On Debian and Ubuntu, the command to install the prerequisites is:

```
root@ubuntu:~# apt-get -y install patch python python-pip libpython-dev
libncurses-dev libreadline-dev git
```

For CentOS, RHEL, and Oracle Linux, the command is:

```
[root@centos ~]# yum install -y patch python python-devel python-pip git
readline-devel
```

Installing nagios-cli also requires some of the prerequisites for building Nagios. If the machine where nagios-cli will be run does not have them, it is recommended that you install them as well. The dependencies for different Linux distributions are described in more details in `Chapter 2`, *Installing Nagios 4*.

The next step is to install the readline Python package by running pip:

```
# pip install readline
```

After that, we can retrieve the nagios-cli source package by running the following command:

```
# git clone https://github.com/tehmaze/nagios-cli.git
```

This will retrieve the latest version of source code in a new directory called nagios-cli. We now need to install it by running:

```
# cd nagios-cli ; python setup.py install
```

This will install the nagios-cli binary into the /usr/local/bin directory. Next, we need to create a configuration file in /etc/nagios/nagios-cli.cfg with the following contents:

```
[nagios]
log                     = /var/nagios
command_file            = %(log)s/rw/nagios.cmd
log_file                = %(log)s/nagios.log
object_cache_file       = %(log)s/objects.cache
status_file             = %(log)s/status.dat
```

This will specify nagios-cli where the Nagios data is kept. Next, we can run the tool using the following command:

```
# nagios-cli -c /etc/nagios/nagios-cli.cfg
```

This will start the interactive shell. The shell accepts commands similar to any other Unix shell, as commands and arguments separated by space. It also supports tab-based expansion of arguments, such as for host and service commands, where it will auto expand host and service names, respectively.

The tool also provides the help command which provides all currently available commands. For example:

```
nagios > help
Global commands:
  ..        EOF       about     configure exit      help      host
license     quit      tail
Local commands:
list        ls
```

We can now issue the ls or list command to list hosts. For example:

```
nagios > ls
linuxbox01   localhost
```

This will list all the hosts currently configured in Nagios. In this example, this includes linuxbox01 and localhost.

To change the context to a specific host, simply call the `host` command by providing the name of a host. The `ls` or `list` command will list all services, and the `service` command can be used for changing the context to a specific service for a specific host. Commands `..` or the `EOF` commands can be used to go back to global context.

For example:

```
nagios > host localhost
nagios (host) localhost> ls
Current-Load     Current-Users     HTTP           PING
Root-Partition   SSH               Swap-Usage     Total-Processes
nagios (host) localhost> service SSH
nagios (host) localhost  SSH> ..
nagios (host) localhost > ..
nagios >
```

When in the context of a host or service, the `status` command will report information about the current host and/or service, as shown here:

```
nagios (host) localhost> status
host name             : localhost
current state         :  OK
plugin output         : PING OK - Packet loss = 0%, RTA = 0.10 ms
(...)
service               : SSH                 OK
service               : Swap Usage          OK
service               : Total Processes     OK
nagios (host) localhost> service SSH
nagios (host) localhost  SSH> status
host name             : localhost
service description : SSH
current state         :  OK
(...)
```

The preceding example shows only partial output from the status commands.

The `check` and `acknowledge` commands can be used to check the current status and acknowledge a problem for the current host or service. For example:

```
nagios (host) localhost  SSH> check
Service check scheduled
nagios (host) localhost  SSH> acknowledge
comment         : Reinstalling service
sticky      [Yn]: n
notify      [Yn]: n
persistent [Yn]: n
Service problem acknowledged
```

The following table shows key commands available in nagios-cli:

Command	Contexts	Description
help	Always	Provides a list of commands valid in the current scope
host	Always	Changes the context to a specific host
service	Host	Changes the context to a specific service in the current host
..	Host or service	Returns to the preceding context, that is from the service context to the host context or from host to global
EOF	Host or service	Returns to the preceding context, that is from the service context to the host context or from host to global
status	Host or service	Prints the detailed status for a host or service
check	Host or service	Forces a check to be made for a host or service
acknowledge	Host or service	Acknowledges a problem for a host or service

Using mobile applications to check the Nagios status

Another interesting aspect of Nagios is its ability to check the status from a mobile device.

While it is possible to use the Nagios built-in web interface from a smartphone or tablet, there are mobile applications that show the status in a more convenient way as well as perform actions, such as adding comments, acknowledging a problem, and scheduling a check.

Usually, Nagios is only run inside local networks and not publicly available. Mobile applications require to communicate with Nagios from external networks. This may require either making the Nagios web server available on a public IP address or preferably using a **Virtual Private Network** (**VPN**) solution. Another option is only to use a Wi-Fi connection that is also local to the Nagios server. For the purpose of this section, we will assume that the mobile device can access the Nagios server.

While mobile interfaces do not usually offer the full functionality of the built-in web interface, it is much more convenient for use on a mobile device, and it is recommended that users especially those who are often on the move and are not always able to access the web interface from a computer, should be familiar with them.

Checking the status on iOS with easyNag

The easyNagapplication is a commercial solution for iOS to check the status for one or more Nagios instances as well as perform basic operations. The application can be found in the App Store and more details about it can be found on the application's website: `http://www.easynag.com/`.

The application communicates with the Nagios web interface. The first thing we need to do after setting it up is to add one or more Nagios instances.

This requires specifying the URL to the Nagios web interface, to be exact, it needs to be the path to `/nagios/cgi-bin/` such as `http://(ip-address)/nagios/cgi-bin/`. We also need to specify the username and password for the Nagios web interface so that the application can properly authenticate with Nagios.

The screenshot was provided as courtesy of the iNag author; `http://idevelop.fullnet.com/iapps /modules/apps/inag.php`.

The application also offers multiple views, such as only showing problems with hosts and services and filtering by many criteria, such as text and status type.

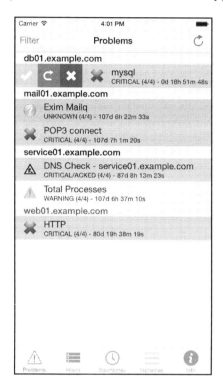

The screenshot was provided courtesy of the iNag author; `http://idevelop.fullnet.com/iapps/m odules/apps/inag.php`

It's also possible to perform basic tasks such as rescheduling a check, acknowledging a problem, and managing downtime. The following screenshot shows service details and the available actions:

This image was provided as courtesy of the iNag author; `http://idevelop.fullnet.com/i` `apps/modules/apps/inag.php`

Working with Nagios on Android using aNag

The aNagapplication is a free tool that can be used to check the Nagios status on Android-based phones and tablets as well as perform basic operations. The application can be found and installed from Google Play by looking it up. More information about it can be found on the aNag author's website: `https://damien.degois.info/android/aNag/`

Similar to easyNag, this application also communicates with the Nagios web interface. After installing it, all that is needed is to go to Settings and add one or more Nagios instances to check. This requires specifying the URL to the Nagios web interface, to be exact it needs to be the path to `/nagios/cgi-bin/` such as `http://(ip-address)/nagios/cgi-bin/`. We also need to specify the username and password for the Nagios web interface so that the application can properly authenticate with Nagios.

After the initial setup, the application will show the status of Nagios instances, hosts, and services as well as it will also allow us to check each instance as well as hosts and services on that instance. A sample overall view is as follows:

This image was provided as courtesy of the aNag author; source: `https://damien.degois.info/android/aNag/`.

The application also allows performing basic actions on the hosts and services, such as rescheduling a check, acknowledging issues, and setting downtimes:

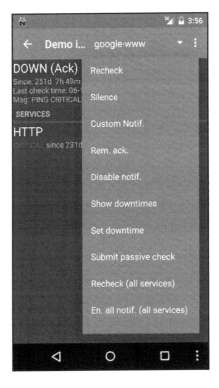

This image was provided as courtesy of the aNag author; source: `https://damien.degois.info/android/aNag/`.

Checking the status on Windows Phone with NagChecker

NagChecker is a Windows Phone 8 and Windows 10 Mobile application for showing the status of your Nagios instance web page.

Similar to easyNag and aNag, all that is required is to provide the URL and credentials to your Nagios instance. For NagChecker, the URL should be the path to status.cgi such as `http://(ip-address)/nagios/cgi-bin/`.

The following image was provided as courtesy of the NagChecker author; source: `http://p rogstudio.pl/en-us/home`

After setting up your instance, NagChecker can be used to see the overall status as well as detailed information about host and service problems. The following screenshot shows an instance overview:

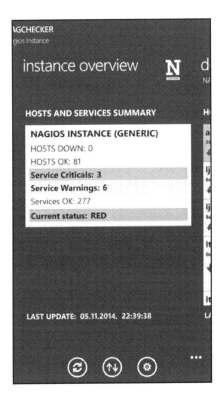

This image was provided as courtesy of the NagChecker author; http://progstudio.pl/en-us/home

Unfortunately, unlike aNag and easyNag, the application only allows us to show the status of hosts and not to perform any actions. It also does not allow adding multiple Nagios instances.

Summary

There are multiple additional interfaces to Nagios that can be used to check the status as well as perform typical operations, such as scheduling checks, acknowledging problems, adding comments, and scheduling downtime.

We have covered the following types of additional web interfaces:

- Dashboards for showing the overall Nagios status
- Visualizing performance data with Nagiosgraph
- Command line interfaces
- Checking the Nagios status from mobile devices

Chapter 6, *Using the Nagios Plugins,*will cover the standard set of Nagios plugins that allow us to perform checks of various services. We will go through monitoring standard services such as e-mail and web and database servers. You will also learn how to monitor resources such as CPU usage, storage, and memory usage.

6
Using the Nagios Plugins

The previous chapters discussed the basic configuration of host and service checking along with the description of the web interface. Nagios can be set up to check if your services are up and running. This chapter describes how these checks work in more detail. It also introduces some of the Nagios plugins that are developed as a part of Nagios and as a part of the **NagiosPlugins** project.

The strength of Nagios comes from its ability to monitor servers and services they offer in a large number of ways. What's more interesting is that all of these ways make sure that your services are provided as functional, are external plugins, and work in quite an easy way. Many of these are even shipped with Nagios, as we mentioned in `Chapter 2`, *Installing Nagios 4*, and `Chapter 3`, *Configuring Nagios*. Therefore, it is possible to either use the existing plugins or write your own.

In this chapter, you will learn the checks that can be made using the Nagios Plugins project, and we will cover the following items:

- Understanding how checks work
- Monitoring using the standard network plugins
- Monitoring the e-mail servers
- Monitoring network services
- Monitoring the database systems
- Monitoring the storage space
- Monitoring the resources
- Monitoring other operations
- Additional and third-party plugins

Understanding checks in Nagios

Nagios is a monitoring tool. It performs checks by running an external command and uses the return code along with output from the command as information on whether the check worked or not. It is the command's responsibility to verify if a host or service is working at the time the command is invoked.

Nagios itself handles all of the internals such as scheduling the commands to be run, storing their results, and determining what the status is for each host and service.

It is required that all plugins follow a specific behavior in order for them to work smoothly. These rules are common for both host and service checks. It requires that each command returns specific result codes, which are outlined in the following table:

Exit code	Status	Description
0	OK	Working correctly
1	WARNING	Working, but needs attention (for example, low resources)
2	CRITICAL	Not working correctly or requires attention
3	UNKNOWN	Plugin was unable to determine the status for the host or service

Standard output from the command is not parsed in any way by Nagios. It is usually formatted in the following way:

```
PLUGIN STATUS - status description
```

Usually, the status description contains human-readable information that is visible using the web interface. Some sample outputs from various plugins and states are as follows:

```
PING OK - Packet loss = 0%, RTA = 0.18 ms
DNS WARNING: 0.015 seconds response time
DISK CRITICAL - free space: /boot 18 MB (8% inode=99%)
```

Nagios plugins use options for their configuration. It is up to the plugin author's host to parse these options. However, most commands that come as part of the Nagios Plugins package use standard options and support the -h or --help command-line switches to provide a full description of all the arguments they accept.

Standard Nagios plugins usually accept the following parameters:

Option	Description
-h, --help	Provide help
-V, --version	Print the exact version of the plugin
-v, --verbose	Make the plugin report more detailed information on what it is doing
-t, --timeout	Timeout (seconds); after this time, plugin will report the CRITICAL status
-w, --warning	Plugin-specific limits for the WARNING status
-c, --critical	Plugin-specific limits for the CRITICAL status
-H, --hostname	Host name, IP address, or Unix socket to communicate with
-4, --use-ipv4	Use IPv4 for network connectivity
-6, --use-ipv6	Use IPv6 for network connectivity

Commands that verify various daemons also have a common set of options. Many of the networking-related plugins use the following options in addition to the preceding standard ones:

Option	Description
-p, --port	TCP or UDP port to connect to
-w, --warning	Response time that will issue a WARNING status (seconds)
-c, --critical	Response time that will issue a CRITICAL status (seconds)
-s, --send	String that will be sent to the server
-e, --expect	String that should be sent back from the server (option might be passed several times; refer to --all for details)
-q, --quit	String to send to the server to close the connection
-A, --all	In case multiple --expect parameters are passed, this option indicates that all responses need to be received; if this option is not present, at least one matching result indicates a success
-m, --maxbytes	The maximum number of bytes to read when expecting a string to be sent back from the server; after this number of bytes, a mismatch is assumed

-d, --delay	Delay in seconds between sending a string to server and expecting a response
-r, --refuse	Status that should be indicated in case the connection is refused (ok, warn, crit; defaults to crit)
-M	Status in case the expected answer is not returned by the server (ok, warn, crit; defaults to warn)
-j, --jail	Do not return output from the server in plugin output text
-D, --certificate	The number of days that the SSL certificate must still be valid; requires -ssl
-S, --ssl	Connect using SSL encryption
-E, --escape	Allows using \n, \r, \t or \\ in send or quit string; must be passed before --send or --quit option

Please note that the option names are case sensitive. For many plugins, there are options that have their abbreviated name the same, but with different cases. For example, both -e and -E as well as -m and -M are valid options for most of the plugins. It is important to distinguish the lower case and upper case options.

All the commands support the --verbose option (or -v for short variant of it) that will print out useful information about the test. It is recommended that you add the -v option whenever you run into issues with getting a plugin to work.

This chapter describes the commands provided by a standard distribution Nagios Plugins and is based on version 2.1.1. Before using specific options for a command, it is recommended that you use the --help option and familiarize yourself with the functionality available on your Nagios installation.

All plugins have their non-standard options and are described in more detail in this chapter. All commands described in this chapter also have a sample configuration for the Nagios check command. Even though some longer definitions might span multiple lines, make sure that you put it on a single line in your configuration. Some of the plugins already have their command counterparts configured with the sample Nagios configuration that is installed along with Nagios. Therefore, it is also worth checking if your commands.cfg file contains a definition for a particular command.

Using standard network plugins

One of the basic roles of a plugin is to monitor local or remote hosts and verify if they are working correctly. There is a choice of generic plugins to accomplish this task.

Standard networking plugins allow hosts to be monitored using ICMP ECHO (ping: refer to `http://en.wikipedia.org/wiki/Ping`). This is used to determine whether a computer is responding to IP requests. It is also used to measure the time that a machine takes to respond and how many packages are lost during the communication. These plugins also try to connect to certain TCP/UDP ports. This is used to communicate with various network-based services to make sure that they are working properly and respond within a defined amount of time.

Testing the connection to a remote host

Checking if a host is alive is a basic test that should be performed on all remote machines. Nagios offers a command that is commonly used to check if a host is alive and plugged into the network. The syntax of the plugin is as follows:

```
check_ping -H <host_address> -w <wrta>,<wpl>% -c <crta>,<cpl>%
[-p packets] [-t timeout] [-4|-6]
```

This command accepts the standard options described in the previous paragraph as well as the following non-standard options:

Option	Description
-p,--packets	Number of packets to send; defaults to 5
-w, --warning	The WARNING status limit in form of RTA, PKTLOSS%
-c, --critical	The CRITICAL status limit in form of RTA, PKTLOSS%

RTA means **RoundTripAverage** and is the average time taken in milliseconds for the package to return. **PKTLOSS** is **Packet Loss**, which is the maximum percentage of packages that can be lost during communication. For example, a value of 100, 20% means that a ping must return within 0.1 seconds on average, and at least four out of five packages have to come back.

A sample command definition for checking if a host is alive is:

```
define command
{
  command_name  check-host-alive
  command_line  $USER1$/check_ping -H $HOSTADDRESS$ -w 3000.0,
    80%  -c 5000.0,100% -p 5
}
```

Testing connectivity using TCP and UDP

In many cases, Nagios is used to monitor services that work over the network. For checking if a service is working properly, it is necessary to make sure that a certain TCP or UDP port is accessible over the network. In such cases, the tests are done by connecting to the service periodically by the plugin, and this may cause entries in the system log regarding connection attempts.

For example, Microsoft SQL Server listens on TCP port 1433. In many cases, it is enough to simply run generic plugins that check whether a service is available on a specified TCP or UDP port. However, it is recommended that you run specialized plugins for various services such as web or e-mail servers, as these commands also try basic communication with the server and/or measure response time.

Internally, as this command is also handling many other checks, the syntax is almost the same. It is designed so that it behaves slightly differently based on the name it is called with. Many other plugins are symbolic links to check_tcp. The check_tcp plugin is mainly intended to test services that do not have a corresponding Nagios check command. The second command check_udp, is also a symbolic link to check_tcp and differs only by communicating over UDP instead of TCP. Its syntax is as follows:

```
check_tcp|check_udp -H host -p port [-w <warning time>]
        [-c <critical time>] [-s <send string>]
        [-e <expect string>] [-q <quit string>]
        [-m <maximum bytes>] [-d <delay>][-t <timeout seconds>]
        [-r <refuse state>] [-M <mismatch state>] [-v] [-4|-6] [-j]
        [-D <warn days cert expire>[,<crit days cert expire>]]
        [-S <use SSL>] [-E]
```

These commands accept several nonstandard options, as follows:

Option	Description
-p, --port	TCP or UDP port to connect to
-w, --warning	Response time that will issue a WARNING status (in seconds)
-c, --critical	Response time that will issue a CRITICAL status (in seconds)

An example to verify whether VMware server (1.x and 2.x) is listening for connections is as follows:

```
define command
{
  command_name   check_vmware
  command_line   $USER1$/check_tcp -H $HOSTADDRESS$ -p 902
     -e "220 VMware"
}
```

Performing UDP-based tests requires specifying both the -s and -e options; UDP requires sending a packet with data and verifying the expected response.

The following example shows how to verify an application server is listening on UDP port 1142:

```
define command
{
  command_name   check_openvpn
  command_line   $USER1$/check_udp -H $HOSTADDRESS$ -p 1142
     -s "PING" -e "PONG"
}
```

The example expects an application on UDP port 1142 to respond to a PING UDP packet with a PONG UDP response.

Monitoring e-mail servers

Making sure that all e-mail-related services are working correctly is something that each hosting company and intranet administrator needs to perform on a daily basis. In order to do this, Nagios can watch these servers and make sure things are working as expected. This can be done by a remote machine to make sure that the services are accessible or can be monitored by the same server that offers these services.

Nagios can make sure that the processes are running and waiting for connections. It is also easy to verify whether a predefined user/password pair is working properly to make sure that a custom authorization system is working properly.

This section describes the commands that check e-mail servers using network connectivity. Plugins that verify specific processes on a server can be used to make sure a particular daemon is up and running as well.

Checking POP3 and IMAP servers

POP3 is a very popular protocol for retrieving e-mail messages from an e-mail client application. It uses TCP port 110 for unencrypted connections and port 995 for SSL encrypted connections. Nagios offers means to verify both unencrypted and encrypted POP3 connections that can be made. Even though POP3 is the most popular e-mail retrieving protocol, another protocol is also very common. IMAP is a protocol that is used to access e-mails on remote servers rather than download them to the user's computer. It uses TCP port 143 for standard connections and port 993 for encrypted connections over SSL. The following plugins are based on `check_tcp` (and are actually symbolic links to `check_tcp`). The syntax is identical to the original plugin:

```
check_pop|check_imap -H host -p port [-w <warning time>]
        [-c <critical time>] [-s <send string>]
        [-e <expect string>] [-q <quit string>]
        [-m <maximum bytes>] [-d <delay>]
        [-t <timeout seconds>] [-r <refuse state>]
        [-M <mismatch state>] [-v] [-4|-6] [-j]
        [-D <warn days cert expire>[,<crit days cert expire>]]
        [-S <use SSL>] [-E]
```

The only difference between this plugin and the standard command is that the port parameter can be omitted for this plugin, and in this case, a default value for both non-SSL and SSL variants is chosen. In order to enable connection over SSL, either pass the `--ssl` option, or invoke the command as `check_spop` instead of `check_pop` and `check_simap` instead of `check_imap`.

The following are sample command definitions that check for a daemon listening on a specified host and verify that a valid POP3 and IMAP welcome message can be retrieved:

```
define command
{
  command_name  check_pop
  command_line  $USER1$/check_pop -H $HOSTADDRESS$
}
define command
{
  command_name  check_imap
  command_line  $USER1$/check_imap -H $HOSTADDRESS$
}
```

However, it seems more useful to verify the actual functionality of the server. It is, therefore, reasonable to also verify that a predefined username and password is accepted by our POP3 daemon. In order to do that, the example uses -E to escape newline characters, -s to send commands that authenticate, and -e to verify that the user has actually been logged in. In addition, the -d option is passed to indicate that the command should wait a couple of seconds before analyzing the output. If this option is not passed, the command will return after the first line. The following examples should work with any POP3/IMAP server, but it may be necessary to customize the response for your particular environment:

```
define command
{
  command_name  check_pop3login
  command_line  $USER1$/check_pop -H $HOSTADDRESS$ -E -s
    "USER    $ARG1$\r\nPASS $ARG2$\r\n" -d 5 -e "logged in"
}
define command
{
  command_name  check_imaplogin
  command_line  $USER1$/check_imap -H $HOSTADDRESS$ -E -s
    "pr01  LOGIN $ARG1 $ARG2$\r\n" -d 5 -e "pr01 OK"
}
```

The value that is passed in the -s option is a string with two lines for POP3 and one line for IMAP4. Each line ends with a newline character (\r\n) that are sent as newline characters because of using the -E option.

For POP3, these lines are the standard protocol commands to log in to an account. The POP3 server should then issue a response stating that the user is authenticated, and this is what the command is expecting to receive,because of the -e option. In addition, $ARG1$ and $ARG2$ will be replaced with a username and a password that is supplied in a service check definition, which allows different usernames and passwords to be specified for different checks.

With IMAP4, there is only a slight difference in the protocol dialect. IMAP requires the sending of only a single LOGIN command in order to authenticate. As for POP3, $ARG1$ and $ARG2$ will be replaced with a username and password. In this way, it is possible to set up checks for different users and passwords with a single command definition. The pr01 string can be replaced by any other text without spaces. It is necessary with the IMAP4 protocol to bind requests with answers provided by the server.

Testing SMTP protocol

SMTP is a protocol for sending e-mails—both from a client application as well as between email servers. Therefore, monitoring it is also very important from the point of view of availability.

Nagios standard plugins offer a command to check whether an SMTP server is listening. Unlike checks for POP3 and IMAP, the command is available only for this particular protocol and therefore, the options are a bit different:

```
check_smtp -H host [-p port] [-4|-6] [-e expect] [-C command]
            [-R response] [-f from addr]
            [-A authtype -U authuser -P authpass] [-w warn]
            [-c crit] [-t timeout] [-q] [-F fqdn] [-S]
            [-D warn days cert expire[,crit days cert expire]] [-v]
```

The plugin accepts most of the standard options. Additional ones are as follows:

Option	Description
-C, --command	SMTP command to execute on the server (option might be repeated)
-R, --response	Response to expect from the server (option might be repeated)
-f, --from	Attempt to set from where the e-mail is originating
-F, --fqdn	Fully-qualified domain name to send during SMTP greeting (defaults to the local hostname if not specified)
-S, --starttls	Use STARTTLS to initialize connection over SMTP

The port can be omitted and defaults to 25. In this case, the -S option also behaves a bit differently and uses the STARTTLS function of SMTP servers instead of connecting directly over SSL. A basic SMTP check command definition looks like this:

```
define command
{
  command_name   check_smtp
  command_line   $USER1$/check_smtp -H $HOSTADDRESS$
}
```

Most of these options are similar to the standard send/expect parameters in the way they work. Therefore, it is quite easy to create a more complex definition that verifies the sending of e-mails to a specific address:

```
define command
{
  command_name   check_smtpsend
  command_line   $USER1$/check_smtp -H $HOSTADDRESS$ -f
      "$ARG1$" - C "RCPT TO:<$ARG2$>" -R "250"
}
```

This check will attempt to send an e-mail from $ARG1$ to $ARG2$, which will be passed from a check definition, and expects to receive the return code 250, which indicates that no error has occurred.

Monitoring network services

Nagios also offers plugins that monitor different network services. These include commands for checking FTP, DHCP protocol, and WWW servers. It is also possible for Nagios to monitor itself.

Checking FTP server

Nagios allows you to verify whether an FTP server is listening for connections using the `check_ftp` command. This plugin is identical to `check_tcp`, with the difference that the port is optional, and by default a valid FTP welcome message is expected:

```
check_ftp -H host -p port [-w <warning time>] [-c <critical time>]
            [-s <send string>] [-e <expect string>]
            [-q <quit string>][-m <maximum bytes>] [-d <delay>]
            [-t <timeout seconds>] [-r <refuse state>]
            [-M <mismatch state>] [-v] [-4|-6] [-j]
            [-D <warn days cert expire>[,<crit days cert expire>]]
            [-S <use SSL>] [-E]
```

The port argument can be omitted and defaults to 21, or 990 for SSL-based connections. A sample command definition for checking FTP accepting connections is as follows:

```
define command
{
  command_name   check_ftp
  command_line   $USER1$/check_ftp -H $HOSTADDRESS$
}
```

Using the `-s` and `-e` flags, it is also possible to verify if a specified username and password is allowed to log in:

```
define command
{
  command_name   check_ftplogin
  command_line   $USER1$/check_ftp -H $HOSTADDRESS$ -E -s
      "USER $ARG1\r\nPASS $ARG2$\r\n" -d 5 -e "230"
}
```

This example is quite similar to POP3 authentication as the commands are the same. The only difference is that the requested response is `230` as this is a code for a successful response to the `PASS` command.

Verifying DHCP protocol

If your network has a server or a router that provides the users with IP addresses via DHCP, it would be wise to make sure that this server is also working correctly. Nagios offers a plugin that attempts to request an IP address via a DHCP protocol, which can be used for this purpose. The syntax is a bit different from other plugins:

```
check_dhcp [-v] [-u] [-s serverip] [-r requestedip] [-t timeout]
           [-i interface] [-m mac]
```

This command accepts the options described in the following table:

Option	Description
-s, --serverip	The IP of the server that needs to reply with an IP (option might be repeated)
-r, --requestedip	Indicates that at least one DHCP server needs to offer the specified IP address
-m, --mac	The MAC address that should be used in the DHCP request
-i, --interface	The name of the interface that is to be used for checking (for example eth0)
-u, --unicast	Unicast, for testing a DHCP relay request; requires -s

Options for DHCP checking are very powerful—they can be used to check if any server is responding to the DHCP requests, for example:

```
define command
{
  command_name   check_dhcp
  command_line   $USER1$/check_dhcp
}
```

This plugin can also be used to verify if specific servers work, if a specified MAC address will receive an IP address, if a specific IP address is returned, or a combination of these check, as shown below:

```
define command
{
  command_name   check_dhcp_mac
  command_line   $USER1$/check_dhcp -s
     $HOSTADDRESS$ -m $ARG1$ -r $ARG2$
}
```

This check will ensure that a specific machine provides a specific IP for requesting a specific MAC address. This allows checks to be created for specific DHCP rules, which is crucial in the case of networks that need to provide specific devices with IP addresses, which other services depend upon.

It is also worth noting that such tests are safe from a network's perspective as the IP received from the server is not acknowledged by the Nagios plugin. Therefore, a check for a specific MAC address can be done even if a network card with the same address is currently connected. DHCP works over broadcast IP requests; therefore, it is not recommended that you set up testing this service often as it might cause excessive traffic for larger networks.

Monitoring Nagios processes

It is possible for Nagios to monitor whether or not it is running on the local machine. This works by checking the Nagios log file for recent entries, as well as reading the output from the `ps` system command to ensure that the Nagios daemon is currently running. This plugin is mainly used in combination with NRPE or SSH, which are described in more detail in `Chapter 10`, *Monitoring Remote Hosts*. However, it can also be deployed to check the same Nagios that is scheduling the command—mainly to make sure that the log files contain recent entries. The syntax and options are as follows:

```
check_nagios -F <status log file> -t <timeout_seconds>        -e
<expire_minutes> -C <process_string>
```

Option	Description
`-F, --filename`	IP of the server that needs to reply with an IP (option might be repeated)
`-e, --expires`	The number of minutes after which the log file is assumed to be stale
`-C, --command`	Command or partial command to search for in the process list

All the preceding arguments listed are required. The check for the `--expires` option is done by comparing the date and time of the latest entry in the log with the current date and time. The log file is usually called `nagios.log` and is stored in the directory that was passed in the `--localstatedir` option during Nagios compilation. For an installation performed according to the steps given in Chapter 2, *Installing Nagios 4*, the path will be `/var/nagios/nagios.log`. The Nagios process for such a setup would be `/opt/nagios/bin/nagios`. An example definition of a command receiving all of the information as arguments is as follows:

```
define command
{
  command_name   check_nagios
  command_line   $USER1$/check_nagios -F $ARG1$ -C
     $ARG2$ -e $ARG3$
}
```

The first argument is the path to the log file, the second is the path to the Nagios daemon binary, and the last one is the maximum acceptable number of minutes since the last log was updated.

Testing websites

Making sure that websites are up and running 24/7 is vital to many large companies. Verifying that the returned pages contain correct data may be even more important for companies conducting e-commerce. Nagios offers plugins to verify that a web server works. It can also make sure that your SSL certificate is still valid and can also verify the contents of specific pages to check that they contain specific text. This command accepts various parameters, as follows:

```
check_http -H <vhost> | -I <IP-address> [-u <uri>] [-p <port>]
           [-J <client certificate file>] [-K <private key>]
           [-w <warn time>] [-c <critical time>] [-t <timeout>]
           [-L] [-E] [-a auth] [-b proxy_auth]
           [-f <ok|warning|critcal|follow|sticky|stickyport>]
           [-e <expect>] [-d string] [-s string] [-l]
           [-r <regex> | -R <case-insensitive regex>]
           [-P string] [-m <min_pg_size>:<max_pg_size>] [-4|-6]
           [-N] [-M <age>] [-A string] [-k string] [-S <version>]
           [--sni] [-C <warn_age>[,<crit_age>]]
           [-T <content-type>] [-j method]
```

The following table lists the options that either differ from their usual behavior or are not common in other commands:

Option	Description
-H, --hostname	The hostname that should be used for the Host http header; the port might be appended, so it is also present in the http header
-I, --IP-address	The IP address to connect to; if not specified, --hostname is used
-u, --url	The URL to GET or POST (defaults to /)
-j, --method	The HTTP method to use, such as GET, HEAD, POST, PUT, and DELETE
-P, --post	Post the encoded http via POST; content is specified as argument
-N, --no-body	Do not wait for the document, only parse the http headers
-M, --max-age	Warn if the document is older than the number of seconds provided; this parameter can also be specified as (for example) "15 m" for minutes, "8 h" for hours, or "7 d" for days
-T,--content-type	Specify the http Content-Type header
-e, --expect	The text to expect in the first line of the http response; If specified, the plugin will not handle status code logic (i.e. won't warn about 404)
-s, --string	Search for the specified text in result html
-r, --ereg	Search for a specified regular expression in html (case sensitive)
-R, --eregi	Search for a specified regular expression in html (case insensitive)
-l, --linespan	Allow the regular expression to span across new lines
--invert-regex	return a state of CRITICAL if the text is found, and OK if it is not found
-a, --authorization	Authorize on the page using the basic authentication type; must be passed in the form of <username>:<password>

`-b, --proxy-authorization`	Authorize for the proxy server; must be passed in the form of `<username>:<password>`
`-A, --useragent`	Pass the specified value as the `User-Agent` http header
`-k, --header`	Add other parameters to be sent in the http header (might be repeated)
`-f, --onredirect`	How to handle redirects; can be one of ok, warning, critical, or follow
`-m, --pagesize`	The minimum and maximum html page sizes in bytes, as `<min>:<max>`
`-C, --certificate`	Specifies how long the certificate has to be valid in days; should be in the form of `critical_days` or `critical_days,warning_days`
`--sni`	Server Name Indication; enables SSL/TLS hostname extension support; this allows verifying SSL-enabled websites with multiple sites on a single IP address

For example, to verify if a main page has at least the specified number of bytes and is returned promptly, the following check can be done:

```
define command
{
  command_name  check_http_basic
  command_line  $USER1$/check_http -H $HOSTADDRESS$ -f
    follow -m $ARG1$:1000000 -w $ARG2$ -c $ARG3$
}
```

More complex tests of the WWW infrastructure should be carried out frequently. For example, to verify if an SSL-enabled page works correctly and quickly, a more complex test might be required. The following command will verify the SSL certificate and the page size and will look for a specific string in the page body:

```
define command
{
  command_name  check_https
  command_line  $USER1$/check_http -H $HOSTADDRESS$ -S
    -C 14 -u $ARG1$ -f follow -m $ARG1$:$ARG2$ -R $ARG3$
}
```

Checking web pages at a higher level is described in more detail in Chapter 13, *Programming Nagios*, and uses plugins custom-written for this purpose.

Monitoring database systems

Databases allow the storage of information that is used often by entire departments or whole companies. Because most systems usually depend on one or more databases, a failure in these databases can cause all of the underlying systems to go down as well. Imagine a business critical database failure that went unnoticed over a weekend, making both the company's website as well as e-mail unavailable. That would be a disaster! A series of scheduled reports that was supposed to be sent out would fail to be generated because of this.

This is why, making sure that databases are working correctly and have enough resources to operate might be essential for many companies. Many enterprise-class databases also have table space capacity management, which should also be monitored—even though a valid user may be able to log in, this does not necessarily mean that a database is up and running correctly.

Checking MySQL

One of the most commonly used database types is MySQL. It is very often used to provide a basic database for PHP-based web applications. It is also commonly used as a database system for client-server applications. Nagios offers two plugins to verify if MySQL is working properly. One of the plugins allows checking of connectivity to the database and checking master-slave replication status. The other one allows the measurement of the time taken to execute a SQL query. The syntax of both commands and the definition of their options are as follows:

```
check_mysql [-d database] [-H host] [-P port] [-s socket]
            [-u user] [-p password] [-S] [-l] [-a cert] [-k key]
            [-C ca-cert] [-D ca-dir] [-L ciphers] [-f optfile]
            [-g group]

check_mysql_query -q SQL_query [-w <warn>] [-c <crit>]
            [-d database] [-H host] [-P port] [-s socket]
            [-u user] [-p password] [-f optfile] [-g group]
```

Option	Description
-s, --socket	Unix socket to use for connection, used if -H option was not specified; does not need to be customized in most cases
-P, --port	The port to use for connections (defaults to 3306)
-d, --database	The database to which an attempt to connect is to be made
-u, --username	Username to log in with
-p, --password	Password to log in with
-S, --check-slave	(check_mysql only) Verify that the slave thread is running; this is used for monitoring replicated databases
-w, --warning	Specifies the warning threshold; dependent on the plugin used
-c, --critical	Specifies the critical threshold; dependent on the plugin used
-q, --query	(check_mysql_query only) Query to perform

For the check_mysql_query command, the -w and -c options specify the limits for the execution time of the specified SQL query. This allows us to make sure that database performance is within acceptable limits.

The definitions of the check commands for both a simple test and running an SQL query within a specified time are as follows:

```
define command
{
  command_name   check_mysql
  command_line   $USER1$/check_mysql -H $HOSTADDRESS$ -u
    $ARG1$ -p $ARG2$ -d $ARG3$ -S -w 10 -c 30
}
define command
{
  command_name   check_mysql_query
  command_line   $USER1$/check_mysql_query -H $HOSTADDRESS$ -u
    $ARG1$ -p $ARG2$ -d $ARG3$ -q $ARG4$ -w $ARG5$ -c $ARG6$
}
```

Both examples need username, password, and dbname as arguments. The second example also requires a SQL query and the warning and critical time limits.

If the -S option is specified, the plugin will also check whether the replication of MySQL databases is working correctly. This check should be run on MySQL slave servers to make sure that the replication with the master server is in place. Monitoring the number of seconds by which the slave server is behind the master server can be done using the -w and -c flags. In this case, if the slave server is more than the specified number of seconds behind the master server in the replication process, a warning or critical status is issued. More information about checking the replication status can be found under the MySQL documentation for the SHOWSLAVESTATUS command (refer to http://dev.mysql.com/doc/refman/5.7/en/show-slave-status.html).

Checking PostgreSQL

PostgreSQL is another open source database that is commonly used in hosting companies. It is also used very often for client-server applications. The Nagios plugins package offers a command to check if the PostgreSQL database is working correctly. Its syntax is quite similar to the MySQL command:

```
check_pgsql [-H <host>] [-P <port>] [-c <critical time>]
            [-w <warning time>] [-t <timeout>] [-d <database>]
            [-l <logname>] [-p <password>] [-q <query>]
            [-C <critical query range>] [-W <warning query range>]
```

The following table describes the options that this plugin accepts:

Option	Description
-P, --port	The port to use for connections (defaults to 5432)
-d, --database	The database to attempt to connect to
-l, --logname	The username to log in with
-p, --password	The password to log in with

A sample check command that expects username, password, and database name as arguments is as follows:

```
define command
{
  command_name   check_pgsql
  command_line   $USER1$/check_pgsql -H $HOSTADDRESS$ -l $ARG1$
    -p $ARG2$ -d $ARG3$
}
```

Checking Oracle

Oracle is a popular enterprise-level database server. It is mainly used by medium- and large-sized companies for business critical applications. Therefore, a failure or even a lack of disk space for a single database might cause huge problems for a company. Fortunately, a plugin exists to verify various aspects of the Oracle database. It even offers the ability to monitor tablespace storage and cache usage. The syntax is quite different from most Nagios plugins as the first argument specifies the mode in which the check should be carried out, and the remaining parameters are dependent on the first one. The syntax is as follows:

```
check_oracle --tns <SID>
             --db <SID>
             --oranames <Hostname>
             --login <SID>
             --cache <SID> <USER> <PASS> <CRITICAL> <WARNING>
             --tablespace < SID> <USER> <PASS>
  <TABLESPACE> <CRITICAL> <WARNING>
```

For all checks, Oracle **System Identifier (SID)** can be specified in the form of `<ip>` or `<ip>/<database>`. Because the plugin automatically adds the username and password to the identifier, an SID in the form of `<username>[/<password>]@<ip>[/<database>]` should not be specified, and in many cases, will not work.

The `--tns` option checks if a database is listening for a connection based on the `tnsping` command. This can be used as a basic check of both local and remote databases.

Verifying that a local database is running can be done using the `--db` option, in which case, a check is performed by running the Oracle process for a specified database.

Verifying a remote Oracle Names server can be done using the `--oranames` mode.

In order to verify if a database is working properly, a `--login` option can be used—this tries to log in using an invalid username and verifies if the `ORA-01017` error is received, in which case, the database is behaving correctly.

Verifying cache usage can be done using the `--cache` option, in which case, the cache hit ratio is checked. If it is lower than the specified warning or critical limits, the respective status is returned. This allows the monitoring of bottlenecks within the database caching mechanism.

Similarly, for tablespace checking, a `--tablespace` option is provided, in which a check is carried out against the available storage for the specified tablespace. If it is lower than the specified limits, a `warning` or `critical` status is returned (as appropriate).

This plugin requires various Oracle commands to be in the binary path (the PATH environment variable). Therefore, it is necessary to have either the entire Oracle installation or the Oracle client installation done on the machine that will perform the checks for the Oracle database. Sample definitions to check the login into the Oracle database and the database cache are as follows:

```
define command
{
  command_name   check_oracle_login
  command_line   $USER1$/check_oracle --login $HOSTADDRESS$
}
define command   {
  command_name   check_oracle_tablespace
  command_line   $USER1$/check_oracle --cache
      $HOSTADDRESS$/$ARG1$ $ARG2$ $ARG3$ $ARG4$ $ARG5$
}
```

The second example requires the passing of the database name, username, password, and critical/warning limits for the cache hit ratio. The critical value should be lower than the warning value.

Checking other databases

Even though Nagios supports verification of some common databases, there are a lot of commonly used databases for which the standard nagios-plugins package does not provide a plugin. For these databases, the first thing worth checking is the Nagios Exchange (refer to http://exchange.nagios.org/), as this has a category for database check plugins with commands for checking various types of databases (such as DB2, Ingres, Firebird, MS SQL, and Sybase).

In some cases, it might be sufficient to use the check_tcp plugin to verify whether a database server is up and running. In other cases, it might be possible to use a dynamic language (such as Python, Perl, or Tcl) to write a small script that connects to your database and performs basic tests. Refer to Chapter 13, *Programming Nagios*, for more information on writing Nagios check plugins.

Monitoring storage space

Making sure that a system is not running out of space is very important. A lack of disk space for basic paths such as /var/spool or /tmp might cause unexpected results throughout the entire system, such as applications failing due to not being able to write temporary files or local e-mail not being delivered due to lack of disk space. Quotas that are not properly set up for home directories might also cause disk space to run out in a few minutes under certain circumstances.

Nagios can monitor storage space and warn administrators before such problems happen. It is also possible to monitor remote shares on other disks without mounting them. This would be useful for easily monitoring disk space on Windows boxes without installing the dedicated Windows Nagios tools described in Chapter 12, *Advanced Monitoring*.

Checking swap space

Making sure that a system is not running out of swap space is essential to the system's correct behavior. Many operating systems have mechanisms that kill the most resource-intensive processes when the system is running out of memory, and this usually leads to many services not functioning properly—many vital processes are not properly respawned in such cases. It is, therefore, a good idea to monitor swap space usage in order to be able to handle low memory issues on critical systems. Nagios offers a plugin to monitor each swap device independently as well as the ability to monitor cumulative values. The syntax and description of these options are as follows:

```
check_swap [-av] -w <percent_free>% -c <percent_free>%   -w <bytes_free> -c
<bytes_free>
```

Option	Description
-a, --all	Compare all swap partitions one by one; if not specified, only total swap sizes are checked

Values for the -w and -c options can be supplied in the <value>% form, in which case the <value> percent must be free in order not to cause an exception to be generated. They can also be supplied in the <value><unit> form (for example, 1000 k, 100 M, and 1 G), and in this case, a test fails if less than the specified amount of swap space is available.

A sample definition of a check is as follows:

```
define command
{
  command_name  check_swap
  command_line  $USER1$/check_swap -w $ARG1$ -c $ARG2$
}
```

Monitoring disk status SMART

Nagios offers a standard plugin that uses **Self-Monitoring, Analysis, and Reporting Technology System** (**SMART**) technology to monitor and report the failure of disk operations. This plugin operates on top of the SMART mechanism and verifies the status of local hard drives. If supported by the underlying IDE and SCSI hardware, this plugin allows the monitoring of hard disk failures. The syntax is as follows:

```
check_ide_smart [-d <device>] [-i] [-q] [-1] [-0] [-n]
```

The following table provides a description of the accepted options:

Option	Description
-d, --device	The device to verify; if this option is set, no other options are accepted
-i, --immediate	Perform offline tests immediately
-q, --quick-check	Return the number of failed tests
-1, --auto-on	Enable automatic offline tests
-0, --auto-off	Disable automatic offline tests
-n, --nagios	Return output suitable for Nagios

A sample definition of a command to monitor a particular device and report failed tests is as follows:

```
define command
{
  command_name  check_ide_smart
  command_line  $USER1$/check_ide_smart -d $ARG1$ -1 -q -n
}
```

Checking disk space

One of the most common checks is checking one or more mounted partitions for available space. Nagios offers a plugin for doing this. This plugin offers very powerful functionality and can be set up to monitor one, several, or all partitions mounted in a system. The syntax for the plugin is as follows:

```
check_disk -w limit -c limit [-W limit] [-K limit]
           {-p path | -x device} [-C] [-E] [-e] [-f]
           [-g group] [-k] [-l] [-M] [-m] [-R path]
           [-r path] [-t timeout] [-u unit] [-v] [-X type]
           [-N type] [-n]
```

The most commonly used options for this plugin are described in the following table:

Option	Description
-w, --warning	Returns a warning status if less than the specified percentage of disk space is free
-c, --critical	Returns a critical status if less than the specified percentage of disk space is free
-W, --iwarning	Returns a warning status if less than the specified percentage of inodes are free
-K, --icritical	Returns a critical status if less than specified percentage of inodes are free
-p, --path	The path or partition to verify (option might be specified multiple times)
-M, --mountpoint	Display the mount point instead of the partition in the result
-l, --local	Check only local filesystems
-A, --all	Verify all mount points
-r, --ereg-path	Regular expression to find paths/partitions (case sensitive)
-R, --eregi-path	Regular expression to find paths/partitions (case insensitive)

Values for the -w and -c options can be supplied in the <value>% form, in which case the <value> percent must be free in order not to cause a state to occur. They can also be specified in the <value><unit> form (for example, 800 k, 50 M, and 4 G), in which case, a test fails if the available space is less than the specified amount. Checks for inode (refer to https://en.wikipedia.org/wiki/inode for more details) availability, with options -W and -K, can only be specified in the <value> form.

It is possible to check a single partition or specify multiple -p, -r, or -R options and check if all matching mount points have sufficient disk space. It is sometimes better to define separate checks for each partition so that if the limits are exceeded on several of these, each one is tracked separately. The sample check commands for a single partition and for all partitions are shown in the following examples:

```
define command
{
  command_name   check_partition
  command_line   $USER1$/check_disk -p $ARG1$ -w $ARG2$ -c $ARG3$
}
define command
{
  command_name   check_local_partitions
  command_line   $USER1$/check_disk -A -l -w $ARG1$ -c $ARG2$
}
```

Both of these commands expect the warning and critical levels, but the first example also requires a partition path or device as the first argument. It is possible to build more complex checks either by repeating the -p parameter or using -r to include several mount points.

Testing free space for remote shares

Nagios offers plugins that allow the monitoring of remote file systems exported over the SMB/CIFS protocol, the standard protocol for file sharing used by Microsoft Windows. This allows you to check whether a specified user is able to log on to a particular file server and to monitor the amount of free disk space on the file server. The syntax of this command is as follows:

```
check_disk_smb -H <host> -s <share> -u <user> -p <password>
-w <warn> -c <crit> [-W <workgroup>] [-P <port>] [-a <IP>]
```

Options specific to this plugin are described in the following table:

Option	Description
-s, --share	SMB share that should be tested
-u, --user	The username to log in to the server as (defaults to guest)
-p, --password	The password to use for logging in
-P, --port	The port to be used for connections; defaults to 139

Values for the -w and -c options can be specified in the `<value>%` form, in which case the `<value>` percent must be free in order to not generate an exception. They can also be specified in the `<value><unit>` form (for example, 800 k, 50 M, and 4 G), in which case, the test fails if the available space is less than the specified amount.

This command uses the smbclient command to communicate over the SMB protocol. It is, therefore, necessary to have the Samba client package installed on the machine where the test will be run.

Sample command definitions to check connectivity to a share without checking for disk space and also to verify disk space over SMB are as follows:

```
define command
{
  command_name   check_smb_connect
  command_line   $USER1$/check_disk_smb -H $HOSTADDRESS$
     -w 100% -c 100% -u $ARG1$ -p $ARG2$ -s $ARG3$
}
define command
{
  command_name   check_smb_space
  command_line   $USER1$/check_disk_smb -H $HOSTADDRESS$
     -u $ARG1$ -p $ARG2$ -s $ARG3$ -w $ARG4$ -c $ARG5$
}
```

Both of the commands require the passing of a username, password, and share name as arguments. The latter example also requires the passing of warning and critical value limits to check. The first example will only issue a `critical` state if a partition has no space left. It is also worth noting that Samba 3.x servers report quota as disk space, if this is enabled for the specified user. Therefore, this might not always be an accurate way to measure disk space.

Monitoring resources

For servers or work stations to be responsive and to be kept from being overloaded, it is also worth monitoring system usage using various additional measures. Nagios offers several plugins to monitor resource usage and to report if the limits set for these checks are exceeded.

Checking system load

The first thing that should always be monitored is the system load, and it is calculated based on the count of the processes running or waiting to be running. This value reflects the number of processes and the amount of CPU capacity that they are utilizing. This means that if one process is using up to 50% of the CPU capacity, the value will be around 0.5; and if four processes try to utilize the maximum CPU capacity, the value will be around 4.0. The system load is measured in three values—the average loads in the last minute, last 5 minutes, and last 15 minutes. The syntax of the command and the description of the option is as follows:

```
check_load [-r] -w wload1,wload5,wload15
-c cload1,cload5,cload15
```

Option	Description
-r, --percpu	Divide the load averages by the number of CPUs

Values for the -w and -c options should be in the form of three values separated by commas. If any of the load averages exceeds the specified limits, a warning, or critical status will be returned. Here is a sample command definition that uses warning and critical load limits as arguments:

```
define command
{
  command_name  check_load
  command_line  $USER1$/check_load -w $ARG1$ -c $ARG2$
}
```

Checking processes

Nagios processes also offer a way to monitor the total number of processes. Nagios can be configured to monitor all processes, only running ones, those consuming CPU, those consuming memory, or a combination of these criteria. The syntax and the description of options are as follows:

```
check_procs -w <range> -c <range> [-m metric] [-s state]
            [-p ppid] [-u user] [-r rss] [-z vsz] [-P %cpu]
            [-a argument-array] [-C command] [-k] [-t timeout] [-v]
```

Option	Description
`-m, --metric`	Select which value to use; one of the following: `PROCS`—Number of processes (the default) `SZ`—Virtual memory size of matching process `RSS`—Resident set memory size of matching process `CPU`—Percentage CPU time of matching process `ELAPSED`—Time elapsed in seconds of matching process
`-s, --state`	Only check processes that have the specified status; this is the same as the status in the `ps` command
`-p, --ppid`	Check the children of the indicated process IDs
`-z, --vsz`	Check processes with a virtual memory size exceeding value
`-r, --rss`	Check processes with the resident set memory exceeding value
`-P, --pcpu`	Check processes with the CPU usage exceeding value
`-u, --user`	Check processes owned by a specified user
`-a, --argument-array`	Check processes whose arguments contain a specified value
`-C, --command`	Check processes with exact matches of the specified value as a command

Values for the `-w` and `-c` options can either take a single value or take the `<min>:<max>` form. In the first case, a `warning` or `critical` status is returned if the value (number of processes by default) exceeds the specified number. In the second case, the appropriate status is returned if the value is lower than `<min>` or higher than `<max>`. Sample commands to monitor the total number of processes and the number of specific processes are as follows:

```
define command
{
  command_name    check_procs_num
  command_line    $USER1$/check_procs -m PROCS -w $ARG1$ -c $ARG2$
}
define command
{
  command_name    check_procs_cmd
  command_line    $USER1$/check_procs -C $ARG1$ -w $ARG1$ -c $ARG2$
}
```

The second code, for example, can be used to check to see if the specific server is running, and has not created too many processes. In this case, the `warning` or `critical` values should be specified ranging from 1.

Monitoring logged-in users

It is also possible to use Nagios to monitor the number of users currently logged in to a particular machine. The syntax is very simple and there are no options, except for the `warning` and `critical` limits:

```
check_users -w limit -c limit
```

A command definition that uses the `warning` or `critical` limits specified in the arguments is as follows:

```
define command
{
  command_name  check_users
  command_line  $USER1$/check_users -w $ARG1$ -c $ARG2$
}
```

Monitoring other operations

Nagios also offers plugins for many other operations that are common to daily system monitoring and activities; this section covers only a few of them. It is recommended that you look for the remaining commands in both the Nagios Plugins package as well as on the Nagios Exchange website.

Checking for updates with APT

Many Linux distributions use **Advanced Packaging Tool** (**APT**) for handling package management (refer to `http://wiki.debian.org/Apt`). This tool is used by default on Debian and its derivatives such as Ubuntu.

It allows the handling of upgrades and download of packages. It also allows the synchronization of package lists from one or more remote sources.

Nagios provides a plugin that allows you to monitor if any upgrades are available and/or perform upgrades automatically. The syntax and the description of the options are as follows:

```
check_apt [-d|-u|-U [<opts>]] [-n] [-t timeout]
          [-i <regex>] [-e <regex>] [-c <regex>]
```

Option	Description
-u, --update	Perform an apt update operation prior to other operations
-U, --upgrade	Perform an apt upgrade operation
-d, --dist-upgrade	Perform an apt dist-upgrade operation
-n, --no-upgrade	Do not run upgrade or dist-upgrade; useful only with -u
-i, --include	Include only packages matching a regular expression
-c, --critical	If any packages match a regular expression, a critical state is returned
-e, --exclude	Exclude packages matching a regular expression

If the -u option is specified, the command first attempts to update apt package information. Otherwise, the package information currently in cache is used. If the -U or -d option is specified, the specified operation is performed. If -n is specified, only an attempt to run the operation is made, without actually upgrading it performs monitoring (and not upgrade) the activities system. The plugin might also be based on daily apt updates/upgrades and only monitor.

The following is a command definition for a simple dist-upgrade, as well as for monitoring available packages and issuing a critical state if the Linux images are upgradeable (that is, if newer packages exist). However, this command does not perform the actual upgrades:

```
define command
{
  command_name   check_apt_upgrade
  command_line   $USER1$/check_apt -u -d
}
define command
{
  command_name   check_apt_upgrade2
  command_line   $USER1$/check_apt -n -u
     -d -c "^linux-(image|restrict)"
}
```

Monitoring UPS status

Another useful feature is that of Nagios being able to monitor the UPS status over the network. This requires the machine with the UPS to have the Network UPS Tools package (refer to `http://www.networkupstools.org/`) installed and running, so that it is possible to query the UPS parameters. It is also possible to monitor local resources using the same plugin. The syntax and the description of the options are as follows:

```
check_ups -H host -u ups [-p port] [-v variable] [-T]
                         [-w <warn time>] [-c <crit time>] [-t <timeout>]
```

Option	Description
-u, --ups	The name of the UPS to check
-p, --port	The port to use for TCP/IP connection; defaults to 3493
-T, --temperature	Report the temperature in Celsius degrees
-v, --variable	Variable to output; one of LINE, TEMP, BATTPCT, and LOADPCT

The name of the UPS is usually defined in the `ups.conf` file on the machine that the command is connecting to. The plugin will return an `ok` state if the UPS is calibrating or running on AC power. A `warning` state is returned if the UPS claims to be running on batteries, and a `critical` state is returned in the case of a low battery or if the UPS is off.

The following is a sample definition of a check command that gets the UPS name passed as an argument:

```
define command
{
  command_name   check_ups
  command_line   $USER1$/check_ups -H $HOSTADDRESS$ -u $ARG1$
}
```

Gathering information from LM sensors

This is a Linux-specific plugin that uses the lm-sensors package (refer to `http://www.lm-sensors.org/`) to monitor hardware health.

The `check_sensors` command issues an `unknown` status if the underlying hardware does not support health monitoring or if the `lm-sensors` package is not installed, a `warning` status if a non-zero error is returned by the `sensors` command, and a `critical` status if the string `ALARM` is found within the output from the command.

The plugin does not take any arguments and simply reports information based on the `sensors` command.

The command definition is as follows:

```
define command
{
  command_name   check_sensors
  command_line   $USER1$/check_sensors
}
```

Using the dummy check plugin

Nagios also offers a dummy checking plugin. It simply takes an exit code from an argument and returns it. It is useful for testing dependencies between hosts and/or services, verifying notifications and can also be used for a service that will be measured using passive checks only. The syntax of this plugin is as follows:

check_dummy <exitcode> [<result string>]

The `result string` object type specifies a message that will be returned and shown in Nagios UI. If it is not specified, the `OK`, `WARNING`, `CRITICAL`, or `UNKNOWN` statuses are returned as messages, based on the exit code to be returned.

The following is a sample command definition that returns an `ok` status without an additional detailed message:

```
define command
{
  command_name   check_dummy_ok
  command_line   $USER1$/check_dummy 0
}
```

The following example also shows how to return a critical status with a more detailed message:

```
define command
{
  command_name  check_dummy_critical
  command_line  $USER1$/check_dummy 2 "Dummy result message"
}
```

Manipulating other plugins' output

Nagios offers an excellent plugin that simply invokes other checks and converts their status accordingly. This might be useful when a failed check from a plugin is actually an indication that the service is working correctly. This can, for example, be used to make sure that non-authenticated users can't send e-mails while valid users can. The syntax and the description of the options are as follows:

```
negate [-t timeout] [-o|-w|-c|-u state] <actual command to run>
```

Option	Description
-o, --ok	State to return to when the actual command returns an ok state
-w, --warning	State to return to when the actual command returns a warning state
-c, --critical	State to return to when the actual command returns a critical state
-u, --unknown	State to return to when the actual command returns an unknown state

The states to return can either be specified as an exit code number or as a string. If no options are specified, only the `ok` and `critical` states are swapped. If at least one status change option is specified, only the specified states are mapped.

Sample command definitions to check that an SMTP server is not listening, and to verify that a user can't log into a POP3 server are as follows:

```
define command
{
  command_name  check_nosmtp
  command_line  $USER1$/negate $USER1$/check_smtp
                -H $HOSTADDRESS$
}
define command
{
  command_name  check_pop3loginfailure
  command_line  $USER1$/negate -o critical -w ok -c critical
```

```
$USER1$/check_pop -H $HOSTADDRESS$ -E
-s "USER $ARG1$\r\nPASS $ARG2$\r\n" -d 5
-e "ogged in"
}
```

The first example does not use state mapping, and the default `ok` for `critical` state replacement is done. The second example maps the states so that if a server is not listening or if the user is actually able to log in, it is considered a `critical` status for the service.

Additional and third-party plugins

So far, we used plugins that are part of the standard Nagios Plugins package. It provides plugins for monitoring typical servers. IT setup often consists of a large variety of hardware and software that have to be monitored. There are many devices and services that should be monitored. In many cases, standard plugins are enough to properly monitor them, such as monitoring using PING, SSH, or HTTP.

There are, however, many applications that require more sophisticated checks, such as applications communicating over a custom protocol that can be checked using `check_udp` or `check_tcp` by specifying handshake to perform an expected response. In addition, many services require more sophisticated checks, such as verifying that the OpenVPN server performs a proper handshake, which cannot easily be done using `check_udp` or `check_tcp`—a check that it is listening can be done, but it could simply be another service running on the same port.

Monitoring network software

Monitoring IT resources often requires verifying that network services are working properly. This can be anything—a web, SSH, or FTP server, as well as many other protocols. There are also a large number of custom protocols that also require monitoring. Popular network services have a working plugin already that can simply be used; however, it is often up to us to create a check.

In many cases, it is sufficient to just use `check_udp` or `check_tcp` and check for the specific string being present. It is often enough to just check the result message, such as with the VMware server. With other services, it may also require sending a specific command.

For example, the following command definition allows monitoring Redis service (refer to ht
tp://redis.io/ for more details), which has a simple line-based protocol:

```
define command
{
  command_name   check_redis
  command_line   $USER1$/check_tcp -H $HOSTADDRESS$ -p 6379
                 -E -s "PING\r\n" -e "+PONG" -w 1 -c 2
}
```

Redis is a key-value based store that is often used by server applications to store
information and communicate between instances. It is commonly used for large web
applications as cache or temporary data storage.

The preceding example connects to the host on port 6379 (which is the port Redis is
listening on) and sends a PING command followed by newline characters, expecting a
+PONG as response. The response time has to be below 1 second for the OK status, otherwise
it is WARNING if it is below 2 seconds, and CRITICAL if it longer than that.

The approach can also be used to also send more complex commands, such as
authenticating to Redis using the AUTH command:

```
define command
{
  command_name   check_redis_auth
  command_line   $USER1$/check_tcp -H $HOSTADDRESS$ -p 6379
                 -E -s "AUTH $ARG1$\r\nSELECT 0\r\n"
                 -e "+OK" -w 1 -c 2
}
```

This check will result in failure if the authentication using a specified password does not
work, as the SELECT command will not return +OK unless the authentication succeeded.

Similarly, a check can be made for memcached (refer to http://memcached.org/ for more
details), which is a cache mechanism often used by web applications as well:

```
define command    {
  command_name   check_memcached
  command_line   $USER1$/check_tcp -H $HOSTADDRESS$ -p 11211
                 -E -s "version\n" -e "VERSION" -w 1 -c 2
}
```

In this case, the only difference is using port 11211 (which is the default port for
memcached) and sending a different command.

The standard check commands can be used for almost all protocols; however, it is a practical solution mainly for text-based protocols, since encoding binary data requires more work, and often it is easier to create a custom plugin for this—especially if a library to communicate over the protocol is available. This approach is described in more detail in Chapter 13, *Programming Nagios*.

Using third-party plugins

There are also many cases where a simple monitoring by sending protocol-specific messages is not enough. For instance, monitoring MySQL replication status requires a dedicated plugin to properly report delays and set a warning or critical status if it exceeds the specified threshold.

In these cases, it is best to use existing plugins if they exist, or write new ones if they don't already. The Nagios Exchange at `http://exchange.nagios.org/` is the best place to start looking for plugins as it is historically the first and the largest directory of additions created by the Nagios community.

The website contains a dedicated category for plugins and at the time of writing the directory contains over 3,000 plugins. They are grouped into categories based on the type of performed checks.

The category with the largest number of plugins is Network Protocols (refer to `http://exch ange.nagios.org/directory/Plugins/Network-Protocols`), and it is over 20% of all the plugins available on the website. It contains ready-to-use plugins for various types of check, such as mail system, VoIP, file, and web protocol checks.

Nagios Exchange also has a section for databases with a lot of plugins available. It provides ready-to-use code for monitoring many types of servers, such as MySQL, PostgreSQL, Oracle, DB2, and SQLServer—some of which do not have a dedicated check in the `nagios-plugins` project. For many databases, there are multiple plugins available ranging from basic service check to more advanced features such as monitoring replication status and disk and memory usage. All the plugins can be found in the Databases section available at `h ttp://exchange.nagios.org/directory/Plugins/Databases`.

The website provides a large number of plugins for monitoring web servers and web applications. This includes checks for common web servers, such as Apache and IIS, but there are also multiple choices for monitoring other web and application servers, such as Nginx, IIS, Tomcat, and JBoss. There are also many plugins for monitoring specific solutions, such as Fast-CGI processes, PHP-FPM (a Fast-CGI-based solution for running PHP applications with many web servers), and Passenger module (used to serve Ruby on Rails and Python/Django applications on top of Apache and Nginx). There are also different plugins aspects of monitoring web servers—number of processes, memory and CPU usage, and many more. The plugins for monitoring web servers can be found in Nagios Exchange under the Web Servers category, available at `http://exchange.nagios.org/directory/Plugins/Web-Servers`.

Nagios Exchange also provides a lot of ready-to-use plugins to monitor a wide range of devices and services. There are multiple plugins for monitoring various operating systems (available at `http://exchange.nagios.org/directory/Plugins/Operating-Systems`), network devices (available at `http://exchange.nagios.org/directory/Plugins/Hardware/Network-Gear`), and network connectivity (available at `http://exchange.nagios.org/directory/Plugins/Network-Connections%2C-Stats-and-Bandwidth`).

Whenever using a third-party plugin—either from Nagios Exchange or downloaded from another website directly—it is important to remember security and licensing issues.

As plugins are run using the same user as Nagios itself, a malicious or erroneous plugin may be able to remove Nagios data files or other important data. It is always best to use a plugin that is in active development and preferably has its source code available. So, in case of problems, it is possible to fix them or get support from the author of the plugin.

Some plugins may have licenses that prevent them from being used in certain environments or require a license in such case. There are also cases where a plugin may depend on libraries of software that require a license for each server it is installed on. For instance, a plugin to monitor a proprietary service may require a client library to connect, which may require additional license.

It is also possible to create your own plugins, and as the plugin interface is very easy it can be done in almost any language—all that is needed is to print the result to standard output and use the appropriate exit code to indicate status. Writing own plugins is described in more details in Chapter 13, *Programming Nagios*.

Summary

The Nagios Plugins package offers a large variety of checks that can be performed to monitor your infrastructure. Whether you are an administrator of an IT company managing a large network, or just want to monitor a small server room, these plugins will allow you to check the majority of the services that you are currently using.

In this chapter, you learned how the plugins report status to Nagios using standard output and exit codes. You also learned about the Nagios Plugins project and the standard options for all the plugins within the package.

We also covered the generic communication plugins for checking remote host connectivity using ping as well as generic TCP and UDP checking plugins.

The chapter also described how to perform checks of standard networking protocols, such as e-mail, FTP, DHCP, website checking as well as Nagios process information.

You also learned about checking various databases and how it can also be used for monitoring the propagation of data to slave databases.

The chapter also covered information about monitoring disk and swap space as well as monitoring system resources and processes.

You also learned how to monitor additional operations, such as APT package management status and UPS and LM sensors. You also learned about using third-party plugins in Nagios.

The next chapter will cover how to create Nagios configuration so that it can be used for monitoring both small and large infrastructure. It also will cover advanced configuration options, such as dependencies, custom variables, inheriting, and flapping.

7
Advanced Configuration

In the previous chapter, we walked through the standard Nagios plugins, which can be used to monitor a large variety of hosts and services. We learned how the plugins can be used to perform specific and generic checking of the IT resources. This chapter describes some guidelines that will help you migrate from small (and increasing) Nagios setups to a flexible model by using templates and grouping effectively. Any experienced administrator knows that there is a huge difference between a working system and a properly configured system. Using this advice will help you and your team survive the switch from monitoring only critical services to checking the health of a majority of your IT infrastructure.

This chapter focuses on how to set up templates, groupings, and the naming structure. However, creating a robust monitoring system involves much more; be sure to read the following chapters, which talk about monitoring other servers and setting up multiple hosts that use Nagios to monitor your network and report to a single central machine, as well as how to monitor hosts running the Microsoft Windows operating system.

In this chapter, we will learn the following:

- Creating maintainable configurations
- Configuring the file structure
- Defining the dependencies
- Using the templates
- Using the custom variables
- Understanding flapping

Creating maintainable configurations

An enormous effort is required to deploy, configure, and maintain a system that monitors your company's IT infrastructure. The configuration for several hundred machines can take months. The effort required will also depend upon the scope of hosts and services that should be tracked; the more precise the checks need to be, the more time is needed to set these up.

If your company plans to monitor a wide range of hosts and services, you should consider setting up a dedicated server solely for running Nagios. Even though a small Nagios installation consumes few resources, as it grows, Nagios will start using more resources. If you set it to run on the same machine as business-critical applications, it can lead to problems. Therefore, it is always best to set up Nagios on a separate machine right from the beginning—even if the machine has fewer resources than a bigger one, shared with other applications.

A good approach is to start with monitoring only critical parts of your network, such as routers and main servers. You can also start off with only making sure that essential services are working—DHCP, DNS, file sharing, and databases are good examples of what is critical. Of course, if your company does not use file servers, or if databases are not critical to the production environment, you can skip these.

The next step would be to set up parenting and start adopting more hosts. At some point, you will also need to start planning how to group hosts and services. In the beginning, the configuration might simply be definitions of people, hosts, and services. After several iterations of setting up more hosts and services to be monitored, you should get to a point where all of the things that are critical to the company's business are monitored. This should be an indication that the initial configuration of Nagios monitoring is complete.

As the number of objects grows, you will need to group them. Contacts need to be defined as groups, because if your team consists of more than one to two people, they will likely rotate over time. This provides a better way to maintain a group than changing the people responsible for each host individually. Hosts and services should be grouped for many reasons. It makes viewing the status and infrastructure topology on the web interface much easier. Also, after you start defining escalations for your objects, it is much easier to manage these using groups.

You should take some time to plan how group hosts and services should be set up. How will you group objects for escalations or for viewing single host groups via the web interface? Learn how you can take advantage of this functionality and then plan how you will approach the setup of your groups.

If your network has common services, it is better to define them for particular groups, and only once— such as the SSH server for all Linux servers and Telnet for all **Advanced Interactive eXecutive (AIX)** machines, which is an IBM operating system that is mainly used by IBM enterprise-level servers. It is possible to define a service only once and tell Nagios to which hosts or host groups the service should be bound. By specifying that all Linux servers offer SSH, and all AIX servers offer Telnet, it will automatically add such services to all of the machines in these groups. This is often more convenient than specifying services for each of the hosts separately.

In such cases, you should either set up a new host group or use an existing one to keep track of the hosts that offer a particular service. Combined with keeping a list of host groups inside each host definition, this makes things much easier to manage; disabling a particular host also takes care of the corresponding service definitions.

Configuring the file structure

A very important issue is how to store all our configuration files. We can put every object definition in a single file, but this will not make it easy to manage. As mentioned in Chapter 3, *Configuring Nagios*, it is recommended to store different types of objects in separate folders.

Assuming your Nagios configuration is in /etc/nagios, it is recommended that you create folders for all types of objects in the following manner:

```
/etc/nagios/commands
/etc/nagios/timeperiods
/etc/nagios/contacts
/etc/nagios/hosts
/etc/nagios/services
```

Of course, these files will need to be added to the nagios.cfg file. After having followed the instructions in Chapter 3, *Configuring Nagios*, these directories should already be added to our main Nagios configuration file.

It would also be worthwhile to use a version control mechanism such as **Git** (http://www.git-scm.com/), **Mercurial** (**Hg**, http://mercurial.selenic.com/) or **Subversion** (**SVN**, http://subversion.tigris.org/) to store your Nagios configuration. While this will add overhead to the process of applying configuration changes, it will also prevent someone from overwriting a file accidentally. It will also keep track of every change in the configuration files, so you will always know what exact change (and who) has broken the monitoring system.

You might consider writing a simple script that will perform an export from the source code repository into a temporary directory; verify that Nagios works fine by using the `nagios -v` command. Only if that did not fail will we then copy the new configuration in place of the older one and restart Nagios. This will make the deployment of configuration changes much easier, especially in cases where multiple people are managing it.

As for naming the files themselves—for time periods, contacts, and commands—it is recommended that you keep single definitions per file, as in `contacts/nagiosadmin.cfg`. This greatly reduces naming collisions and also makes it much easier to find particular object definitions. This does not prevent an object from referencing another object—for instance, it is fine for a time period to use an `exclude` option referencing a time period from another file.

Storing hosts and services might be done in a slightly different way—host definitions should go to the `hosts` subdirectory, and the file should be named the same as the hostname, for example, `hosts/localhost.cfg`. Services can be split into two different types and stored, depending on how they are defined and used.

Services that are associated with more than one host should be stored in the services subdirectory. A good example is the SSH service, which will be available on the majority of hosts. In this case, it should go to `services/ssh.cfg`, and host groups should be used to associate it with the hosts that actually offer connection over this protocol.

Services that are specific to a single host should be handled differently. It's best to store them in the same file as the host definition. A good example might be checking the disk space on partitions that might be specific to a particular machine, such as checking the `/oracle` partition on a host that's dedicated to Oracle databases.

For handling groups, it is recommended to create files called `groups.cfg` and define all groups in it, without any members. Then, whenever you deifne a contact, host, or group, you can define to which groups it belongs by using the `contactgroups`, `hostgroups`, or `servicegroups` directives accordingly. This way, if you disable a particular object by deleting or commenting out its definition, the definition of the group itself will still work.

If you plan on having a large number of both check command and notify command definitions, you may want to split these into two separate directories— `checkcommands` and `notifycommands`. You can also use a single commands subdirectory, prefix the file names, and store the files in a single directory, for example, `commands/check_ssh.cfg` or `commands/notify_jabber.cfg`.

Defining object dependencies

It is a very common scenario that computers, or the applications they offer, depend on other objects to function properly. A typical example is that a web based application will depend on a database server. Another is a host behind a private network that depends on an OpenVPN service to work. As a system administrator, your job is to know these relations—if you plan to reinstall a database cluster, you need to let people know there will be downtime for almost all applications. Nagios should also be aware of such relations.

In such cases, it is very useful for system monitoring software to consider these dependencies. When analyzing which hosts and services are not working properly, it is good to analyze such dependencies and discard things that are not working because of other failures. This way, it will be easier for you to focus on the real problems. Therefore, it allows you to get to the root cause of any malfunction much faster.

Nagios allows you to define how hosts and services depend on each other. This allows for very flexible configurations and checks. Nagios provides very flexible mechanisms for checking hosts and services—it will take all dependencies into account. This means that if a service relies on another one to function properly, Nagios will perform checks to make sure that all dependent services are working properly. In case a dependent service is not working properly, Nagios may or may not perform checks and may or may not send out any notifications, depending on how the dependency is defined. This is logical, because the service will probably not work properly if a dependent object is not working.

Nagios also offers the ability to specify parents for hosts. This is, in a way, similar to dependencies, as both specify that one object depends on another object. The main difference is that parents are used to define the infrastructure hierarchy. Parent definitions are also used by Nagios to skip checks for hosts that will obviously be down. Dependencies, on the other hand, can be used to suppress notifications about the problems that are occurring due to dependent services being down, but they do not necessarily cause Nagios to skip checking a particular host or service. Another difference is that parents can only be specified for hosts, whereas dependencies can be set up between hosts and services.

Dependencies also offer more flexibility in terms of how they are configured. It is possible to specify which states of the dependent host or service will cause Nagios to stop sending out notifications. You can also tell Nagios when it should skip performing checks based on the status of the dependent object.

To aid in describing how objects depend on each other, Nagios documentation uses two terms—*master* and *dependent* objects. When defining dependency, a master object is the object that needs to be working correctly in order for the other object to function. Similarly, the dependent object is the one that needs another object in order to work. This terminology will be used throughout this section, to avoid confusion.

Creating host dependencies

Let's start with host dependency definitions. These are objects that have several attributes, and each dependency can actually describe one or more dependencies, for example, it is possible to tell Nagios that 20 machines rely on a particular host in a single dependency definition.

Here is an example of a dependency specifying that during maintenance, a Windows backup storage server in another branch depends upon a VPN server:

```
define hostdependency
{
  dependent_host_name          backupstorage-branch2
  host_name                    vpnserver-branch1
  dependency_period            maintenancewindows
}
```

The following table describes all of the available directives for defining a host dependency. Items in bold are required when specifying a dependency:

Option	Description
dependent_host_name	Defines hostnames that are dependent on the master hosts, separated by commas
dependent_hostgroup_name	Defines the host group names whose members are dependent on the master hosts, separated by commas
host_name	Defines the master hosts, separated by commas
hostgroup_name	Defines the host groups whose members are to be the master hosts, separated by commas
inherits_parent	Defines whether a dependency should inherit dependencies of the master hosts

Option	Description
execution_failure_criteria	Specifies which master host states should prevent Nagios from checking the dependent hosts, separated by commas; it can be one or more of the following: n - none, checks should always be executed p - pending state (no check has yet been done) o - host UP state d - host DOWN state u - host UNREACHABLE state
notification_failure_criteria	Specifies which master host states should be prevented from generating notifications about the dependent host's status changes, separated by commas; it can be one or more of the following: n - none, notification should always take place p - pending state (no check has yet been done) o - host UP state d - host DOWN state u - host UNREACHABLE state
dependency_period	Specifies the time periods during which the dependency will be valid; if not specified, the dependency is always valid

The question is where to store such dependency files. As for service definitions, it is recommended that you store dependencies specific to a particular host in the file containing the definition of the dependent host. For the previous example, we would put it in the `hosts/backupstorage-branch2.cfg` file.

When defining a dependency that will describe a relationship between more than one master or dependent host, it's best to put these into a generic file for dependencies—for example, we can put it in `hosts/dependencies.cfg`. Another good option is to put the dependency definitions that only affect a single master host in the master host's definition.

If you are defining a dependency that covers more than one master or dependent host, it is best to use host groups to manage the list of hosts that should be included in the dependency's definition. This can be one or more host group names, and very often, these groups will also be the same as for the service definitions.

Creating service dependencies

Service dependencies work in a similar way to host dependencies. For hosts, you need to specify one or more master hosts and one or more dependent hosts; for services, you need to define a master service and a dependent service.

Service dependencies can be defined only for a single service, but on multiple hosts. For example, you can tell Nagios that IMAP services on the `emailservers` host group depend on the LDAP service on the `ldapserver` host.

Here is an example of how to define such a service dependency:

```
define servicedependency
{
  host_name                      ldapserver
  service_description            LDAP
  dependent_hostgroup_name       emailservers
  dependent_service_description  IMAP
  execution_failure_criteria     c,u
  notification_failure_criteria  c,u,w
}
```

The following table describes all available directives for defining a service dependency. Items in bold are required when specifying a dependency:

Option	Description
dependent_host_name	Defines the hostnames whose services should be taken into account for this dependency, separated by commas
dependent_hostgroup_name	Defines the host group names whose members' services should be taken into account for this dependency, separated by commas
dependent_service_description	Defines the service that should be the dependent service for all the specified dependent hosts
host_name	Defines the master hosts whose services should be taken into account by this dependency, separated by commas
hostgroup_name	Defines the master host groups whose members' services should be taken into account by this dependency, separated by commas

Option	Description
service_description	Defines the service that should be the master service for all the provided master hosts
inherits_parent	Specifies whether this dependency should inherit the dependencies of the master hosts
execution_failure_criteria	Specifies which master service states should prevent Nagios from checking the dependent services, separated by commas; it can be one or more of the following: n - none, checks should always be executed p - pending state (no check has yet been done) o - service OK state w - service WARNING state c - service CRITICAL state u - service UNKNOWN state
notification_failure_criteria	Specifies which master service states should be prevented from generating notifications for the dependent service status changes, separated by commas; it can be one or more of the following: n – none, checks should always be executed p – pending state (no check has yet been done) o – service OK state w – service WARNING state c – service CRITICAL state u – service UNKNOWN state
dependency_period	Specifies the time periods during which the dependency will be valid; if not specified, the dependency is always valid

As is the case for host dependencies, there is a question of where to store the service dependency definitions. A good answer to this is to store dependencies in the same files that the dependent service definitions are kept in. If you are following the previous suggestions regarding how to keep services in the file structure, then for a service bound to a single host, both service and the related dependencies should be kept in the same file as the host definition itself. If a service is used by more than one host, it is kept in a separate file. In this case, dependencies related to that service should also be kept in the same file as the service.

Using templates

Templates in Nagios allow you to create a set of parameters that can then be used in the definitions of multiple hosts, services, and contacts. The main purpose of templates is to keep parameters that are generic to all objects or a group of objects in one place. In this way you can avoid putting the same directives in hundreds of objects and your configuration is more maintainable.

 Nagios allows an object to inherit from single or multiple templates. Templates can also inherit from other templates. This allows for the creation of very simple templates, where objects inherit from a single template, as well as a complex templating system, where actual objects (such as services or hosts) inherit from multiple templates. It is recommended to start with a simple template. Multiple templates are more useful when monitoring a larger numbers of hosts and services across multiple sites.

It is also good to try using templates for hosts and services and decide how they should be used. Sometimes, it's better to have one template, inherit another, and create a hierarchical structure. In many cases, it is more reasonable to create hosts so that they use multiple templates. This functionality allows the inheritance of some options from one template and some parameters from another.

The following is an illustration of how the templates can be structured using both techniques:

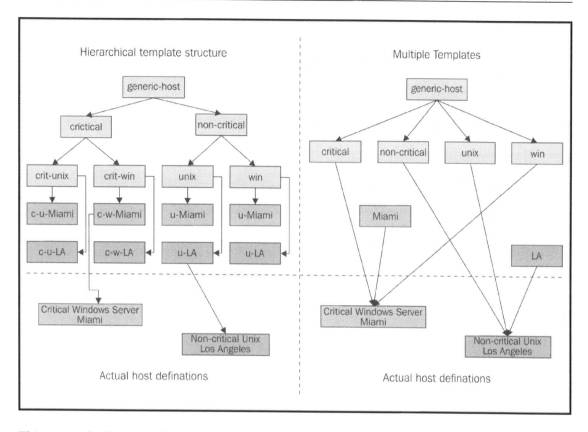

This example illustrates how the templates can be structured using both hierarchy and multiple templates inheritance. It shows how to use templates for host definitions, but similar rules apply for services as well; the inheritance structure may be a lot different, though.

In both methods shown in the preceding diagram, there's a distinction between `critical` and `non-critical` servers. Hosts are also split into ones that are Unix-based and ones that are Windows-based. There is also a distinction between the two branches that are configured— `Miami` and `LA` (Los Angeles). Furthermore, there is also a `generic-host` template that is used by every other template.

Usually, such distinctions make sense, as Windows and Unix hosts might be checked differently as well as have services checked by default. Based on the operating system and the location of the machine, different people should be assigned as contacts in case of problems. There may also be different time periods during which these hosts should be checked.

The example on the left shows the inheritance of one type of parameter at a time. First, a distinction is made between `critical` and `non-critical` machines. Usually, both types have different values for the notification and check intervals, as well as the number of checks to perform before generating a notification for a problem. The next step is to differentiate between Windows and Unix-based servers; this might involve the `check` command to verify that a server is up. The last step is to define templates for each system in both of the branches (`Miami` and `LA`). The actual host definition inherits from one template in the final set of templates.

The example on the right uses a slightly different approach. It first defines different templates for Unix and Windows systems. Next, a pair of templates for `critical` and `noncritical` machines is also defined. Finally, a set of templates defines the branches `Miami` and `LA`. The actual host definition inherits templates for the operating system, for the level of criticality, and for the branch to which it belongs. The actual host definitions then inherit parts of parameters from each of the templates.

In both cases, attributes that are passed at different levels are the same, even though the approach is different. Usually, templates that define the operating system also define how a host check should be done. They might also indicate the time period over which a host should be checked as well as host groups the host should be a member of by default.

Templates for `critical` and `noncritical` machines usually specify how notifications should be carried out. If a host is crucial to infrastructure, its owners should be notified in a more aggressive way. Similarly, machines that are not affecting business directly do not need that much attention.

Templates for locations usually define the owners of the machines. The locations are not always branches, as in this example; they can be branches, floors, or even network connection types. Locations can also point machines to their parent hosts; usually, computers located in the same place that are connected to the same router.

Creating templates

Defining the templates in Nagios is very similar to defining actual objects. You simply define the template as the required object type. The only difference is that you need to specify the `register` directive and specify a value of for it. This will tell Nagios that it should not treat this as an actual object, but as a template. You will also need to use the `name` directive for defining template names. You do not need to specify other directives for naming objects, such as `host_name`, `contact_name`, or `service_description`.

When defining an object, simply include the `use` directive and specify all of the templates to be used as its value. If you want to inherit from multiple templates, separate all of them with commas.

The following is an example of defining a template for a Linux server and then using this in an actual host definition:

```
define host   {
  register              0
  name                  generic-servers
  check_period          24x7
  retry_interval        1
  check_interval        15
  max_check_attempts    5
  notification_period   24x7
  notification_interval 60
  notification_options  d, r
}
define host
{
  register              0
  use                   generic-servers
  name                  linux-servers
  check_command         check-host-alive
  contact_groups        linux-admins
}
define host
{
  use                   linux-servers
  host_name             ubuntu1
  address               192.168.2.1
}
```

As mentioned earlier, templates use `name` for defining the template, and the actual host uses the `host_name` directive.

Inheriting from multiple templates

Nagios allows us to inherit from multiple templates and the templates using other (nested) templates. It's good to know how Nagios determines the order in which every directive is looked for in each of the templates. When inheriting attributes from more than one template, Nagios tries to find the directive in each of the templates, starting from the first one. If it is found in the first template, that value is used; if not, Nagios checks for a value in the second one. This cycle continues until the last template in the list. If any of the templates is also inheriting from another template, then a check for the second level of templates is done recursively. This means that checking for a directive will perform a recursive check of all of the templates that are inherited from the currently checked one.

The following illustration shows an example of this situation. The actual host definition inherits three templates— B, F, and G. Template B inherits A, F inherits D and E, and finally, D inherits attributes from template C :

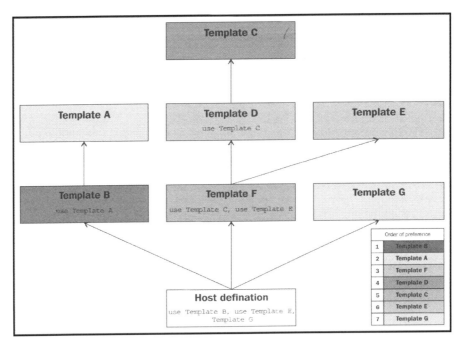

If Nagios tries to find any directive related to this host, the first thing that will be checked is the actual host definition. If the host does not include the directive, Nagios will first look under B, as this is the first template that should be used. If it is not found in B, Nagios will, recursively, try to find the attribute in A, as it is used by template B. The next step is to look in F along with all of the templates it is using. F inherits D and E. The first one to check is B along with all parent templates; this means that D, C, and the next E should now be checked. If the attribute is still not found, then template G is used. Let's assume that the following directives (among others) are defined for the previous illustration:

```
define host
{
    register                0
    name                    A
    check_period            workinghours
    retry_interval          1
    check_interval          15
}
define host
{
    register                0
    use                     A
    name                    B
    check_period            24x7
}
define host
{
    register                0
    name                    D
    use                     C
    max_check_attempts      4
}
define host
{
    register                0
    name                    E
    max_check_attempts      3
}
define host
{
    register                0
    use                     D,E
    name                    F
    notification_interval   30
}
define host
{
    use                     B,F,G
```

```
    host_name           ubuntu1
    address             192.168.2.1
    notification_interval  20   }
```

For this particular example, the values for the `address` and `notification_interval` directives are taken directly from the host `ubuntu1` definition. Even though `notification_interval` is also defined in F, it is overwritten by the actual host definition.

The value for `max_check_attempts` is taken from template D, regardless of whether it is also defined in C. Even though template E also defines a value for it, as D is put before E, the values defined in both of them are taken from D.

The value for `check_period` is taken from B, which overwrites the value defined for template A. Values for `retry_interval` and `check_interval` are taken from A.

Even though the preceding examples mention host configurations, templates for other types of objects work in the same way. Templates are often used extensively for service definitions. They usually use a similar approach as the one for hosts. It is a good idea to define templates for branches depending on the priority or type of service, such as a template common for all services in a specific branch. One template could be used for all services for web, mail, and other applications. Another template could be used for critical, non-critical, or backup servers. This increases the maintainability of the configurations, especially for the larger setups. It is much easier to change contact address or notification settings for all the critical applications if that info is defined in the template used by all services. In this case, our configuration may have several templates, and most of the service definitions will just re-use existing templates, perhaps only specifying how checks for those services should be made.

Contacts, on the other hand, usually use only a couple of templates. They depend on the working hours and the notification preferences. The remaining parameters can be kept in an individual contact's definition. Very often, users may have their own preferences on how they should be notified, so it's best not to try and design templates for that.

Using the custom variables

The custom variables allow you to include your own directives when defining objects. These can then be used in commands. This allows you to define objects in a more concise way and define service checks in a more general fashion.

The idea is that you define directives that are not standard Nagios parameters in host, service, or contact objects, and they can be accessed from all commands, such as check commands, notifications, and event handlers. This is very useful for complex Nagios configurations, where you might want commands to perform nontrivial tasks for which they will require additional information.

Let's assume we want Nagios to check that the hosts have correct MAC addresses. We can then define a service once and use that custom variable for the check command. When defining an object, a custom variable needs to be prefixed with an underscore and written in uppercase.

The custom variables are accessible as the following macros:

- $_HOST<variable>$: This is used for directives defined within a host object
- $_SERVICE<variable>$: This is used for directives defined within a service object
- $_CONTACT<variable>$: This is for directives defined within a contact object

For the preceding example, a macro definition would be $_HOSTMAC$.

These variables can be used for command definitions, notifications, or time periods. The following is an example of a contact and notification command that uses a custom variable for the Jabber address:

```
define contact
{
  contact_name              jdoe
  alias                     John Doe
  host_notification_commands host-notify-by-jabber
  _JABBERID                 jdoe@jabber.yourcompany.com
}
define command
{
  command_name      host-notify-by-jabber
  command_line      $USER1$/notify_via_jabber $_CONTACTJABBERID$
                    "Host $HOSTDISPLAYNAME$ changed state to
$HOSTSTATE$"
}
```

Of course, you will also need a plugin to send notifications over Jabber. This can be downloaded from the Nagios project on SourceForge (http://nagios.sf.net/download/ contrib/notifications/notify_via_jabber). The previous example will work with any other protocol you might be using. All that's needed is a plugin that will send commands over such a protocol.

A major benefit of custom variables is that they can also be changed on the fly over an external command pipe. This way, the custom variables' functionality can be used in more complex configurations. Event handlers may trigger changes in the attributes of other checks.

An example might be that a ping check with 50 ms and 20 percent packet loss limits is made to ensure that the network connectivity is working correctly. However, if the main router is down and a failover connection is used, the check is set to a more relaxed limit of 400 ms and 50 percent packet loss.

An example configuration might be as follows:

```
define service
{
  host_name              router2
  service_description PING
  check_command          check_ping_limits
  _LIMITS                50.0,20%
}
define command
{
  command_name           check_ping_limits
  command_line           $USER1$/check_ping -H $HOSTADDRESS$
                         -w $_SERVICELIMITS$ -c $_SERVICELIMITS$

}
```

When a service checks if the main router is up (that is, it is in a critical state), an event handler will invoke a change in the limits by sending a CHANGE_CUSTOM_SVC_VAR command (documented here: http://www.nagios.org/developerinfo/externalcommand s/commandinfo.php?command_id=14) over the external commands pipe to set the _LIMITS custom variable. Chapter 8, *Notifications and Events,* covers event handlers and external commands pipe in more detail. It will also show how to change custom host and service variables to a Nagios instance.

Understanding state flapping

State flapping is a situation where a host or service changes states very rapidly, constantly switching between working correctly and not working. This can happen due to various reasons; a service might crash after a short period of operating correctly or due to some maintenance work being done by system administrators.

Nagios can detect that a host or service state is flapping if it is configured to do so. It does so by analyzing previous results in terms of how many state changes have taken place within a specific period of time. Nagios keeps a history of the 21 most recent checks and analyzes changes within that history.

The following is a screenshot illustrating the 21 most recent check results, which means that Nagios can detect up to 20 state changes in the recent history of an object. It also shows how Nagios detects state transitions:

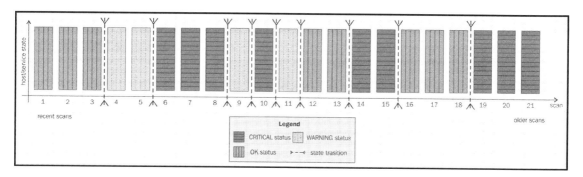

Nagios then finds all of the changes between different states and uses them to determine if a host or service state is flapping. It checks to see if a state is the same as the result from the previous check, and if it has changed, a state transition is counted at this place. In the preceding example, we have nine transitions.

Nagios calculates a flapping threshold based on this information. The value reflects how many of the state changes have occurred recently. If there are no changes in the last 21 state checks, the value would be 0 percent. If all checks have different states, the flapping threshold would be 100 percent.

In our case, if Nagios would only take the number of transitions into account, the flapping threshold would be 45 percent. The weighted algorithm used in Nagios would calculate the flapping threshold as more than 45 percent because there have been many changes in the more recent checks.

Nagios takes threshold values into consideration when estimating whether a host or service has started or stopped flapping. The configuration for each object allows the definition of high and low flapping thresholds.

If an object state was not flapping previously, and the current flapping threshold is equal to or greater than the high flap threshold, Nagios assumes that the object has just started flapping. If an object was flapping previously and the current threshold is lower than the low flap threshold, Nagios assumes the object has just stopped flapping.

The following chart shows how the flapping threshold for an object has changed over time and when Nagios flapping detection assumes it has been flapping. In this case, the high flap threshold is set to 40 percent and the low flap threshold is set to 25 percent. The vertical lines indicate when Nagios assumed the flapping to have started and stopped, and the gray area shows where the service was assumed to be flapping:

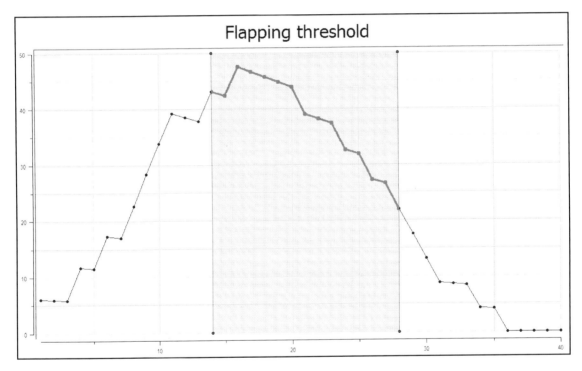

It is worth noting that the low flap threshold should be lower than the high flap threshold. This prevents the situation where, after one state transition, flapping would be detected, and the next check would tell Nagios that the object has stopped flapping. If both the attributes are set to the same value, an object might be identified as having started and stopped flapping often. This can happen when the flapping threshold changes from below threshold to above threshold or vice versa. This might cause Nagios to send out a large number of notifications and cause its performance to degrade.

Summary

When creating or extending Nagios configuration to monitor a large number of resources, spend some time planning the layout of your configuration. Some people recommend one file for each single definition, while others recommend storing things in a single file per host. We recommend keeping similar things in the same file and maintaining a directory-based set of files.

In this chapter we have learned the following things:

- Setting up efficient directory structure and file naming standards
- Where to put objects depending on the type and hosts it is configured for
- How to define dependencies so that Nagios can then detect root causes of problems
- Using templates to ease defining a large number of objects
- Accessing host, service, or contact-specific information with custom variables
- What state flapping is and how Nagios detects when flapping occurs

The next chapter describes notifications and events in more detail. It will help us set up an efficient way to let the IT department know about errors, and when things are working normally. It will also show how event handlers can be used to proactively fix problems before anyone is notified.

8
Notifications and Events

We already know how notifications work in Nagios. The previous chapters described how Nagios sends information to the users when a problem occurs and how it decides to notify people. Previously, our examples were limited to sending an e-mail 24 hours a day or only during working days.

In this chapter, we will cover the following items:

- Creating effective notifications
- Understanding escalations
- Sending commands to Nagios
- Creating event handlers
- Using adaptive monitoring

Creating effective notifications

This section covers notifications in more depth and describes the details of how Nagios can tell other people about what is happening. We will discuss both simple as well as more complex approaches on how notifications can make your life easier.

In many cases, a plain e-mail notification about a problem may not always be the right thing to do. As people's inboxes get cluttered with e-mails, the usual approach is to create rules to move certain messages that they don't even look at to separate folders. There's a pretty good chance that if people start getting a lot of notifications that they won't need to react to, they'll simply ask their favorite mailing program to move these messages into a *do not look in here unless you have plenty of time* folder. Moreover, in such cases, if there is an issue they should be handling, they will most probably not even see the notification e-mail.

This section talks about the things that can be implemented in your company to make notifications more convenient for the IT staff. Limiting the amount of irrelevant information sent to various people tends to decrease their response time, as they will have much less information to filter out.

Using multiple notifications

The first issue that many Nagios administrators overlook is the ability to create more than one notification command. In this way, Nagios can try to notify you on both instant messaging (such as HipChat, Slack, Jabber, Twitter, or Telegram) and e-mail. It can also send you an SMS. A disadvantage is that at some point, you might end up receiving text messages at 2 AM about an outage of a machine that may well be down for the next three days and is not critical.

At this point, it's worth mentioning that there's another easy solution. The approach is to create multiple contacts for a single person. For example, you can set up different contacts when you're at work, when you're offline, and define a profile to not to disturb you too much during the night.

For example, you can set up the following contacts to handle various times of the day in a different fashion:

- `jdoe-workhours` would be a contact that will only receive notifications during working hours; notifications will be carried out using both the corporate IM system and an e-mail
- `jdoe-daytime` would be a contact that will only receive notifications between 7 AM and 10 PM, excluding working hours; notifications will be sent as a text or a pager message, and an e-mail
- `jdoe-night` would be a contact that will only receive notifications between 10 PM and 7 AM; notifications will only be sent out as an e-mail

All entries would also contain contact groups pointing to the same groups that the single jdoe contact entry used to contain. This way, the other objects such as hosts, services, or contact groups related to this user would not be affected. All entries would also reside in the same file, for example, contacts/jdoe.cfg.

The main drawback of this approach is that logging on to the web interface would require using one of the users above or keeping the jdoe contact without any notifications, just to be able to log on to the interface.

The example above combined both the creation of multiple contacts and use of multiple notification commands to achieve a convenient way of getting notified about a problem. Using only multiple contacts also works fine. Another approach to the problem is to define different contacts for different ways of being notified—for example, jdoe-e-mail, jdoe-sms, and jdoe-jabber. This way, you can define different contact methods for various time periods—instant messages during working hours, text messages while on duty, and an e-mail when not at work.

Another important issue is to make sure that few people as possible are notified of the problem. Imagine there is a host without an explicit administrator assigned to it. A notification about a problem gets sent out to 20 different people. In such a case, either each of them will assume that someone else will resolve the problem, or people will run into a communication problem over discussing who will actually handle it.

Teams that cooperate tightly with each other usually solve these issues naturally—knowledgeable people start discussing a solution and a natural person to solve the issue comes out of the discussion. However, the teams that are distributed across various locations or that have problems with efficient communication within their team will run into problems in such cases.

This is why it is a good idea to either nominate a coordinator who will assign tasks as they arise or try to maintain a short list of people responsible for each machine. If you need to make sure that other people will investigate the problem if the original owner of the machine cannot do it immediately, then it is a good idea to use escalations for this purpose. These are described later in this chapter.

Previously, we mentioned that notifications only via e-mail may not always be the best thing to do. For example, they don't work well for situations that require fast response times. There are various reasons behind this. Firstly, e-mails are slow—even though the e-mail lands on your mail server in a few seconds, people usually only poll their e-mails every few minutes. Secondly, people tend to filter e-mails and skip those that they are not interested in.

Another good reason why e-mails should not always be used is that they stay on your e-mail account until you actually fetch and read them. If you have been on a 2-week vacation and a problem has occurred, should you still be worried when you read it after you get back? Has the issue been resolved already?

If your team needs to react to problems promptly, using e-mail as the basic notification method is definitely not the best choice. Let's consider what other possibilities exist to notify users of a problem effectively.

As already mentioned, a very good choice is to use instant messaging or **Short Message Service** (**SMS**) messages as the basic means of notification, and only use e-mail as a last resort. Some companies might also use the client/server approach to notify the users of the problems, perhaps integrated with showing Nagios status only for particular hosts and services. Nagios Exchange has plenty of available solutions you can use for handling notifications effectively. Visit `http://exchange.nagios.org/` for more details.

Sending instant messages via Jabber

The first and the most powerful option is to use Jabber (`http://www.jabber.org/`) for notifications. There is an existing script for this that is available in the contributions repository on the Nagios project website (directly available at `http://nagios.sf.net/download/contrib/notifications/notify_via_jabber`).

This is a small Perl script that sends messages over Jabber. You may need to install additional system packages to handle Jabber connectivity from Perl.

On Ubuntu, this requires running the following command:

```
root@ubuntu1:~# apt-get install libnet-jabber-perl
```

When using **Central Perl Archive Network** (**CPAN**), which is the source for Perl modules and documentation; visit `http://www.cpan.org/`) to install Perl packages, run the following command:

```
root@ubuntu1:~# cpan install Net::Jabber
```

In order to use the notification plugin, you will need to customize the script—change the `SERVER`, `PORT`, `USER`, and `PASSWORD` parameters to an existing account. Our recommendation is to create a separate account to use only for Nagios notifications—you will need to set up authorization for each user that you want to send notifications to.

After modifying the script, it can be used for notifications as follows:

```
define command{
        command_name     notify-host-by-jabber
        command_line     /path/to/notify_via_jabber $_CONTACTJABBERID$
"Nagios Host Notification Type: $NOTIFICATIONTYPE$ Host: $HOSTNAME$\nState:
$HOSTSTATE$ Address: $HOSTADDRESS$ Info: $HOSTOUTPUT$ "
        }

define command{
        command_name     notify-service-by-jabber
        command_line     /path/to/notify_via_jabber $_CONTACTJABBERID$
```

```
"Nagios Service Notification Type: $NOTIFICATIONTYPE$ Service:
$SERVICEDESC$ Host: $HOSTALIAS$ Address: $HOSTADDRESS$ State:
$SERVICESTATE$ Additional Info: $SERVICEOUTPUT$"
        }
```

The commands above can be used for host and service notifications and will send a descriptive message using Jabber to the specified user. The `$_CONTACTJABBERID$` text will be replaced with the current contact's `_JABBERID` custom variable.

Please note that due to how Jabber works, the best approach is for the `notify_via_jabber` script to use the same Jabber server as the client for receiving notifications.

As you plan to monitor servers and potentially even outgoing Internet connectivity, it would not be wise to use public Jabber servers for reporting errors. Therefore, it would be a good idea to set up a private Jabber server, probably on the same host on which the Nagios monitoring system is running.

There are multiple desktop clients for the Jabber protocol that can be used to receive Nagios notifications in a convenient way. Pidgin, available from `http://www.pidgin.im/` is a cross-platform instant messaging client with multiple protocol support and includes support for Jabber.

Notifying users with text messages

There are also very useful packages for sending SMS (the text messages in mobile phones). There are multiple interfaces for sending SMS information over the Internet—such as `http://www.twilio.com/`, which offers a service to send SMS to phones in a large number of countries.

Using Twilio to send notifications from Nagios is straightforward. Download the twilio-sms command line from `https://www.twilio.com/labs/bash/sms`. It also requires creating a configuration file that specifies account information for Twilio. For an installation performed according to the steps given in `Chapter 2`, *Installing Nagios 4,*the location for the file is `/opt/nagios/.twiliorc`.

Next, create a Nagios command that uses the twilio-sms command directly—such as:

```
define command{
        command_name    notify-host-by-twilio
        command_line    echo "Nagios $NOTIFICATIONTYPE$ Host: $HOSTNAME$
State: $HOSTSTATE$" | /path/to/twilio-sms $_CONTACTSMSNUMBER$
        }
define command{
        command_name    notify-service-by-twilio
        command_line    echo "Nagios $NOTIFICATIONTYPE$ Svc: $SERVICEDESC$
Host: $HOSTALIAS$ State: $SERVICESTATE$" | /path/to/twilio-sms
$_CONTACTSMSNUMBER$
        }
```

The downside of using Internet-based notification services is that if Internet connectivity is down, it is not possible for Nagios to send notifications. This may be a problem for Internet providers, which need to be sure their customers are online all the time.

Another possibility for sending notifications is to use GSM terminals or USB modems that offer a convenient way to send SMS notifications. Both GSM terminals and USB modems can be used to send text messages over regular SIM cards—which only require GSM coverage and do not require Internet access. These devices are usually connected via USB or serial port.

There are multiple tools that allow managing GSM terminals/modems—such as Gammu (`http://wammu.eu/gammu/`) and Gnokii (`http://www.gnokii.org/`).

Both are very common applications, and when setting up a GSM terminal it is best to check both for how well the specific hardware is supported and choose the program that supports this specific GSM terminal better. Depending on the exact hardware used, additional steps to set up drivers and/or configure Gammu/Gnokii may be needed—it is recommended to check with the documentation for both Gammu/Gnokii as well as the GSM terminal's documentation.

After setting up, both Gammu and Gnokii provide command line tools for sending SMS messages. The example below shows how to send messages using Gammu:

```
define command{
        command_name    notify-host-by-gammu
        command_line    echo "Nagios $NOTIFICATIONTYPE$ Host: $HOSTNAME$
State: $HOSTSTATE$" | /path/to/gammu --sendsms TEXT $_CONTACTSMSNUMBER$
        }
define command{
        command_name    notify-service-by-gammu
        command_line    echo "Nagios $NOTIFICATIONTYPE$ Svc: $SERVICEDESC$
Host: $HOSTALIAS$ State: $SERVICESTATE$" | /path/to/gammu --sendsms TEXT
```

```
$_CONTACTSMSNUMBER$
            }
```

Current mobile phones also offer cheap Internet connectivity, and smart devices offer the possibility to write custom applications in Java, .NET, and many other languages including Ruby, Python, and Tcl. Therefore, you can also make a client/server application that queries the server for the status of selected hosts and services. It can even be unified with a notification command that pushes the changes down to the application immediately.

Integrating with HipChat

There are also multiple specialized tools for communication within organizations—such as HipChat, (http://www.hipchat.com/). It is a popular online service for group and direct communication within a company. The service has extensive APIs and is commonly used for sending notifications in addition to regular messaging.

HipChat offers rooms for group communications, which are often used for receiving notifications as well—such as a room for Nagios notifications, where IT staff reside and receive notifications instantly. The chat can then also be used to quickly and informally assign tasks to individual people.

There is a ready to use freely available solution for integrating Nagios with HipChat called hipsaint, which is available from https://github.com/hannseman/hipsaint.

To use it, simply download the source code and run the installation script:

```
$ python setup.py install
```

Next, create new commands to send notifications to specific rooms:

```
define command {
    command_name     notify-host-by-hipchat
    command_line     hipsaint --token=tokenid --room=roomid --type=host --
inputs="$HOSTNAME$|$LONGDATETIME$|$NOTIFICATIONTYPE$|$HOSTADDRESS$|$HOSTSTA
TE$|$HOSTOUTPUT$" -n
}

define command {
    command_name     notify-service-by-hipchat
    command_line     hipsaint --token=tokenid --room=roomid --type=service -
-
inputs="$SERVICEDESC$|$HOSTALIAS$|$LONGDATETIME$|$NOTIFICATIONTYPE$|$HOSTAD
DRESS$|$SERVICESTATE$|$SERVICEOUTPUT$" -n
}
```

All of the above are ways to send notifications about host/service statuses that are more convenient than regular e-mails. Letting the IT staff know about problems (and once things are resolved) and being able to communicate to other people in your team/company is essential. Using e-mail may be a good solution in many cases; however, it is a good idea to spend some time on researching for a convenient and non-intrusive way to use for Nagios notifications.

Aside from the examples mentioned above, there are many more ready to use solutions available online. Many of them are listed on Nagios Exchange at `http://exchange.nagios` `.org/directory/Addons/Notifications`.

Slack integration

Slack (`https://slack.com`) is a very popular communication tool. Aside from regular chat based communication, it allows sending messages both to the channel and directly to other users.

The easiest way to post a message to Slack from an external service such as Nagios is to use the incoming webHook concept (`https://api.slack.com/incoming-webhooks`). Essentially, it boils down to sending an HTTP POST with specific JSON content to a WebHook URL, which can be uniquely generated for your Slack's team. Once we have Slack configured and a WebHook URL generated, we can proceed with setting up commands to send notifications:

```
define command{
        command_name     notify-host-by-slack
        command_line     /usr/bin/curl -X POST --data-urlencode
```

```
'payload={"channel": "#general", "username": "Nagios", "text": "Nagios Host
Notification Type: $NOTIFICATIONTYPE$ Host: $HOSTNAME$ State: $HOSTSTATE$
Address: $HOSTADDRESS$ Info: $HOSTOUTPUT$"}' WEBHOOK_URL
        }

define command{
        command_name    notify-service-by-slack
        command_line    /usr/bin/curl -X POST --data-urlencode
'payload={"channel": "#general", "username": "Nagios", "text": "Nagios
Service Notification Type: $NOTIFICATIONTYPE$ Service: $SERVICEDESC$ Host:
$HOSTALIAS$ Address: $HOSTADDRESS$ State: $SERVICESTATE$ Additional Info:
$SERVICEOUTPUT$"}' WEBHOOK_URL
        }
```

As we can see, it is enough to have the `curl` command installed, and the good news is that, most probably, it is already present in the system. Replace the `WEBHOOK_URL` string with the correct value, similar to

`https://hooks.slack.com/services/T00000000/B00000000/XXXXXXXXXXXXXXXXXXXXXXXX`

and you are ready to go. A sample message sent from Nagios to Slack is shown in the following diagram:

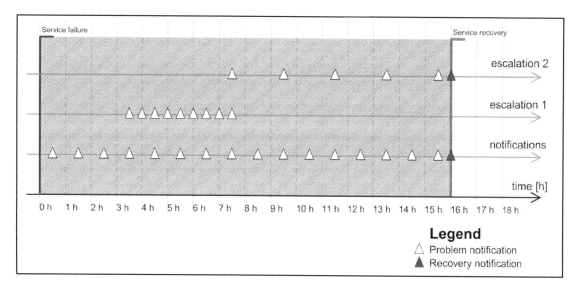

The message's JSON payload is well described in Slack's documentation; here is a quick recap of the most important fields:

Option	Description
text	Message text
channel	Specifies a target of the message. It can be both a channel (in the form #channelName) or user (@userName)
username	String that will be displayed on Slack as message sender
icon_url	URL to icon that will be displayed along with the message
icon_emoji	Code of Slack's built-in emoji emoticons, for example, :warning:

Although the provided example of Nagios-Slack integration is rather simple and straightforward, it can be enhanced in many ways. For example, by specifying an icon that would reflect service state or selecting the appropriate user/channel to send a message to based on notification parameters. One interesting example is available here: http://matthewcmcmillan.blogspot.com/2013/12/simple-way-to-integrate-nagios-with.html, where the author decided to put message formatting logic into a separate shell script.

Please note that at the time of writing the script did not include full support for notifications regarding host and/or service status acknowledgements—the notifications will still be sent properly, but may lack information about the user that has acknowledged the problem and comment.

Understanding escalations

A common problem with resolving problems is that a host or a service may have blurred ownership. Often there is no single person responsible for a host or service, which makes things harder. It is also typical to have a service with subtle dependencies on other things, which by themselves are small enough not to be monitored by Nagios. In such a case, it is good to include lower management in the escalations so that they are able to focus on problems that haven't been resolved in a timely manner.

Here is a good example—a database server might fail because a small Perl script that is run prior to actual start to clean things up has entered an infinite loop. The owner of this machine gets notified. But the question is, who should be fixing it? The script owner? Or perhaps the database administrator? Often this may end up in different teams assuming someone else should resolve it—programmers waiting on database administrators and vice versa.

In such cases, escalations are a great way to solve such complex problems. In the previous example, if the problem has not been resolved after two hours, the IT team coordinator or manager would be notified. Another hour later, he would get another e-mail. At that point, he would schedule an urgent meeting with the developer who owns the script, and the database admin to discuss how this could be solved.

Of course, in real-world scenarios, escalating to management alone would not solve all problems. However, often, situations need a coordinator that will take care of communicating issues between teams and try to find a company-wide solution. Business-critical services also require much higher attention. In such cases, it is a real benefit for the company if it has an escalation ladder that can be followed for all major problems.

Setting up escalations

Nagios offers many ways to set up escalations, depending on your needs. Escalations do not need to be sent out just after a problem occurs, which would create confusion and prevent smaller problems from being solved. Usually, escalations are set up so that additional people are informed only if a problem has not been resolved after a certain amount of time.

From a configuration point of view, all escalations are defined as separate objects. There are two types of objects—`hostescalation` and `serviceescalation`. Escalations are configured so that they start and stop being active along with the normal host or service notifications. This way, if you change the `notification_interval` directive in host or service definition, the times at which escalations start and stop will also change.

A sample escalation for a company's main router is as follows:

```
define hostescalation   {
    host_name               mainrouter
    contactgroups           it-management
    first_notification      2
    last_notification       0
    notification_interval   60
    escalation_options      d,u,r
}
```

This will define an escalation for host `mainrouter`. The escalation will cause the `it-management` contact group to also start being notified starting with the second notification. The escalation will cause notifications about the host being in DOWN and UP state as well as when it recovers. Details of how escalations work are defined in the next section of the chapter.

The following table describes all available directives for defining a host escalation. Items in bold are required when specifying an escalation.

Option	Description
host_name	Specifies a list of all hosts that the escalation should be defined for; separated by commas
hostgroup_name	Specifies a list of all host groups that the escalation should be defined for; all hosts inside said host groups will have the escalation defined for them; separated by commas
contacts	List of all contacts that should receive notifications related to this escalation; separated by commas; at least one contact or contact group needs to be specified for each escalation
contactgroups	List of all contact groups that should receive notifications related to this escalation, separated by commas; at least one contact or contact group needs to be specified for each escalation
first_notification	The number of notifications after which this escalation becomes active; setting this to 0 causes notifications to be sent until the host recovers from the problem; how Nagios handles notifications and escalations is described in more detail later in the next section of the chapter
last_notification	The number of notifications after which this escalation stops being active; how Nagios handles notifications and escalations is described in more detail later in the chapter

Option	Description
`notification_interval`	Specifies the number of minutes between sending notifications related to this escalation
`escalation_period`	Specifies the time period during which this escalation should be valid; if not specified, this defaults to 24 hours a day, 7 days a week
`escalation_options`	Specifies the host states for which notification types should be sent, separated by commas; this can be one or more of the following: d - host DOWN state u – host UNREACHABLE state r – host recovery (UP state)

Service escalations are defined in a very similar way to host escalations. You can specify one or more hosts or host groups, as well as a single service description. Service escalation will be associated with this service on all hosts mentioned in the host_name and hostgroup_name attributes.

The following is an example of a service escalation for an OpenVPN check on the company's main router:

```
define serviceescalation
{
  host_name              mainrouter
  service_description    OpenVPN
  contactgroups          it-management
  first_notification     2
  last_notification      0
  notification_interval 60
  escalation_options     w,c,r
}
```

This will define an escalation for service OpenVPN running on host mainrouter. The escalation will cause it-management contact group to also start being notified starting with second notification. The escalation will cause notifications about service being in WARNING and CRITICAL state as well as when it recovers. Details of how escalations work are defined in the next section of the chapter.

The following table describes all available directives for defining a service escalation. Items in bold are required when specifying an escalation.

Option	Description
host_name	Specifies a list of all hosts that the escalation should be defined for; separated by commas
hostgroup_name	Specifies a list of all host groups that the escalation should be defined for; all hosts inside said host groups will have the escalation defined for them; separated by commas
service_description	The service for which the escalation is being defined
contacts	List of all contacts that should receive notifications related to this escalation, separated by commas; at least one contact or contact group needs to be specified for each escalation
contactgroups	List of all contact groups that should receive notifications related to this escalation, separated by commas; at least one contact or contact group needs to be specified for each escalation
first_notification	The number of notifications after which this escalation becomes active; how Nagios handles notifications and escalations is described in more detail later in the chapter
last_notification	The number of notifications after which this escalation stops being active; setting this to 0 causes notifications to be sent until the service recovers from the problem; how Nagios handles notifications and escalations is described in more detail later in the chapter
notification_interval	Specifies the number of minutes between sending notifications related to this escalation
escalation_period	Specifies the time period during which escalation should be valid; if not specified, this defaults to 24 hours a day, 7 days a week
escalation_options	Specifies which notification types for service states should be sent, separated by commas; this can be one or more of the following: r - service recovers (OK state) w - service WARNING state c - service CRITICAL state u - service UNKNOWN state

Understanding how escalations work

Let's consider the following configuration—a service along with two escalations:

```
define service
{
   use                    generic-service
   host_name              mainrouter
   service_description    OpenVPN
   check_command          check_openvpn_remote
   check_interval         15
   max_check_attempts     3
   notification_interval 30
   notification_period    24x7
}
# Escalation 1
define serviceescalation   {
   host_name              mainrouter
   service_description    OpenVPN
   first_notification     4
   last_notification      8
   contactgroups          it-escalation1
   escalation_options     w,c
   notification_period    24x7
   notification_interval 15
}
# Escalation 2
define serviceescalation   {
   host_name              mainrouter
   service_description    OpenVPN
   first_notification     8
   last_notification      0
   contactgroups          it-escalation2
   escalation_options     w,c,r
   notification_period    24x7
   notification_interval 120
}
```

In order to show how the escalations work, let's take an example—a failing service. A service fails for a total of 16 hours and then recovers—for the clarity of the example, we'll skip the soft and hard states and the timing required for hard state transitions.

Service notifications are set up so that the first notification is sent out 30 minutes after failure. Later on, they are repeated every 60 minutes and then the next notification is sent 1.5 hours after the actual failure and so on. The service also has two escalations defined for it.

`Escalation 1` is first triggered along with the fourth service notification that is sent out. The escalation stops being active after the eighth service notification on the failure. It only sends out reports about problems, not recovery; the `escalation_options` is set to `w`, `c`, which is `WARNING` and `CRITICAL` state. The interval for this escalation is configured to be 15 minutes.

`Escalation 2` is first triggered along with the eighth service notification and never stops—the `last_notification` directive is set to 0. It sends out reports about problems and recovery—the `escalation_options` is set to `w`, `c`, `r`, which is WARNING and CRITICAL state as well as recovery. The interval for this escalation is configured to two hours.

The diagram below shows when both escalations are sent out:

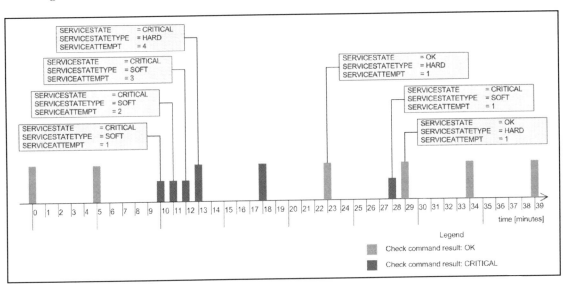

Notifications for the service itself are sent out 0.5, 1.5, 2.5, 3.5 … hours after the occurrence of the initial service failure.

`Escalation 1` becomes active after 3.5 hours—which is when the fourth service notification is sent out. The last notification related to `Escalation 1` is sent out 7.5 hours after the initial failure—this is the time when the eighth service notification is sent out. It is sent every 30 minutes; so a total of nine notifications related to `Escalation 1` are sent out.

`Escalation 2` becomes active after 7.5 hours—which is when the eighth service notification is sent out. The last notification related to `Escalation 2` is sent out when the problem is resolved, and concerns the actual problem resolution. It is sent every two hours, so a total of four notifications related to `Escalation 2` are sent out.

Escalations can be defined to be independent of each other—there is no reason why `Escalation 2` cannot start after the sixth service notification is sent out. There are also no limits on the number of escalations that can be set up for a single host or service.

The main point is that escalations should be defined reasonably, so that they don't bloat management or other teams with problems that would be solved without their interference anyway.

Escalations can also be used to contact different people for a certain set of objects, based on time periods. If an escalation has the `first_notification` option set to 1 and the `last_notification` option set to 0, then all notifications related to this escalation will be sent out exactly in the same way as notifications for the service itself.

For example, normal IT staff may be handling problems normally, but during holidays, if notifications about problems should also go to the `CritSit` team, then you can simply define an escalation saying that during the `holidays` time period, the `CritSit` group should also be notified about problems when the first notification is sent out. The following is an example that is based on the `OpenVPN` service defined earlier:

```
define serviceescalation
{
    host_name              mainrouter
    service_description    OpenVPN
    first_notification     1
    last_notification      0
    contactgroups          CritSit
    notification_period    holidays
    notification_interval  30
    escalation_options     w,c,r
}
```

The definitions above specify both the service and its escalation. Please note that the `notification_interval` option is set to the same value in both the object and the escalation.

Sending commands to Nagios

Nagios offers a very powerful mechanism for receiving events and commands from external applications—the external commands pipe. This is a pipe file created on a filesystem that Nagios uses to receive incoming messages. The name of the file is `rw/nagios.cmd` and it is located in the directory passed as the `localstatedir` option during compilation. If you have followed the compilation and installation instructions given in `Chapter 2`, *Installing Nagios 4*, of this book, the filename will be `/var/nagios/rw/nagios.cmd`.

The communication does not use any authentication or authorization—the only requirement is to have write access to the pipe file. An external command file is usually writable by the owner and the group; the usual group used is `nagioscmd`. If you want a user to be able to send commands to the Nagios daemon, simply add that user to this group.

A small limitation of the command pipe is that there is no way to get any results back and so it is not possible to send any query commands to Nagios. Therefore, by just using the command pipe, you have no verification that the command you have just passed to Nagios has actually been processed, or will be processed soon. It is, however, possible to read the Nagios log file and check if it indicates that the command has been parsed correctly, if necessary.

An external command pipe is used by the web interface to control how Nagios works. The web interface does not use any other means to send commands or apply changes to Nagios. This gives a good understanding of what can be done with the external command pipe interface.

From the Nagios daemon perspective, there is no clear distinction as to who can perform what operations. Therefore, if you plan to use the external command pipe to allow users to submit commands remotely, you need to make sure that the authorization is in place as well so that it is not possible for unauthorized users to send potentially dangerous commands to Nagios.

The syntax for formatting commands is easy. Each command must be placed on a single line and end with a newline character. The syntax is as follows:

```
[TIMESTAMP] COMMAND_NAME;argument1;argument2;...;argumentN
```

TIMESTAMP is written as Unix time—that is the number of seconds since 1970-01-01 00:00:00. This can be created by using the date +%s system command. Most programming languages also offer the means to get the current Unix time. Commands are written in uppercase. This can be one of the commands that Nagios should execute, and the arguments depend on the actual command.

All of the commands that can be sent to Nagios using the external command pipe are defined in the documentation available at http://www.nagios.org/developerinfo/exter nalcommands/commandinfo.php.

Adding comments to hosts and services

One of the commands that can be sent to Nagios via the external pipe are commands for adding a comment for a host or service.

For example, to add a comment to a host stating that it has passed a security audit, one can use the following shell command:

```
echo "[`date +%s`] ADD_HOST_COMMENT;somehost;1;Security Audit;       This
host has passed security audit on `date +%Y-%m-%d`"
>/var/nagios/rw/nagios.cmd
```

This will send an ADD_HOST_COMMENT command to Nagios over the external command pipe. Nagios will then add a comment to the host, somehost, stating that the comment originated from Security Audit. The first argument specifies the hostname to add the comment to; the second tells Nagios if this comment should be persistent. The next argument describes the author of the comment, and the last argument specifies the actual comment text.

Similarly, adding a comment to a service requires the use of the ADD_SVC_COMMENT command. The command's syntax is very similar to the ADD_HOST_COMMENT command except that the command requires the specification of the hostname and service name.

For example, to add a comment to a service stating that it has been restarted, you should use the following:

```
echo "[`date +%s`] ADD_SVC_COMMENT;router;OpenVPN;1;nagiosadmin;
Restarting the OpenVPN service" >/var/nagios/rw/nagios.cmd
```

The first argument specifies the hostname to add the comment to; the second is the description of the service to which Nagios should add the comment. The next argument tells Nagios if this comment should be persistent. The fourth argument describes the author of the comment, and the last argument specifies actual comment text.

You can also delete a single comment or all comments using the DEL_HOST_COMMENT, DEL_ALL_HOST_COMMENTS, DEL_SVC_COMMENT ,or DEL_ALL_SVC_COMMENTS commands.

Scheduling host and service checks

Other commands worth mentioning are related to scheduling checks on demand. Very often, it is necessary to request that a check must be carried out as soon as possible; for example, when testing a solution.

This time, let's create a script that schedules a check of a host, all services on that host, and a service on a different host, as follows:

```
#!/bin/sh

NOW=`date +%s`

echo "[$NOW] SCHEDULE_HOST_CHECK;somehost;$NOW" \
     >/var/nagios/rw/nagios.cmd
echo "[$NOW] SCHEDULE_HOST_SVC_CHECKS;somehost;$NOW" \
     >/var/nagios/rw/nagios.cmd
echo "[$NOW] SCHEDULE_SVC_CHECK;otherhost;Service Name;$NOW" \
     >/var/nagios/rw/nagios.cmd

exit 0
```

The commandsSCHEDULE_HOST_ and SCHEDULE_HOST_SVC_CHECKS accept a hostname and the time at which the check should be scheduled. The SCHEDULE_SVC_CHECK command requires the specification of a service description as well as the name of the host to schedule the check on.

Normal scheduled checks, such as the ones scheduled above, might not actually take place at the time that you scheduled them. Nagios also needs to take allowed time periods into account as well as checking whether checks were disabled for a particular object or globally for the entire Nagios.

Here are cases when you'll need to force Nagios to do a check-in such cases, you should use `SCHEDULE_FORCED_HOST_`, `SCHEDULE_FORCED_HOST_SVC_CHECKS`,and `SCHEDULE_FORCED_SVC_CHECK` commands. They work in exactly the same way as described above, but make Nagios skip the checking of time periods, and ensure that the checks are disabled for this particular object. This way, a check will always be performed, regardless of other Nagios parameters.

Modifying custom variables

Other commands worth using are related to the custom variables feature, which is described in more detail in `Chapter 7`, *Advanced Configuration*. When you define a custom variable for a host, service, or contact, you can change its value on the fly with the external command pipe.

As these variables can then be directly used by check or notification commands and event handlers, it is possible to make other applications or event handlers change these attributes directly without modifications to the configuration files.

A good example would be an application the IT staff uses for receiving notifications—such as Growl (a notification system for OS X and Windows; visit `http://growl.info/` and `http://www.growlforwindows.com/` for more details).

It is then possible for a helper application to also periodically send information about the latest known IP address, and that information is then passed to Nagios assuming that the person is in the office. This can then be passed to the notification command to use that specific IP address while sending a message to the user.

Assuming that the username is `jdoe` and the custom variable name is `DESKTOPIP`, the message that would be sent to the Nagios external command pipe would be as follows:

    [1206096000] CHANGE_CUSTOM_CONTACT_VAR;jdoe;DESKTOPIP;12.34.56.78

This would cause a later use of `$_CONTACTDESKTOPIP$` to return a value of `12.34.56.78`.

Nagios offers the `CHANGE_CUSTOM_CONTACT_`, `CHANGE_CUSTOM_HOST_VAR`,and `CHANGE_CUSTOM_SVC_VAR` commands for modifying custom variables in contacts, hosts, and services, accordingly.

The commands explained above are just a very small subset of the full capabilities of the Nagios external command pipe. For a complete list of commands, visit `http://www.nagios.org/developerinfo/externalcommands/commandlist.php`, where the **External Command List** can be seen.

External commands are usually sent from event handlers or from the Nagios web interface. You will find external commands most useful when writing event handlers for your system, or when writing an external application that interacts with Nagios.

Creating event handlers

Event handlers are commands that are triggered whenever the state of a host or service changes. They offer functionality similar to notifications. The main difference is that the event handlers are called for each type of change and even for each soft state change. This provides the ability to react to a problem before Nagios notifies it as a hard state and sends out notifications about it. Another difference is what the event handlers should do. Instead of notifying users that there is a problem, event handlers are meant to carry out actions automatically.

For example, if a service defined with `max_check_attempts` is set to 4, the `retry_interval` is set to 1, and `check_interval` is set to 5, then the following example illustrates when event handlers would be triggered, and with what values, for $SERVICESTATE$, $SERVICESTATETYPE$, and $SERVICEATTEMP$ macro definitions:

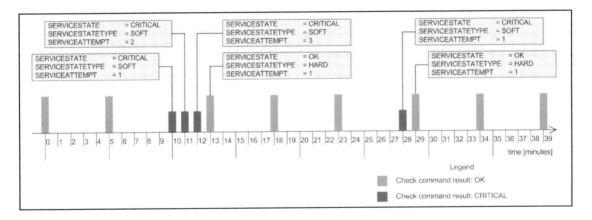

Event handlers are triggered for each state change—for example, in minutes, 10, 23, 28, and 29. When writing an event handler, it is necessary to check whether an event handler should perform an action at that particular time or not. See the preceding example for more details.

Event handlers are also triggered for each soft check attempt. It is also triggered when the host status becomes hard (when `max_check_attempts` attempts of checks have been made and service has not recovered). In this example, these occur at minutes 11, 12, and 13. It's important to know that the events will not be run if no state changes have occurred, and the object is in a hard state—for example, no events are triggered in minutes 5, 18, 34, and 39.

Restarting services automatically

A typical example might be that your web server process tends to crash once a month. Because this is rare enough, it is very difficult to debug and resolve it. Therefore, the best way to proceed is to restart the server automatically until a solution to the problem is found.

If your configuration has `max_check_attempts` set to 4, as in the example above, then a good place to try to restart the web server is after the third soft failure check-in the previous example, this would be minute 12.

Assuming that the restart has been successful, the diagram shown above would look like this:

Nagios BOT 3:03 PM
Nagios Service Notification Type: PROBLEM Service: HTTP Host: localhost Address: 127.0.0.1 State: CRITICAL Additional Info: connect to address 127.0.0.1 and port 80: Connection refused

Please note that no hard critical state has occurred since the event handler resolved the problem. If a restart cannot resolve the issue, Nagios will only try it once, as the attempt is done only in the third soft check.

Event handlers are defined as commands, similar to check commands. The main difference is that the event handlers only use macro definitions to pass information to the actual event handling script. This implies that the $ARGn$ macro definitions cannot be used and arguments cannot be passed in the host or service definition by using the ! separator.

In the previous example, we would define the following command:

```
define command
{
  command_name restart-apache2
  command_line $USER1$/events/restart_apache2
              $SERVICESTATE$ $SERVICESTATETYPE$ $SERVICEATTEMPT$
}
```

The command would need to be added to the service. For both hosts and services, this requires adding an event_handler directive that specifies the command to be run for each event that is fired. In addition, it is good to set event_handler_enabled to 1 to make sure that event handlers are enabled for this object.

The following is an example of a service definition:

```
define service
{
  host_name               localhost
  service_description     Webserver
  use                     apache
  event_handler           restart-apache2      event_handler_enabled      1
}
```

Finally, a short version of the script is as follows:

```
#!/bin/sh

# use variables for arguments
SERVICESTATE=$1
SERVICESTATETYPE=$2
SERVICEATTEMPT=$3

# we don't want to restart if current status is OK
if [ "$SERVICESTATE" != "OK" ] ; then

  # proceed only if we're in soft transition state
  if [ "$SERVICESTATETYPE" == "SOFT" ] ; then
```

```
# proceed only if this is 3rd attempt, restart
if [ "$SERVICESTATEATTEMPT" == "3" ] ; then

  # restarts Apache as system administrator
  sudo service apache2 restart
fi

  fi

fi

exit 0
```

As we're using `sudo` here, obviously the script needs an entry in the `sudoers` file to allow the user `nagios` to run the command without a password prompt. An example entry for the `sudoers` file would be as follows:

```
nagios ALL=NOPASSWD: /usr/sbin/service
```

This will tell `sudo` that the command `/usr/sbin/service` can be run by the user `nagios` and that asking for passwords before running the command will not be done.

According to our script, the restart is only done after the third check fails. Assuming that the restart went correctly, the next Nagios check will notify that Apache is running again. As this is considered a soft state, Nagios has not yet sent out any notifications about the problem.

If the service would not restart correctly, the next check will cause Nagios to set this failure as a hard state. At this point, notifications will be sent out to the object owners.

You can also try performing a restart in the second check. If that did not help, then during the third attempt, the script can forcefully terminate all Apache2 processes using the `killall` or `pkill` command. After this has been done, it can try to start the service again. For example:

```
# proceed only if this is 3rd attempt, restart
if [ "$SERVICESTATEATTEMPT" == "2" ] ; then

  # restart Apache as system administrator
  sudo service apache2 restart
fi

# proceed only if this is 3rd attempt, restart
if [ "$SERVICESTATEATTEMPT" == "3" ] ; then
  # try to terminate apache2 process as system administrator
  sudo pkill apache2
```

```
    # starts Apache as system administrator
    sudo service apache2 start
fi
```

Similar to the previous example, it requires adding an entry in the sudoers file. In addition to the previous line it also requires adding the pkill command, the whole path to the command is /usr/bin/pkill:

```
nagios ALL=NOPASSWD: /usr/bin/pkill
nagios ALL=NOPASSWD: /usr/sbin/service
```

Another common scenario is to restart one service if another one has just recovered—for example, you might want to restart e-mail servers that use a database for authentication if the database has just recovered from a failure state. The reason for doing this is that some applications may not handle disconnected database handles correctly—this can lead to the service working correctly from the Nagios perspective, but not allowing some of the users in due to internal problems.

If you have set this up for hosts or services, it is recommended that you keep flapping enabled for these services. It often happens that due to incorrectly planned scripts and the relations between them, some services might end up being stopped and started again.

In such cases, Nagios will detect these problems and stop running event handlers for these services, which will cause fewer malfunctions to occur. It is also recommended that you keep notifications set up so that people also get information on when flapping starts and stops.

Modifying notifications

Nagios also offers the ability to change various parameters related to notifications. These parameters are modified via an external command pipe, similar to a few of the commands shown in the previous section.

A good example would be when Nagios contact persons have their workstations connected to the local network only when they are actually at work (which is usually the case if they are using notebooks), and turn their computers off when they leave work. In such a case, a ping check for a person's computer could trigger an event handler to toggle that person's attributes.

Let's assume that our user jdoe has two actual contacts—jdoe-e-mail and jdoe-jabber, each for different types of notifications. We can set up a host corresponding to the jdoe workstation. We will also set it up to be monitored every five minutes and create an event handler. The handler will change the jdoe-jabber's host and service notification time period to none on a hard host down state. On a host up state change, the time period for jdoe-jabber will be set to 24x7. This way, the user will only get Jabber notifications if they are at work.

Nagios offers commands to change the time periods during which a user wants to receive notifications. The commands for this purpose are:
CHANGE_CONTACT_HOST_NOTIFICATION_TIMEPERIOD and
CHANGE_CONTACT_SVC_NOTIFICATION_TIMEPERIOD. Both commands take the contact and the time period name as their arguments.

An event handler script that modifies the user's contact time period based on state is as follows:

```sh
#!/bin/sh

NOW=`date +%s`
CONTACT=$1-jabber
if [ "$2,$3" = "DOWN,HARD" ] ; then
    TP=none
else
    TP=24x7
fi
echo "[$NOW] CHANGE_CONTACT_HOST_NOTIFICATION_TIMEPERIOD;
$CONTACT;$TP" \
    >/var/nagios/rw/nagios.cmd
echo "[$NOW] CHANGE_CONTACT_SVC_NOTIFICATION_TIMEPERIOD;
$CONTACT;$TP" \
    >/var/nagios/rw/nagios.cmd
exit 0
```

The command should pass $CONTACTNAME$, $SERVICESTATE$, and
$SERVICESTATETYPE$ as parameters to the script.

In case you need a notification about a problem sent again, you should use the
SEND_CUSTOM_HOST_NOTIFICATION or SEND_CUSTOM_SVC_NOTIFICATION command.
These commands take host or host and service names, additional options, author name, and
comments that should be put in the notification.

The additional options allow specifying if the notification should also include all escalation
levels (a value of 1), if Nagios should skip time periods for specific users (a value of 2), as
well as if Nagios should increment notifications counters (a value of 4). Options are stored
bitwise, so a value of 7 (1+2+4) would enable all of these options. The notification would be
sent to all people including escalations; it will be forced, and the escalation counters will be
increased. Option value 3 means it should be broadcast to all escalations as well, and the
time periods should be skipped.

To send a custom notification about the main router to all users including escalations, you
should send the following command to Nagios:

```
[1206096000] SEND_CUSTOM_HOST_NOTIFICATION;router1;3;jdoe;RESPOND ASAP
```

Using adaptive monitoring

Nagios provides a very powerful feature called adaptive monitoring that allows the
modification of various check-related parameters on the fly. This is done by sending a
command to the Nagios external command pipe.

The first thing that can be changed on the fly is the command to be executed by Nagios,
along with the attributes that will be passed to it-an equivalent of the check_command
directive in the object definition. In order to do that we can use the
CHANGE_HOST_CHECK_COMMAND or CHANGE_SVC_CHECK_COMMAND command. These require
the hostname, or the hostname and service description, and the check command as
arguments.

This can be used to actually change how hosts or services are checked, or to only modify parameters that are passed to the check commands-for example, a check for ping latency can be modified based on whether a primary or a backup connection is used. An example to change a check command of a service, which changes the command and its specified parameters, is as follows:

```
[1206096000] CHANGE_SVC_CHECK_COMMAND;linux1;PING;check_ping!500.0,50%
```

A similar possibility is to change the custom variables that are used later in a check command. An example where the following command and service are used is:

```
define command
{
  command_name          check-ping
  command_line          $USER1$/check_ping -H $HOSTADDRESS$
                        -p $_SERVICEPACKETS$
                        -w $_SERVICEWARNING$
                        -c $_SERVICECRITICAL$
}
define service
{
  host_name             linux2
  service_description   PING
  use                   ping
  check_command         check-ping
  _PACKETS              5
  _WARNING              100.0,40%
  _CRITICAL             300.0,60%
}
```

This example is very similar to the one we saw earlier. The main benefit is that parameters can be set independently—for example, one event handler might modify the number of packets to send while another one can modify the warning and/or critical state limits.

The following is an example to modify the warning level for the ping service on a linux1 host:

```
[1206096000] CHANGE_CUSTOM_SVC_VAR;linux1;PING;_WARNING;500.0,50%
```

It is also possible to modify event handlers on the fly. This can be used to enable or disable scripts that try to resolve a problem. To do this, you need to use the CHANGE_HOST_EVENT_HANDLER and CHANGE_SVC_EVENT_HANDLER commands.

In order to set an event handler command for the Apache2 service mentioned previously in this section, you need to send the following command:

```
[1206096000] CHANGE_SVC_EVENT_HANDLER;localhost;webserver; restart-apache2
```

Please note that setting an empty event handler disables any previous event handlers for this host or service. The same comment also applies for modifying the check command definition. In case you are modifying commands or event handlers, please make sure that the corresponding command definitions actually exist; otherwise, Nagios might reject your modifications.

Another feature that you can use to fine-tune the execution of checks is the ability to modify the time period during which a check should be performed. This is done with the CHANGE_HOST_CHECK_TIMEPERIOD and CHANGE_SVC_CHECK_TIMEPERIOD commands. Similar to the previous commands, these accept the host, or host and service names, and the new time period to be set. See the following example:

```
[1206096000] CHANGE_SVC_CHECK_TIMEPERIOD;localhost;webserver; workinghours
```

As is the case with command names, you need to make sure that the time period you are requesting to be set exists in the Nagios configuration. Otherwise, Nagios will ignore this command and leave the current check time period.

Nagios also allows modifying intervals between checks—both for the normal checks, and retrying during soft states. This is done through the CHANGE_NORMAL_HOST_CHECK_, CHANGE_RETRY_HOST_CHECK_INTERVAL, CHANGE_NORMAL_SVC_CHECK_INTERVAL,and CHANGE_RETRY_SVC_CHECK_INTERVAL commands. All of these commands require passing the host, or the host and service names, as well as the intervals that should be set.

A typical example of when intervals would be modified on the fly is when the priority of a host or service relies on other parameters in your network. An example might be a failover server—which will only be run if the primary server is down.

Making sure that the host and all of the services on it are working properly is very important before actually performing scheduled backups. During idle time, its priority might be much lower. Another issue might be that monitoring the failover server should be performed more often in case the primary server fails.

An example to modify the normal interval for a host to every 15 minutes is as follows:

```
[1206096000] CHANGE_NORMAL_HOST_CHECK_INTERVAL;backupserver;15
```

There is also the possibility to modify how many checks need to be performed before a state is considered to be hard. The commands for this are CHANGE_MAX_HOST_CHECK_ATTEMPTS and CHANGE_MAX_SVC_CHECK_ATTEMPTS

The following is an example command to modify max retries for a host to 5:

```
[1206096000] CHANGE_MAX_HOST_CHECK_ATTEMPTS;linux1;5
```

There are many more commands that allow the fine tuning of monitoring and check settings on the fly. It is recommended that you get acquainted with all of the external commands that your version of Nagios supports, as mentioned in the section introducing the external commands pipe.

Summary

In this chapter, we have learned how to use the notifications mechanism more effectively—sending information about host and service status using multiple protocols such as SMS or instant messaging. This can be used to reduce the number of e-mails sent and reduce chances of information about failure getting caught by spam or e-mail filters.

We have also learned about escalations and how those can be used to automatically let additional people know when a problem has not been resolved in a timely manner. This can be especially important in large organizations or when there is no clear ownership of one or more resources.

The chapter also covers sending commands to Nagios and how they can be used to add information about hosts and services, scheduling checks, and changing custom variables.

We have also learned how to create event handlers and how those can be used to automatically attempt to restart a service and/or change notification settings.

The chapter also covers adaptive notifications and how events or external applications can fine-tune the checking of settings for hosts and services.

To sum up, in this chapter, we have learned the following items:

- How to use multiple protocols such as instant messaging or SMS to send notifications
- What escalations are and how to use them to ensure problem resolution
- Learned how to send commands to Nagios
- What event handlers and adaptive monitoring are

The next chapter covers passive checks and **Nagios Remote Data Processor** (**NRDP**). These can be used to notify Nagios about host and service status from external applications or from other Nagios instances, including sending the information over the network.

9
Passive Checks and NRDP

Nagios is a very powerful platform because it is easy to extend. The previous chapters talked about the check command plugins and how they can be used to check any host or service that your company might be using. Another great feature that Nagios offers is the ability for third-party software or other Nagios instances to report information on the status of services or hosts. This way Nagios does not need to schedule and run checks by itself; other applications can report information as it is available to them.

In this chapter, we will cover the following topics:

- Understanding passive checks
- Using NRDP

Understanding passive checks

The previous parts of this book often mentioned Nagios performing checks on various software and machines. In such cases, Nagios decides when a check is to be performed, runs the check, and stores the result. These types of checks are called **active checks**.

Nagios also offers another way to let Nagios know about the status of hosts and services. It is possible to configure Nagios so that it will receive status information sent over a command pipe.

In such cases, other programs can either perform checks or report the current monitoring status by sending the current host or service status to Nagios. These types of checks are called **passive checks**. Nagios will still handle all notifications, event handlers, and dependencies between hosts and services.

Introducing active and passive checks

Active checks are the most common way to perform checks of services. They have a lot of advantages and some disadvantages. One of the problems is that such checks can take only a few seconds to complete; a typical timeout for an active check to complete is 10 or 30 seconds. While this timeout is configurable (with the global option `service_check_timeout` set in main Nagios configuration file—`nagios.cfg`), the idea behind Nagios is to run checks that take a few seconds to complete and return status.

In many cases, the time taken is not enough as some checks need to be performed over a longer period of time to have satisfactory results—such as if a test takes several hours to complete. In this case, it does not make sense to raise the check timeout. Instead, a better solution is to schedule these checks outside of Nagios and only report the results back after the checks are complete.

There are also different types of checks including external applications or devices that want to report information directly to Nagios. This can be done to gather all critical errors in a single, central place.

For example, when a web application cannot connect to the database, it can let Nagios know about it immediately. It can also send reports after a database recovery, or periodically, even if connectivity to the database has consistently been available so that Nagios has an up to date status. This can be done in addition to active checks to identify critical problems earlier.

Another example is where an application already processes information such as network bandwidth utilization. In this case, adding code that reports current utilization along with the `OK/WARNING/CRITICAL` state to Nagios seems much easier than using active checks for the same job.

Often, there are situations where active checks obviously fit better. In other cases, passive checks are the way to go. In general, if a check can be done quickly and does not require long-running processes, it should definitely be done as an active service. If the situation involves reporting problems that will be sent independently by Nagios from other applications or machines, it is definitely a use case for a passive check. In cases where the checks require the deployment of long-running processes or monitoring information constantly, this should be done as a passive service.

Another difference is that active checks require much less effort to be set up when compared to passive checks. In the first case, Nagios takes care of the scheduling, and the command only needs to perform the actual checks and mark the results as OK/WARNING/CRITICAL based on how a check command is configured. Passive checks require all the logic related to what should be reported and when it should be checked to be put in an external application. This usually calls for some effort.

The following diagram shows how both active and passive checks are performed by Nagios. It shows what is performed by Nagios in both cases and what needs to be done by the check command or an external application for passive checks:

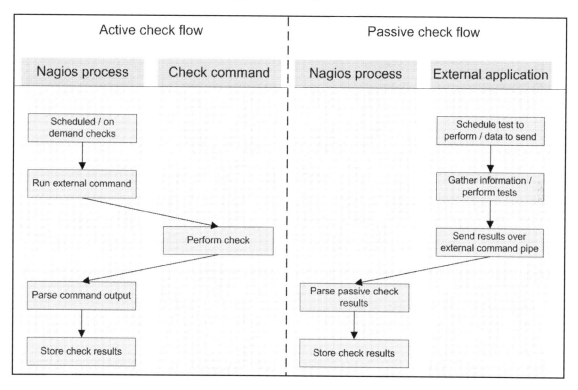

Nagios also offers a way of combining the benefits of both active and passive checks. Often, you have situations where other applications can report if a certain service is working properly or not. But if the monitoring application is not running or some other issue prevents it from reporting, Nagios can use active checks to keep the service status up to date.

A good example would be a server that is a part of an application, processing job queues using a database. It can report each problem when accessing the database. We want Nagios to monitor this database, and as the application is already using it, we can add a module that reports this to Nagios.

The application can also periodically let Nagios know if it succeeded in using the database without problems. However, if there are no jobs to process and the application is not using it, there will be no up to date information about the database status. In this case Nagios would simply run a check on its own.

Configuring passive checks

The first thing that needs to be done in order to use passive checks for your Nagios setup is to make sure that you have the following options in your main Nagios configuration file—such as /etc/nagios/nagios.cfg if Nagios was set up according to instructions from Chapter 2, *Installing Nagios 4*:

```
accept_passive_service_checks=1
accept_passive_host_checks=1
```

It is also good to enable the logging of incoming passive checks; this makes determining the problem of not processing a passive check much easier. The following directive enables it:

```
log_passive_checks=1
```

Setting up hosts or services for passive checking requires an object to have the passive_checks_enabled option set to 1 for Nagios to accept passive check results over the command pipe. If only passive checks will be sent to Nagios, it is also advised that you disable active checks by setting the active_checks_enabled option to 0. The following is an example of the required configuration for a host that accepts passive checks and has active checks disabled:

```
define host
{
  use                     generic-host
  host_name               linuxbox01
  address                 10.0.2.1
  active_checks_enabled   0
  passive_checks_enabled  1
}
```

Configuring services is exactly the same as with hosts. For example, to set up a very similar service, all we need to do is to use the same parameters as those for the hosts:

```
define service
{
  use                        ping-template
  host_name                  linuxbox01
  service_description        PING
  active_checks_enabled      0
  passive_checks_enabled     1
}
```

In this case, Nagios will never perform any active checks on its own and will only rely on the results that are passed to it.

We can also configure Nagios so that if no new information has been provided within a certain period of time, it will perform active checks to get the current status of the host or service. If up to date information has been provided by a passive check during this period, then no active checks will be performed.

To do this, we need to enable active checks by setting the active_checks_enabled option to 1 without specifying the normal_check_interval directive. For Nagios to perform active checks when there is no up to date result from passive checks, you need to set the check_freshness directive to 1 and set freshness_threshold to the duration after which a check should be performed. The time specified in the freshness_threshold option is specified in seconds.

The first parameter tells Nagios that it should check whether the results from the checks are up to date. The next parameter specifies the number of seconds after which Nagios should consider the results to be out of date. Attributes can be used for both hosts and services.

A sample definition for a host that runs an active check if there has been no result provided within the last two hours is as follows:

```
define host
{
  use                        generic-host
  host_name                  linuxbox02
  address                    10.0.2.2
  check_command              check-host-alive
  check_freshness            1
  freshness_threshold        7200
  active_checks_enabled      1
  passive_checks_enabled     1
}
```

The following is a diagram showing when Nagios will invoke active checks:

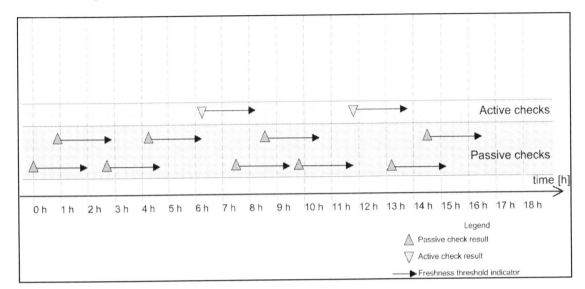

Each time there is at least one passive check result that is still valid (a result that was received within the past two hours), Nagios will not perform any active checks.

However, two hours after the last passive or active check result is received, Nagios will perform an active check to keep the results up to date.

Sending passive check results for hosts

Nagios allows applications and event handlers to send out passive check results for host objects. In order to use them, the host needs to be configured to accept passive check results. In order to be able to submit passive check results, we need to configure Nagios to allow the sending of passive check results and set the host objects to accept them.

Submitting passive host check results to Nagios requires sending a command to the Nagios external command pipe. This way, other applications on your Nagios server can report the status of the hosts.

All commands sent to the Nagios command pipe are sent as a single line of text and use a specific format:

```
[<time>] <command_id>;<command_arguments>
```

The `time` should be put in square brackets and has to be a Unix timestamp (which is number of seconds since January 1st 1970). The command and all of its arguments are separated using a semicolon.

The format is described in more detail in the external command documentation available at: `http://assets.nagios.com/downloads/nagioscore/docs/nagioscore/4/en/extcommands.html`.

The command to submit passive checks is `PROCESS_HOST_CHECK_RESULT` (visit `http://assets.nagios.com/downloads/nagioscore/docs/nagioscore/4/en/passivechecks.html` for more details on the command). This command accepts the hostname and status code. The host status code should be 0 for an UP state, 1 for DOWN, and 2 for an UNREACHABLE state.

The syntax is:

```
[<time>] PROCESS_HOST_CHECK_RESULT;<host>;<status>;<plugin_output>
```

The following is a sample script that will accept the hostname, status code, and output from a check and will submit these to Nagios:

```
#!/bin/sh

NOW=`date +%s`
HOST=$1
STATUS=$2
OUTPUT=$3

echo "[$NOW] PROCESS_HOST_CHECK_RESULT;$HOST;$STATUS;$OUTPUT" \
    >/var/nagios/rw/nagios.cmd

exit 0
```

As an example of the use of this script, the command sent to Nagios for `host01`, status code 2 (UNREACHABLE), and output `router 192.168.1.2 down` would be as follows:

```
[1206096000] PROCESS_HOST_CHECK_RESULT;host01;2;router  192.168.1.2 down
```

While submitting results, it is worth noting that Nagios might take some time to process them, depending on the intervals between checks of the external command pipe in Nagios. Unlike active checks, Nagios will not take network topology into consideration by default. This is very important in situations where a host behind a router is reported to be down because the router is actually down.

By default, Nagios handles results from active and passive checks differently. When Nagios plans and receives results from active checks, it takes the actual network topology into consideration and return as an UNREACHABLE state.

When a passive result check comes in to Nagios, Nagios expects that the result already has a network topology included. When a host is reported to be DOWN as a passive check result, Nagios does not perform a translation from DOWN to UNREACHABLE. Even if its parent host is currently DOWN, the child host state is also stored as DOWN.

How Nagios handles passive check results can be defined in the main Nagios configuration file. In order to make Nagios treat passive host check results in the same way as active check results, we need to enable the following option:

```
translate_passive_host_checks=1
```

By default, Nagios treats host results from passive checks as hard results. This is because, very often, passive checks are used to report host and service statuses from other Nagios instances. In such cases, only reports regarding hard state changes are propagated across Nagios servers. If you want Nagios to treat all passive check results for hosts as if they were soft results, you need to enable the following option in the main Nagios configuration file:

```
passive_host_checks_are_soft=1
```

Sending passive check results for services

Passive service checks are very similar to passive host checks. In both cases, the idea is that Nagios receives information about host statuses over the external command pipe. As with passive checks of hosts, all that is needed is to enable the global Nagios option to accept passive check results and to also enable this option for each service that should allow the passing of passive check results.

The results are passed to Nagios in the same way as they are passed for hosts. The command to submit passive checks is PROCESS_SERVICE_CHECK_RESULT. This command accepts the hostname, service description, status code, and the textual output from a check. Service status codes are the same as those for active checks— 0 for OK, 1 for WARNING, 2 for CRITICAL, and 3 for an UNKNOWN state.

The syntax is:

```
[<time>] PROCESS_SERVICE_CHECK_RESULT;<host>;<svc>;<status>;<output>
```

The following is a sample script that will accept the hostname, status code, and output from a check and submit these to Nagios:

```
#!/bin/sh

CLOCK=`date +%s`
HOST=$1
SVC=$2
STATUS=$3
OUTPUT=$4

echo "[$CLOCK] PROCESS_SERVICE_CHECK_RESULT;$HOST;$SVC;$STATUS;
$OUTPUT" >/var/nagios/rw/nagios.cmd

exit 0
```

As a result of running the script, the command that is sent to Nagios for host01, service PING, status code 0 (OK), and output RTT=57 ms is as follows:

```
[1206096000] PROCESS_SERVICE_CHECK_RESULT;host01;PING;0;RTT=57 ms
```

A very common scenario for using passive checks is a check that takes a very long time to complete. When submitting results, it is worth noting that Nagios might take some time to process them, depending on the intervals between checks of the external command pipe in Nagios.

A major difference between hosts and services is that service checks differentiate between soft and hard states. When new information regarding a service gets passed to Nagios via the external command pipe, Nagios treats it in the same way as if it had been received by an active check. If a service is set up with a max_check_attempts directive of 5, then the same number of passive check results would be needed in order for Nagios to treat the new status as a hard state change.

The passive service checks are often used to report the results of long lasting tests that were run asynchronously. A good example of such a test is checking whether there are bad blocks on a disk. This requires trying to read the entire disk directly from the block device (such as /dev/sda1) and checking if the attempt has failed. This can't be done as an active check as reading the device takes a lot of time and larger disks might require several hours to complete. For this reason, the only way to perform such a check is to schedule it from the system, for example, by using the cron daemon (visit http://linux.die.net/man/8/cron). The script should then post results to the Nagios daemon.

The following is a script that runs the dd system command (visit http://linux.die.net/man/1/dd) to read an entire block device. Based on whether the read was successful or not, the appropriate status code along with the plugin output is sent out:

```
#!/bin/sh

SVC=$1
DEVICE=$2
TMPFILE=`mktemp`
NOW=`date +%s`
PREFIX="[$NOW] PROCESS_SERVICE_CHECK_RESULT;localhost;$SVC"

# try to read the device
dd bs=1M if=$DEVICE of=/dev/null >$TMPFILE 2>&1
CODE=$?
RESULT=`grep copied <$TMPFILE`
rm $TMPFILE

if [ $CODE == 0 ] ; then
    echo "$PREFIX;0;$RESULT"
else
    echo "$PREFIX;2;Error while checking device $DEVICE"
fi

exit 0
```

If the check fails, then a `critical` status along with text stating that there was a problem checking the specific device is sent out to Nagios. If the check was successful, an output mentioning the number of bytes and the speed of transfer is sent out to Nagios. A typical output would be something like this:

```
254951424 bytes (255 MB) copied, 9.72677 seconds, 26.2 MB/s
```

The hostname is hardcoded to `localhost`. Using this script requires configuring a service to have active checks disabled and passive checks enabled. As the checks will be done quite rarely, it's recommended that you set `max_check_attempts` to 1. It is also possible to use the `badblocks` (please visit http://linux.die.net/man/8/badblocks for more details) command to check for bad blocks on a hard drive.

Troubleshooting errors

It's not always possible to set up passive checks correctly the first time. In such cases, it is a good thing to try to debug the issue one step at a time in order to find any potential problems. Sometimes, the problem could be a configuration issue, while in other cases it could be an issue such as the mistyping of the host or service name.

One thing worth checking is whether the Web UI shows changes after you have sent the passive result check. If it doesn't, then at some point, things were not working correctly. The first thing you should start with is enabling the logging of external commands and passive checks. To do this, make sure that the following values are enabled in the main Nagios configuration file:

```
log_external_commands=1
log_passive_checks=1
```

In order for the changes to take effect, a restart of the Nagios process is needed. After this has been done, Nagios will log all commands passed via the command pipe and log all of the passive check results it receives.

A very common problem is that the application or script cannot write data to the Nagios command pipe. In order to test this, simply try to write to the Nagios external command pipe in the same manner that the application/script's user is running.

For example if the application or script is running as daemon, you can run the following as root:

```
root@ubuntuserver:# su -s/bin/sh daemon
$ echo TEST >/var/nagios/rw/nagios.cmd
```

The su command will switch the user to the specified user. The next line is run as the user daemon and an attempt to write to the Nagios external command pipe is made. The -s flag for the su command forces /bin/sh as the shell to use. It is useful in cases where the user's default shell is not a proper shell, that is, it is set to /bin/false for security reasons to prevent the account from interactive shell access.

If the preceding command runs fine and no errors are reported, then your permissions are set up correctly. If an error shows up, you should add the user to the nagioscmd group as described in Chapter 2, *Installing Nagios 4*. The following command will add the user daemon to the nagioscmd group:

```
root@ubuntuserver:# adduser daemon nagioscmd
```

The next thing to do is to manually send a passive check result to the Nagios command pipe and check whether the Nagios log file was received and parsed correctly. To do this, run the following command as the same user that the application or script is running as:

```
root@ubuntuserver:# su -s/bin/sh daemon
$ echo "[`date +%s`] PROCESS_HOST_CHECK_RESULT;host1;2;test" \
  >/var/nagios/rw/nagios.cmd
```

The name `host1` needs to be replaced with an actual hostname from your configuration. A few seconds after running this command, the Nagios log file should reflect the command that we have just sent. You should see the following lines in your log:

```
EXTERNAL COMMAND: PROCESS_HOST_CHECK_RESULT;host1;2;test
[1220257561] PASSIVE HOST CHECK: host1;2;test
```

If both of these lines are in your log file, then we can conclude that Nagios has received and parsed the command correctly. If only the first line is present, then it means either that the option to receive passive host check results are disabled globally or that it is disabled for this particular object.

If this is the case, first thing you should do is to make sure that your main Nagios configuration file contains the following line:

```
accept_passive_host_checks=1
```

Next, you should check your configuration to see whether the host definition has passive checks enabled as well. If not, simply add the following directive to the object definition:

```
passive_checks_enabled  1
```

If you have misspelled the name of the host object, then the following will be logged:

```
Warning:  Passive check result was received for host 'host01',
but the host could not be found!
```

In this case, make sure that your hostname is correct. Similar checks can also be done for services. You can run the following command to check if a passive service check is being handled correctly by Nagios:

```
root@ubuntuserver:# su -s/bin/sh daemon
$ echo "[`date +%s`] PROCESS_SERVICE_CHECK_RESULT;host1;APT;0;test" \
  >/var/nagios/rw/nagios.cmd
```

Again, `host1` should be replaced by the actual hostname, and `APT` needs to be an existing service for that host.

After a few seconds, the following entries in the Nagios log file (`/var/nagios/nagios.log`) will indicate that the result has been successfully parsed:

```
EXTERNAL COMMAND: PROCESS_SERVICE_CHECK_RESULT;host1;APT;0;test
PASSIVE SERVICE CHECK: host1;APT;0;test
```

If the second line is not in the log file, there are two possible reasons for this.

One is that the global option to accept service passive checks by Nagios is disabled. You should start by making sure that your main Nagios configuration file (`/etc/nagios/nagios.cfg`) contains the following line:

```
accept_passive_service_checks=1
```

The other possibility is that the host does not have passive checks enabled. You should make sure that the service definition has passive checks enabled as well, and if not, add the following directive to the object definition:

```
define host
{
    host_name                    host1
    passive_checks_enabled       1
}
```

If you have misspelled the name of the host or service, then the following information will be logged in the Nagios log file:

```
Warning:  Passive check result was received for service 'APT' on host
'host1', but the service could not be found!
```

Using NRDP

Passive checks are sent to Nagios via the external command pipe, which can only be accessed on the same machine where Nagios is running. Very often passive checks are carried out on one or more remote hosts. This requires a mechanism to pass results from the machines that perform the tests to the computers running the Nagios daemon, which will process the results.

NRDP is a technology that allows sending results to a Nagios instance remotely. It provides a simple API to send the results to a Nagios instance using the HTTP protocol and leveraging existing web servers such as Apache web server that we have installed in `Chapter 2`, *Installing Nagios 4*.

NRDP consists of two parts-server and client. The part responsible for receiving check results from remote hosts and passing them to Nagios is the server. Once installed and added into the Apache configuration, it will accept requests, validate the token used to authenticate the request and pass the information to Nagios. The client part gets the data to be sent as command line arguments and sends a HTTP or HTTPS request to the NRDP server.

The following diagram shows how data is sent using NRDP as the protocol and what is performed on the machine that is sending the data as well as how the data is passed to the Nagios server:

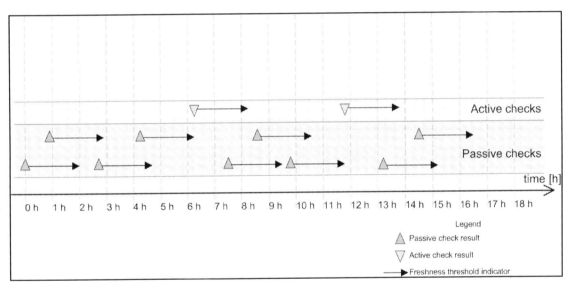

 NRDP is a successor to the **Nagios Service Check Acceptor** (**NSCA**) technology and it is recommended to migrate to it if currently using NSCA. NRDP is implemented in PHP, uses standard HTTP protocol and can easily be integrated with Apache serving the Nagios web interface. To upgrade, all that is needed is to install NRDP, change how other services and/or machines send data to Nagios, and then disable NSCA.

Installing the NRDP server

NRDP is an open source solution that can be downloaded from Nagios Exchange at the following URL: `https://exchange.nagios.org/directory/Addons/Passive-Checks/NRDP-2D-Nagios-Remote-Data-Processor/details`. Both client and server are simply a set of PHP scripts and do not need to be compiled.

NRDP requires the web server to be running and PHP to be available. NRDP should be set up on the same machine where Nagios is running. If you have followed the steps in `Chapter 2`, *Installing Nagios 4*, PHP should already be available and configured. If not, we recommend going back and following the manual installation steps related to installing Apache, PHP as well as enabling PHP in the web server configuration.

We will also need to set up a temporary directory inside the Nagios subdirectory that Nagios and NRDP will use to create files in. We'll use permissions 0775 and change the directory group to be nagioscmd so that both Nagios and NRDP can use the directory:

```
root@ubuntuserver:~# mkdir -p /opt/nagios/var/tmpp
root@ubuntuserver:~# chmod 0775 /opt/nagios/var/tmp
root@ubuntuserver:~# chgrp nagioscmd /opt/nagios/var/tmp
```

In order to install the NRDP server, simply unpack the ZIP archive and copy the `server` subdirectory from the contents of the ZIP file to the target directory-such as `/opt/nagios/nrdp`. For example:

```
root@ubuntuserver:~# unzip nrdp.zip
root@ubuntuserver:~# cp -pfR nrdp/server /opt/nagios/nrdp
```

Next, let's edit the configuration file `/opt/nagios/nrdp/config.inc.php`. NRDP comes with a sample configuration file, but we'll need to customize it a bit.

The lines configuring `$cfg['authorized_tokens']` should be modified to contain one or more tokens that can be used by clients to validate the request—such as:

```
$cfg['authorized_tokens'] = array(
        "cu8Eiquasoomeiphahpa",
        );
```

A tool for random passwords can be used to generate tokens—such as `pwgen`, which is available both in many Linux distributions as well as a JavaScript based online version available from `http://8-p.info/pwgen/`.

Next we'll need to specify the name of the system group that both Nagios and web server are members of—in our case it is `nagioscmd`. To do this, we'll need to modify the line with the `$cfg["nagios_command_group"]` option—such as:

```
$cfg["nagios_command_group"]="nagioscmd";
```

We'll also need to modify `$cfg["command_file"]` and `$cfg["check_results_dir"]` options to point to the `nagios.cmd` pipe and results directory respectively:

```
$cfg["command_file"]="/var/nagios/rw/nagios.cmd";
$cfg["check_results_dir"]="/var/nagios/spool/checkresults";
```

The last option that needs to be modified is `$cfg["tmp_dir"]` to point to the newly created temporary directory:

```
$cfg["tmp_dir"]="/opt/nagios/var/tmp";
```

After that, the NRDP server is now configured.

The next step is to update the web server configuration to include NRDP specific settings. We can reuse the file that was created in Chapter 2, *Installing Nagios 4*, which is either `/etc/apache2/conf-available/nagios.conf` or `/etc/httpd/conf.d/nagios.conf`, depending on Linux distribution.

Simply add the following to the configuration file:

```
<Directory "/opt/nagios/nrdp">
Options None
AllowOverride None
Order allow,deny
Require all granted
Allow from all
</Directory>
Alias /nrdp "/opt/nagios/nrdp"
```

And restart Apache—one of the following commands will successfully restart it:

```
# apachectl restart
# service apache2 restart
# service httpd restart
```

Next we can go to `http://(ip-address)/nrdp/` and manually submit a check result using the **Submit Check Data** form. First we need to specify the same token that was added in the configuration file, for the Check Data field, we can pass the following to send host check results for `localhost`:

```
<?xml version='1.0'?>
<checkresults>
    <checkresult type='host'>
        <hostname>localhost</hostname>
        <state>0</state>
        <output>EVERYTHING_OK|perfdata</output>
    </checkresult>
</checkresults>
```

The result should be a report similar to the XML below:

```
<result>
  <status>0</status>
  <message>OK</message>
  <meta>
    <output>1 checks processed.</output>
  </meta>
</result>
```

This indicates that the result was successfully processed and it should be visible in the Nagios web interface soon. After a few seconds the details page for the localhost host should show the `EVERYTHING_OK` message in the `Status Information` field.

Using the NRDP client

Now that we have set up the NRDP server, we can proceed to configuring the NRDP client and sending events remotely to our Nagios instance. The NRDP client is a single PHP script that can be run from the command line or Nagios to send data to the server.

In order to use the NRDP client, PHP must be present on the system. For a machine that has the Nagios server already installed based on the steps in `Chapter 2`, *Installing Nagios 4*, PHP should already be available and configured.

In all other cases, for Debian and Ubuntu Linux distributions, the following command will install PHP CLI tools:

```
apt-get -y install php5-cli
```

Similarly, the package list is also the same for all distributions that use the `rpm` package format. To install all the prerequisites we need to run the following command:

```
yum -y install php-cli
```

The NRDP client is located in the `clients` directory of the `nrdp.zip` archive. Simply copy it to any location such as to `/opt/nagios/bin` and change its permissions to make the script executable. It is as follows:

```
root@ubuntuserver:~# cp nrdp/clients/send_nrdp.php /opt/nagios/bin/
root@ubuntuserver:~# chmod 0755 /opt/nagios/bin/send_nrdp.php
```

In order to ensure the script works with all Linux distributions and PHP versions, it is best to replace the first two lines of the script with the following:

```
#!/usr/bin/php -q
<?php
```

This will ensure the script works properly in cases where PHP requires the entire `<?php` opening tag for using PHP code rather than the `<?` opening tag. The second form is only available if PHP is configured with the `short_open_tag` option enabled, which may be disabled in some Linux distributions. The issue is described in more details in PHP documentation: `http://php.net/manual/en/language.basic-syntax.phpmode.php`.

We can now use the script to send a result for the host localhost to Nagios:

```
root@ubuntuserver:~# /opt/nagios/bin/send_nrdp.php \
  --url=http://127.0.0.1/nrdp/ \
  --token=cu8Eiquasoomeiphahpa \
  --host=localhost \
  --state=0 \
  --output=EVERYTHING_OK
```

The `127.0.0.1` should be replaced with the IP address of your Nagios instance if the script is not running locally. Also the value for `--token` should be set to the actual, valid token that was added in the NRDP server configuration.

Similar to the previous test, after a few seconds the Nagios web interface details page for the `localhost` host should show the `EVERYTHING_OK` message in the `Status Information` field.

Securing the NRDP communication

NRDP is a protocol that can often be used over potentially insecure connections—such as if NRDP is used to send passive check results over the Internet.

By default, the NRDP server will accept connections on all protocols that the web server is configured for; it includes both HTTP and HTTPS protocols. The first is an unencrypted protocol and all the data, including the security token, is transmitted in plain text. The second provides SSL/TLS based encryption.

If NRDP is to be used on untrusted networks—such as over Internet—it is advisable to use HTTPS protocol only. This can be enabled in the web server itself and varies depending on web server.

For example, for an Apache web server a good idea may be to use the rewrite engine to redirect such requests to HTTPS, as described in the following documentation: `https://wiki.apache.org/httpd/RewriteHTTPToHTTPS`. The downside of this is that HTTP based requests that do not use encryption, are redirected, but handled properly.

If we want to be sure communication is not handled properly over HTTP, NRDP can be configured to require the HTTPS protocol. To do this, simply enable the `require_https` option in the NRDP server configuration file (which can be found at `/opt/nagios/nrdp/config.inc.php` if the installation was done according to the instructions earlier in this chapter).

For example:

```
$cfg["require_https"]=false;
```

After this option is set, the NRDP server will return an error to all API calls that are using the HTTP protocol and only accept requests over the HTTPS protocol.

Summary

Nagios allows both the monitoring of services on its own and the receipt of information about computer and service statuses from other applications. Being able to send results directly to Nagios creates a lot of opportunities for extending how Nagios can be used.

In this chapter we have learned the following items:

- What are passive checks and how they differ from Nagios performing active checks
- Submitting passive check results to Nagios
- How to troubleshoot errors with sending passive checks
- What is NRDP and how it can be used to submit passive checks remotely
- Configuring NRDP server and client

The next chapter will cover how to monitor remote hosts and how the SSH protocol can be used to run checks remotely in a secure way. It will also cover **Nagios Remote Plugin Executor** (**NRPE**), which is a client-server protocol that allows running checks remotely.

10
Monitoring Remote Hosts

Nagios offers various ways of monitoring computers and services. The previous chapter talked about passive checks and how they can be used to submit results to Nagios. It also discussed NRDP, which can be used to send check results from other machines to the Nagios server.

This chapter talks about another approach to check the service status. It uses Nagios active checks that run the actual check commands on different hosts. This approach is most useful in cases where resources local to a particular machine are to be checked, such as monitoring disk and memory usage as well as checking if your operating system is up to date. This type of data cannot be checked without running commands on the target computer.

Remote checks are usually used in combination with the Nagios plugins package that use either SSH or NRPE to run the plugins on the remote machine. This makes monitoring remote systems very similar to monitoring a local computer, with a difference only in the actual running of the commands on the remote machine. In this chapter, we will cover the following topics:

- Monitoring over SSH
- Monitoring using NRPE
- Comparing NRPE and SSH
- Alternatives to SSH and NRPE

Monitoring over SSH

Nagios is often used to monitor computer resources such as CPU utilization, memory, and disk space. One way in which this can be done is to connect over SSH and run a Nagios check plugin.

Automating the authentication process requires setting up SSH to authenticate using public keys. This works because the Nagios server has an SSH private key and the target machine is configured to allow users with that particular key to connect without prompting for a password.

Nagios offers a `check_by_ssh` plugin that takes the hostname and the actual command to run on the remote server. It then connects using SSH, runs the plugin, and returns both output and exit code from the actual check performed on the remote machine to Nagios running on the local server. Internally it runs the SSH client to connect to the server and runs the actual command to run along with its attributes on the target machine. After the check has been performed, the output along with the check command's exit code is returned to Nagios.

This way any Nagios plugin can be run from the same machine as the Nagios daemon as well as remotely over SSH without any changes to the plugins. Using the SSH protocol also means that the authorization process can be automated using the key-based authentication so that each check is done without any user activity. This way Nagios is able to log in to remote machines automatically without using any passwords. The following is an illustration of how such a check is performed:

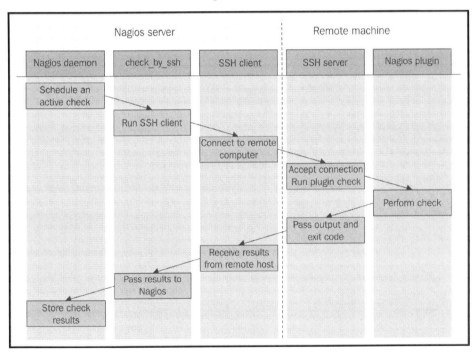

Once Nagios schedules an active check to be performed, the `check_by_ssh` plugin runs the `ssh` command to connect to the remote host's SSH server. It then runs the actual plugin, which has to be present on the remote host, and waits for the result. The SSH client passes the standard output as well as exit code to the `check_by_ssh` plugin that also prints the output and exits with the same code as the plugin.

Even though the scenario might seem a bit complicated, it works quite efficiently and requires very little setup to work properly. It also works with various flavors of Unix systems such as the SSH protocol, clients, and the shell syntax for commands used by the `check_by_ssh` plugin is the same on all Unix-based systems.

Configuring the SSH connection

SSH provides multiple ways for a user to authenticate. One of them is password-based authentication, which means that the user specifies a password; the SSH client sends it to the remote machine, and the remote machine checks if the password is correct.

Another form of verifying whether a user or program can access the remote machine is public key-based authentication. It uses asymmetric cryptography (visit `http://en.wikipe dia.org/wiki/Public-key_cryptography` for more detail) to perform the authentication and provides a secure way to authenticate without specifying any credentials. It requires the user to generate an authentication key, which consists of a public and private key. By default, the filename is `~/.ssh/id_rsa` for the private key and `~/.ssh/id_rsa.pub` for the public key. The public key is then put on the remote machines and it allows the remote machine to authenticate the user. The SSH protocol then takes care of the authentication, it only requires the client machine to have the private key and the remote machine to be configured to accept it by adding the public key to the remote user's SSH authorized keys file, which is located in `~/.ssh/authorized_keys` in most cases.

Setting up remote checks over SSH requires a few steps. The first step is to create a dedicated user for performing checks on the machine on which the remote checks will be run. We will also need to set up directories for the user. The steps to create directory structure on the remote machine are very similar to the steps performed for the Nagios installation itself.

The first thing that needs to be performed on the Nagios server is the creation of a private and public key pair that will be used to log in to all the remote machines without using passwords. We will need to execute the `ssh-keygen` command to generate it. For example:

```
root@nagiosserver:~# su -s /bin/bash nagios
nagios@nagiosserver:~$ ssh-keygen
Generating public/private rsa key pair.
File in which to save the key (/opt/nagios/.ssh/id_rsa): <enter>
Created directory '/opt/nagios/.ssh'.
Enter passphrase (empty for no passphrase): <enter>
Enter same passphrase again: <enter>
Your identification has been saved in /opt/nagios/.ssh/id_rsa.
Your public key has been saved in /opt/nagios/.ssh/id_rsa.pub.
The key fingerprint is:
c9:68:47:bd:cd:6e:12:d3:9b:e8:0d:cf:93:bd:33:98 nagios@nagiosserver
nagios@nagiosserver:/root$
```

We used the `su` command to switch users along with the `-s` flag to force the shell to be `/bin/bash`; this is because in most setups the `nagios` user usually does not have shell access. The `<enter>` text means that the question was answered with the default reply. The private key is saved as `/opt/nagios/.ssh/id_rsa`, and the public key has been saved in the `/opt/nagios/.ssh/id_rsa.pub` file.

At this point our Nagios server is set up.

Next we need to set up the remote machines that we will monitor. All the following commands should be executed on the remote machine that is to be monitored, unless explicitly mentioned. First, let's create a user and group named `nagios`:

```
root@remotehost:~# groupadd nagios
root@remotehost:~# useradd -g nagios -d /opt/nagios nagios
```

We do not need the `nagioscmd` group as we will only need the account to log in to the machine. The computer that only performs checks does not have a full Nagios installation along with the external command pipe that needs a separate group.

The next thing that needs to be done is the compiling of the Nagios plugins. You will probably also need to install the prerequisites that are needed for Nagios. Detailed instructions on how to do this can be found in `Chapter 2`, *Installing Nagios 4*. For the rest of the section, we will assume that the Nagios plugins are installed in the `/opt/nagios/plugins` directory, similar to how they were installed on the Nagios server.

It is best to install plugins in the same directory on all the machines they will be running. In this case, we can use the $USER1$ macro definition when creating the actual check commands in the main Nagios configuration. The USER1 macro points to the location where Nagios plugins are installed in the default Nagios installations. This is described in more detail in Chapter 2, *Installing Nagios 4*.

Next, we will need to create the /opt/nagios directory and set its permissions:

```
root@remotehost:~# mkdir /opt/nagios
root@remotehost:~# chown nagios:nagios /opt/nagios
root@remotehost:~# chmod 0700 /opt/nagios
```

You can make the /opt/nagios directory permissions less restrictive by setting the mode to 0755. However, it is recommended not to make the users' home directories readable for all users.

We will now need to add the public key from the nagios user on the remote machine that is running the Nagios daemon, as shown in the following command snippet:

```
root@remotehost:~# mkdir /opt/nagios/.ssh
root@remotehost:~# echo 'ssh-rsa ... nagios@nagiosserver' \
    /opt/nagios/.ssh/authorized_keys

root@remotehost:~# chown Nagios:nagios \
    /opt/nagios/.ssh /opt/nagios/.ssh/authorized_keys
root@remotehost:~# chmod 0700 \
    /opt/nagios/.ssh /opt/nagios/.ssh/authorized_keys
```

You need to replace the text ssh-rsa ... nagios@nagiosserver with the actual contents of the /opt/nagios/.ssh/id_rsa.pub file on the server that is running Nagios.

If your machine is maintained by more than one person, you might replace the nagios@nagiosserver string to a more readable comment such as Nagios on nagiosserver SSH check public key.

Make sure that you change the permissions for both the .ssh directory and the authorized_keys file, as many SSH server implementations ignore public key-based authorization if the files can be read or written to by other users on the system.

In order to configure multiple remote machines to be accessible over ssh without a password, you will need to perform all the steps mentioned earlier, except the key generation at the computer running the Nagios server, as a single private key will be used to access multiple machines.

Assuming everything was done successfully, we can now move on to testing if the public key-based authorization actually works. In order to check that our connection can now be successfully established, we need to try to connect to the remote machine from the computer that has the Nagios daemon running. We will use the `ssh` client with the verbose flag to make sure that our connection works properly:

```
nagios@nagiosserver:~$ ssh -v nagios@192.168.2.1
OpenSSH_6.6.1, OpenSSL 1.0.1f 6 Jan 2014
debug1: Reading configuration data /etc/ssh/ssh_config
debug1: Applying options for *
debug1: Connecting to 192.168.2.1 [192.168.2.1] port 22.
debug1: Connection established.
debug1: identity file /opt/nagios/.ssh/id_rsa type 1
(...)
debug1: SSH2_MSG_KEXINIT sent
debug1: SSH2_MSG_KEXINIT received
debug1: kex: server->client aes128-cbc hmac-md5 none
debug1: kex: client->server aes128-cbc hmac-md5 none
debug1: SSH2_MSG_KEX_DH_GEX_REQUEST(1024<1024<8192) sent
debug1: expecting SSH2_MSG_KEX_DH_GEX_GROUP
debug1: SSH2_MSG_KEX_DH_GEX_INIT sent
debug1: expecting SSH2_MSG_KEX_DH_GEX_REPLY
The authenticity of host '192.168.2.1 (192.168.2.1)' can't be
established.
RSA key fingerprint is cf:72:1e:40:03:a4:e0:9b:6c:84:4e:e1:2d:ea:56:fc.
Are you sure you want to continue connecting (yes/no)? yes
Warning: Permanently added '192.168.2.1' (RSA) to the list of known
hosts.
debug1: ssh_rsa_verify: signature correct
debug1: SSH2_MSG_NEWKEYS sent
debug1: expecting SSH2_MSG_NEWKEYS
debug1: SSH2_MSG_NEWKEYS received
debug1: SSH2_MSG_SERVICE_REQUEST sent
debug1: SSH2_MSG_SERVICE_ACCEPT received
debug1: Authentications that can continue: publickey,password
debug1: Next authentication method: publickey
debug1: Offering public key: /opt/nagios/.ssh/id_rsa
debug1: Server accepts key: pkalg ssh-rsa blen 277
debug1: read PEM private key done: type RSA
debug1: Authentication succeeded (publickey).
debug1: channel 0: new [client-session]
debug1: Entering interactive session.
debug1: Sending environment.
debug1: Sending env LANG = en_US.UTF-8
$
```

As we were connecting to the remote machine for the first time, the `ssh` command asked whether to accept the connection so that SSH can continue and store the remote machine's key to a list of known hosts. This is only done once for each host.

Also, note that we need to test the connection from the Nagios account so that the keys that are used for authentication as well as the list of known hosts are the same ones that will be used by the Nagios daemon later.

Assuming that we have the Nagios plugins installed on the remote machine in the `/opt/nagios/plugins` directory, we can try to use the `check_by_ssh` plugin from the computer running Nagios to the remote machine by running the following command:

```
nagios@nagiosserver:~$ /opt/nagios/plugins/check_by_ssh \
    -H 192.168.2.1 -C "/opt/nagios/plugins/check_apt"
APT OK: 0 packages available for upgrade (0 critical updates).
```

We are now sure that the checking itself works fine, and we can move on to how `check_by_ssh` can be used and what its syntax is.

Using the check_by_ssh plugin

As mentioned earlier, Nagios uses a separate check command that connects to a remote machine over SSH and runs the actual check command on it.

The command has multiple features and can be used to query a single service status by using active checks. It can also be used to perform and report multiple checks at once as passive checks.

The syntax of the plugin is as follows:

```
check_by_ssh -H <host> -C <command> [-fqv] [-1|-2] [-4|-6]
             [-S [lines]] [-E [lines]] [-t timeout] [-i identity]
             [-l user] [-n name] [-s servicelist] [-O outputfile]
             [-p port] [-o ssh-option]
```

The following table describes all the options accepted by the plugin. Items required are marked in bold:

Option	Description
-H, --hostname	This provides the hostname or IP address of the machine to connect to; this option must be specified
-C, --command	This provides the full path of the command to be executed on the remote host along with any additional arguments; this option must be specified
-l, --logname	This lets you log in as a specific user; if omitted, it defaults to the current user (usually nagios) or any other user specified in the per-user SSH client configuration file
-I, --identity	This specifies the path to the SSH private key to be used for authorization; if omitted, then ~/.ssh/id_rsa is used by default
-o, --ssh-option	This allows passing SSH-specific options that will be passed as the -o option to the ssh command
-q, --quiet	This stops SSH from printing warning and information messages
-w, --warning	This specifies the time in seconds after which the connection should be terminated and a warning should be issued to Nagios
-c, --critical	This specifies the time in seconds after which the connection should be terminated and a critical should be issued to Nagios
-t, --timeout	This specifies the time in seconds after which the connection should be terminated and checks should be stopped; defaults to 10 seconds
-p, --port	This specifies the port to connect over SSH; defaults to 22
-1, --proto1	This will let you use the SSH protocol Version 1
-2, --proto2	This will let you use the SSH protocol Version 2; this is the default
-4	This will let you use IPv4 protocol for SSH connectivity
-6	This will let you use IPv6 protocol for SSH connectivity
-S, --skip-stdout	This will let you ignore all or the provided number of lines from the standard output
-E, --skip-stderr	This will let you ignore all or the provided number of lines from the standard error

Option	Description
-f	This tells SSH to work in the background just after connecting, instead of using a terminal

The only required flags are -H to specify the IP address or hostname to connect and -C to specify the command to run. The remaining parameters are optional. If they are not passed, SSH defaults and the timeout of 10 seconds will be used.

The -S and -E options are used to skip messages that are written by the SSH client or the remote machine, regardless of the commands executed. For example, to properly check machines printing MOTD, even for non-interactive sessions, skipping it by using one of the options is required.

When specifying commands, they usually need to be enclosed in single or double quotation marks. This is because the entire command that should be run needs to be passed to check_by_ssh as a single argument. If one or more arguments contain spaces, single quote characters will have to be used.

For example, when checking for disk usage remotely, we need to quote the entire command as well; this is because it's safer to quote the path to the drive we're checking, as shown here:

```
nagios@nagios1:~$ /opt/nagios/plugins/check_by_ssh -H 192.168.2.1 -C \
    "/opt/nagios/plugins/check_disk -w 15% -c 10% -p '/'"
DISK OK - free space: / 243 MB (17% inode=72%)
```

The example above is a typical usage of the check_by_ssh plugin as an active check. It performs a single check and returns the status directly using the standard output and exit code. This is how it is used as an active check within Nagios.

If you want to use check_by_ssh to deploy checks locally on the same machine as the one on which Nagios is running, you will need to add the SSH key from id_rsa.pub to the authorized_keys file on that machine as well. In order to verify that it works correctly, try logging in to the local machine over SSH.

Now that the plugin works when invoked manually; we need to configure Nagios to make use of it.

Usually, for commands that will be performed both locally and remotely, the approach is to create a duplicate entry for each command with a prefix, for example, _by_ssh.

For example a command that checks swap usage locally may be defined as follows:

```
define command
{
  command_name  check_swap
  command_line  $USER1$/check_swap -w $ARG1$ -c $ARG2$
}
```

Then, assuming that we will also check the swap usage on remote machines, we need to define the following remote counterpart:

```
define command
{
  command_name  check_swap_by_ssh
  command_line  $USER1$/check_by_ssh -H $HOSTADDRESS$ -C
                "$USER1$/check_swap -w $ARG1$ -c $ARG2$"
}
```

Usually services are defined for groups of hosts. For example, a service to check swap space usage may be defined to be performed on all the Linux servers. It is more convenient to always use the `check_swap_by_ssh` command in this case—both for local Nagios as well as all remote machines. The overhead for performing checks over SSH is relatively small and can be ignored in most cases.

However, this requires that a server running Nagios accepts SSH connections, which is not always the case. It is also possible to simply define two types of service – one that is run over SSH and one locally and define that localhost should not use the SSH based check—such as:

```
define service
{
  use                  generic-service
  host_name            localhost
  service_description  SWAP
  check_command        check_swap
}

define service
{
  use                  generic-service
  host_name            !localhost
  hostgroup_name       linux-servers
  service_description  SWAP
  check_command        check_swap_by_ssh
}
```

This way `localhost` will use the `check_swap` command and all the remaining machines that are part of the `linux-servers` host group will use the `check_swap_by_ssh` check command.

Performing multiple checks

The `check_by_ssh` plugin can also run multiple plugins at once and report their results to Nagios using the external command pipe. The reason for this approach is that the SSH protocol negotiations introduce a lot of overhead related to the protocol itself. For hosts with heavy load or for machines with connectivity issues, it is more efficient to run all the checks using a single SSH session instead of performing every check individually.

As the results are reported as passive checks, using this functionality requires that those services allow receiving passive check results over the command pipe.

One of the main issues with doing multiple checks is that it is not trivial to schedule these directly from Nagios. A typical approach to passive checks is to schedule checks from an external application such as cron (http://linux.die.net/man/8/cron).

An alternate approach is to create a dummy service in Nagios that will launch passive checks in the background. The actual result for this service would also be to check whether running the tests was successful or not. An upside of this approach is that the checks will be performed even if the `cron` daemon is currently disabled, as Nagios will still take care of scheduling the checks done by it.

When using `check_by_ssh` to report multiple results as passive checks, the following options need to be specified:

Option	Description
-n, --name	This provides the short name of the host that the tests refer; this is the name of the host that will be used when sending the results over the external command pipe
-s, --services	These are the names of the services that the tests refer, separated by a colon; these are the names of services that will be used when sending results over the external pipe
-O, --output	This is the path to the external command pipe to which the results of all the checks should be sent

The options above are specific to performing multiple checks only and are not all of the options that the plugin accepts when running multiple checks. The remaining options described earlier must also be specified—especially the −H and −C options.

The −C option needs to be specified multiple times, each for one check. The number of parameters must match the number of entries in the −s parameter so that each result can be mapped to a service name.

The following example runs a disk space check for three partitions:

```
/opt/nagios/plugins/check_by_ssh -H 192.168.2.1 -O /tmp/out1 \
    -n ubuntu1 -s "DISK /:DISK /usr:DISK /opt" \
    -C "/opt/nagios/plugins/check_disk -w 15% -c 10% -p /" \
    -C "/opt/nagios/plugins/check_disk -w 15% -c 10% -p /usr" \
    -C "/opt/nagios/plugins/check_disk -w 15% -c 10% -p /opt"
```

This command will put the output into /tmp/out1, similar to the following example:

```
[1462485600] PROCESS_SERVICE_CHECK_RESULT;ubuntu1;DISK /:DISK
CRITICAL...
    [1462485600] PROCESS_SERVICE_CHECK_RESULT;ubuntu1;DISK /usr:DISK OK
...
    [1462485600] PROCESS_SERVICE_CHECK_RESULT;ubuntu1;DISK /opt:DISK OK
...
```

As mentioned earlier in this section, it is very common to write a script that is run as an active check and will perform passive checks.

The following is a sample script that runs several tests and reports their results back to Nagios:

```
#!/bin/sh

COMMANDFILE=$1
HOSTNAME=$2
HOSTADDRESS=$3
PLUGINPATH=$4

$PLUGINPATH/check_by_ssh -H $HOSTADDRESS -t 30 \
    -o $COMMANDFILE -n $HOSTNAME \
    -s "SWAP:Root Partition:Processes:System Load" \
    -C "$PLUGINPATH/check_swap -w 20% -c 10%" \
    -C "$PLUGINPATH/check_disk -w 20% -c 10% -p /" \
    -C "$PLUGINPATH/check_procs -w 100 -c 200" \
    -C "$PLUGINPATH/check_load -w 5,3,2 -c 10,8,7" \
        (
        echo "BYSSH CRITICAL problem while running SSH"
```

```
    exit 2
  )

echo "BYSSH OK checks launched"
exit 0
```

For the remaining part of the section we'll assume that the script is in the `/opt/nagios/plugins` directory and is called `check_linux_services_by_ssh`.

The script will perform several checks, and if any of them fail, it will return a critical result as well. Otherwise, it will return an `OK` status and the remaining results will be passed as passive check results. We will also need to configure Nagios, both services that will receive their results as passive checks, and the service that will actually schedule the checks properly.

All the services that are checked via the `check_by_ssh` command itself have a very similar definition—accept passive checks and not have any active checks scheduled.

The following is a sample definition for the SWAP service:

```
define service
{
  use                    generic-service
  host_name              !localhost
  hostgroup_name         linux-servers
  service_description    SWAP
  active_checks_enabled  0
  passive_checks_enabled 1
}
```

All other services will also need to have a very similar definition.

We might also define a template for such services and only create services that use it. This will make the configuration more readable.

We'll need to define a command definition that will launch the passive check script written earlier:

```
define command
{
  command_name    check_linux_services_by_ssh
  command_line    $USER1$/check_linux_services_by_ssh
                  "$COMMANDFILE$" "$HOSTNAME$" "$HOSTADDRESS$" "$USER1$"
}
```

All the parameters that are used by the script are passed directly from the Nagios configuration. This makes reconfiguring paths to Nagios plugins or command pipe easier.

The next step is to define an actual service that will run these checks:

```
define service
{
  use                      generic-service
  host_name                !localhost
  hostgroup_name           linux-servers
  service_description      Check Services By SSH
  active_checks_enabled    1
  passive_checks_enabled   0
  check_command            check_linux_services_by_ssh
  check_interval           30
  check_period             24x7
  max_check_attempts       1
  notification_interval    30
  notification_period      24x7
  notification_options     c,u,r
  contact_groups           linux-admins
}
```

This will cause the checks to be scheduled every 30 minutes. It will also notify the Linux administrators if any problem occurs with the scheduling of the checks.

An alternative approach is to use the `cron` daemon to schedule the launch of the previous script. In such a case, the `Check Services By SSH` service is not needed. In this case, scheduling of the checks is not done in Nagios, but we will still need to have the services for which the status will be reported.

In such a case, we need to make sure that `cron` is running to have up-to-date results for the checks. Such verification can be done by monitoring the daemon using Nagios and the `check_procs` plugin.

The first thing that needs to be done is to adapt the script to not print out the results in case everything worked fine and hardcode paths to the Nagios files:

```
#!/bin/sh

COMMANDFILE=/vat/nagios/rw/nagios.cmd
PLUGINPATH=/opt/nagios/plugins
HOSTNAME=$1
HOSTADDRESS=$2

$PLUGINPATH/check_by_ssh -H $HOSTADDRESS -t 30 \
    -o $COMMANDFILE -n $HOSTNAME \
```

```
       -s "SWAP:Root Partition:Processes:System Load" \
       -C "$PLUGINPATH/check_swap -w 20% -c 10%" \
       -C "$PLUGINPATH/check_disk -w 20% -c 10% -p /" \
       -C "$PLUGINPATH/check_procs -w 100 -c 200" \
       -C "$PLUGINPATH/check_load -w 5,3,2 -c 10,8,7" \
       || (
          echo "BYSSH CRITICAL problem while running SSH"
          exit 2
       )
   exit 0
```

The main changes are that COMMANDFILE and PLUGINPATH variables are hardcoded as they are not passed from Nagios anymore. Also, by default the script does not print anything on standard output – this is because cron sends an e-mail with the script output if any is written or exit code is not 0.

The next step is to add an entry to the Nagios user, crontab. This can be done by running the crontab -e command as the nagios user or the crontab -u nagios -e command as the administrator.

Assuming that the check should be performed every 30 minutes, the crontab entry should be as follows:

```
       */30 * * * * /opt/nagios/plugins/check_linux_services_by_ssh
```

For more details on how an entry in crontab should look, please consult its manual page available at http://linux.die.net/man/5/crontab.

Troubleshooting the SSH-based checks

If you have followed the steps from the previous sections carefully, then everything should be working properly. However, in some cases, performing checks over SSH might not be working properly and troubleshooting needs to be done to understand the root cause of the problem.

The first thing that you should start with is using the check_ssh plugin to make sure that SSH is accepting connections on the host that we are checking. For example, we can run the following command:

```
       root@ubuntu1:~# /opt/nagios/plugins/check_ssh -H 192.168.2.51
       SSH OK - OpenSSH_4.7p1 Debian-8ubuntu1.2 (protocol 2.0)
```

Where `192.168.2.51` is the name of the IP address of the remote machine we want to monitor. If no SSH server is set up on the remote host, the plugin will return `Connection refused` status, and if it failed to connect, the result will state `No route to host`. In these cases, you need to make sure that the SSH server is working and all routers and firewalls do not reject communications over SSH, which is TCP port 22.

Assuming that the SSH server is accepting connections, the next thing that can be checked is whether the SSH key-based authorization works correctly. To do this, switch to the user the Nagios process is running as. Next, try to connect to the remote machine. The following are sample commands to perform this check:

```
root@ubuntu1:~# su nagios -
$ ssh -v 192.168.2.51
```

This way you can check the connectivity as the same user as that which Nagios is using to run checks. You can also analyze the logs that will be printed to the standard output, as described earlier in this chapter.

If the SSH client prompts you for a password, then your keys are not set up properly. It is a common mistake to set up keys on the `root` account instead of setting them up on the `nagios` account. If this is the case, then create a new set of keys as the correct user and verify whether these keys are working correctly now.

Assuming this step worked fine, the next thing to be done is checking whether invoking an actual check command produces correct results. For example:

```
root@ubuntu1:~# su nagios -
$ ssh 192.168.2.51 /opt/nagios/plugins/check_procs
PROCS OK: 51 processes
```

This way, you will check the connectivity as the same user at which Nagios is running checks.

The last check is to make sure that the `check_by_ssh` plugin also returns correct information. For example by doing:

```
root@ubuntu1:~# su nagios -
$ /opt/nagios/plugins/check_by_ssh -H 192.168.2.1 \
    /opt/nagios/plugins/check_procs
PROCS OK: 52 processes
```

If the last step also worked correctly, it means that all check commands are working correctly.

If you still have issues with the running of the checks, then the next thing you should investigate is if Nagios has been properly configured and whether all commands, hosts, and services are set up in the correct way.

Monitoring using NRPE

NRPE is a client-server solution for running check commands on remote computers. It is designed explicitly to allow the central Nagios server to trigger checks on other machines in a secure manner.

NRPE offers a very good security mechanism along with encryption mechanisms. It is possible to specify a list of machines that can run checks via NRPE and which plugins can be run along with aliases that should be used by the central Nagios server.

The main difference is that the communication overhead is much smaller than for running checks over the SSH protocol. This means that both the central Nagios server and the remote machine need less CPU time to perform a check. This is mainly important for Nagios servers that deal with a lot of checks that are performed remotely on machines. If the SSH overhead compared to NRPE is 1 second per each test that has to be run, then when performing 20,000 checks it maps to 5.5 hours that would be spent on SSH overhead.

NRPE also allows running only specific commands to perform specific checks—so it is not possible to use the NRPE protocol to run arbitrary commands. While the same is possible with SSH by configuring it properly, NRPE provides this by default.

NRPE uses the TCP protocol with SSL encryption on top of it. Enabling encryption is optional, but it is highly recommended. By default, NRPE communicates on port 5666. The connection is always made from the machine running the Nagios daemon to the remote machine. If your company has firewalls set up for local connectivity, make sure that you allow communications from port 5666 of your Nagios server.

The following is an illustration of how such a check is performed:

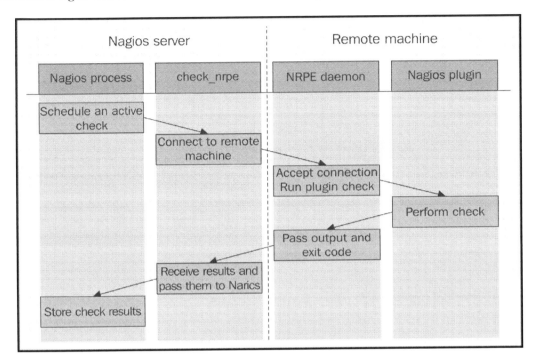

Nagios determines that an active check should be performed. It runs the `check_nrpe` plugin that connects to the remote host's NRPE daemon. After the NRPE daemon accepts this as a valid host to send commands to, `check_nrpe` sends the command to be run along with any parameter to the remote machine.

Next, the NRPE daemon translates these into the actual system command to be run. In case the specified command is not allowed, the NRPE daemon will reject this request. Otherwise it will run the command and pass the results back to `check_nrpe` on the machine hosting the Nagios daemon. This information is then passed back to the Nagios daemon and stored in the data files and/or databases.

The NRPE package consists of two parts: the NRPE daemon and the NRPE check command. The first one needs to be running on all remote machines that are to be monitored using this method. The NRPE check command (`check_nrpe`) is a Nagios plugin to perform active checks and needs to be installed on the machine on which the Nagios daemon is running.

Obtaining NRPE

NRPE is a core add-on for Nagios and it is maintained by the Nagios development team. NRPE can be downloaded as both source code and binary packages with multiple Linux distributions.

The NRPE source package can be downloaded from the Nagios download page (`https://www.nagios.org/downloads/nagios-core-addons/`). The actual downloads are hosted on SourceForge and the NRPE sources can be retrieved from `https://sourceforge.net/projects/nagios/files/nrpe-2.x/nrpe-2.15/`—version 2.15 is the latest version at the time of writing.

For Ubuntu Linux, the package names are `nagios-nrpe-server` and `nagios-nrpe-plugin` for the daemon and client, respectively. For Ubuntu, the command to install the client and the server is as follows:

```
apt-get install nagios-nrpe-server nagios-nrpe-plugin
```

For RHEL, CentOS, and Fedora systems that have `yum` installed, the package names are `nagios-nrpe` and `nagios-plugins-nrpe` for the daemon and the client, respectively. The command to install both client and server is as follows:

```
yum install nagios-nrpe nagios-plugins-nrpe
```

Microsoft Windows version of the NRPE daemon can be found in the **NRPE_NT** project on SourceForge (`http://sourceforge.net/projects/nrpent/`). It offers the same functionality as its Unix version and is configured in the same way.

The Nagios plugins do not provide the Windows version, so you will need to compile Nagios plugins using the Cygwin package (visit `http://www.cygwin.com/`). You can also provide only your own check commands and set up NRPE_NT to use those. In the case of Microsoft Windows, it is important to remember that your plugins need to be command-line tools and cannot be created as GUI-based tools.

Monitoring Microsoft Windows-based machines and using the NRPE protocol for performing the checks is described in more detail in Chapter 12, *Advanced Monitoring*.

Compiling NRPE

If you are using NRPE from prebuilt packages, you can skip this section and resume with the NRPE configuration information. Compiling NRPE requires a standard compiler, linker, and similar tools to be present on your system. It also needs the OpenSSL package along with the actual openssl command line, which is used to generate the Diffie-Hellman key for each instance.

On an Ubuntu Linux system, installing the prerequisite packages can be done by performing the following command:

```
apt-get install gcc make binutils cpp pkg-config libc6-dev \
        libssl-dev openssl
```

For other Linux distributions and operating systems, the commands and package names may vary, but should be very similar.

More information on what packages should be installed on other operating systems and how to do this can be found in Chapter 2, *Installing Nagios 4*.

Now that our packages are set up, the next step is to run the configure script that will set up the NRPE parameters and create the Diffie-Hellman key.

For standard paths and users that were used in Chapter 2, *Installing Nagios 4*, the command is as follows:

```
sh configure \
    --sysconfdir=/etc/nagios \
    --libexecdir=/opt/nagios/plugins \
    --prefix=/opt/nagios \
    --localstatedir=/var/nagios \
    --with-nrpe-user=nagios \
    --with-nrpe-group=nagios \
    --with-nagios-user=nagios \
    --with-nagios-group=nagios \
    --enable-ssl
```

If the configuration step has failed, one common reason is that the SSL library could not be found even if it was installed properly in the system. This is due to a configuration script sometimes not locating the libraries, especially on 64bit Linux systems.

What you can do is add the `--with-ssl-lib` option and point to the proper directory. First we'll need to find `libssl.so` —such as follows:

```
# find /usr -name libssl.so
/usr/lib/x86_64-linux-gnu/libssl.so
```

This means the directory is `/usr/lib/x86_64-linux-gnu` and `--with-ssl-lib` should be set to that—for example:

```
sh configure \
    --sysconfdir=/etc/nagios \
    --libexecdir=/opt/nagios/plugins \
    --prefix=/opt/nagios \
    --localstatedir=/var/nagios \
    --with-nrpe-user=nagios \
    --with-nrpe-group=nagios \
    --with-nagios-user=nagios \
    --with-nagios-group=nagios \
    --with-ssl-lib=/usr/lib/x86_64-linux-gnu \
    --enable-ssl
```

If running the `configure` script still fails, it is probably because one or more of the required packages are missing. If this happens, verify whether all the packages mentioned earlier in the chapter have been installed, and then try again. Also, if you know that the package is properly installed, it may require additional options to be passed. In such cases, it is recommended to check for the exact error code on the Internet.

The next step is to actually build the NRPE client and daemon. To do this, run the following command:

```
make all
```

This command will build both the binaries and then create the sample configuration files for the NRPE daemon.

It is a very common problem that the build fails, claiming that the `get_dh512` function could not be found. The problem is not obvious. In this case, please make sure that the `openssl` command is installed, the directory where it is located is added to the `PATH` environment variable, and then run all of the steps again—starting with the `configure` script.

The problem is that the `configure` script tries to generate a Diffie-Hellman key if a problem exists during this step. Then the script itself does not fail to complete, but the build process eventually fails. Please make sure that somewhere at the end of the output from the `configure` script, a text similar to the one that follows is printed out:

```
*** Generating DH Parameters for SSL/TLS ***
Generating DH parameters, 512 bit long safe prime, generator 2
This is going to take a long time
+..............+...........+.......++*+++*+++*++*++*++*
```

If the `openssl` command is not present, the following error will show up instead:

```
*** Generating DH Parameters for SSL/TLS ***
configure: line 6703: /usr/bin/openssl: No such file or directory
```

If the compilation process fails for any other reason, it is most probably due to the missing libraries or header files. In this case, installing the packages mentioned earlier will help.

Assuming that the build succeeded, the next step is to install either the NRPE client or the daemon. On the machine that is running the Nagios daemon, we need to install the client `check_nrpe` command. To do this, type the following command:

```
make install-plugin
```

This command will copy the `check_nrpe` command to the `/opt/nagios/plugins` directory. NRPE does not require any configuration file for the NRPE client, and hence, no additional file needs to be copied. For all of the remaining machines, please run the following command to install the NRPE daemon:

```
make install-daemon
```

This command will copy the `nrpe` binary to the `/opt/nagios/bin` directory.

Because the NRPE daemon requires configuration, it is recommended that you copy the `sample-config/nrpe.cfg` file as `/etc/nagios/nrpe.cfg`.

Configuring the NRPE server

Our NRPE daemon is now built and ready to be deployed on remote machines. We need to configure it and set up the system so that it accepts connections from other computers. The following steps should be applied to all machines where NRPE should be running.

First we need to create a user and a group named `nagios` that NRPE daemon will be running as:

```
groupadd nagios
useradd -g nagios -d /opt/nagios nagios
```

We also need to create a home directory for the user, and it is a good idea to lock out access for that user if no checks are to be performed over SSH. To do this, run the following commands:

```
mkdir /opt/nagios
chown nagios:nagios /opt/nagios
passwd -l nagios
```

This was needed as the machine is not the same as where the Nagios server itself is running.

There are many ways of setting this up—NRPE can work either as a standalone process that handles incoming connections using init.d or system approach. It can also be run as part of the `inetd` setup (`http://en.wikipedia.org/wiki/inetd`) or the `xinetd` (`http://www.xinetd.org/`) setup. In all cases, a configuration file is needed. This file specifies the commands to be used and the additional options to run the NRPE daemon standalone.

To run NRPE as a standalone process, which is the preferred way in most cases, all that is needed is to create a script called `/etc/init.d/nrpe` containing the following:

```
#!/bin/sh
#
### BEGIN INIT INFO
# Provides:              nrpe
# Required-Start:        $local_fs $syslog $network
# Required-Stop:         $local_fs $syslog $network
# Short-Description:     Starts and stops the NRPE server
# Description:           Starts and stops the NRPE server
### END INIT INFO

is_running() {
  pgrep -u nagios nrpe >/dev/null
}

case "$1" in
  start)
    echo -n "Starting NRPE: "
    if ! is_running ; then
      /opt/nagios/bin/nrpe -d -c /etc/nagios/nrpe.cfg
    fi
    echo "done."
    ;;
```

```
stop)
  echo -n "Stopping NRPE: "
  if is_running ; then
    pkill -u nagios nrpe
    sleep 1
    pkill -u nagios -9 nrpe
  fi
  echo "done."
  ;;
restart)
  $0 stop
  sleep 2
  $0 start
  ;;
status)
  if is_running ; then
    echo "NRPE is running"
    exit 0
  else
    echo "NRPE is NOT running"
    exit 1
  fi
  ;;
esac
```

The script has to be set to be executable—which we can do by running:

```
# chmod 0755 /etc/init.d/nrpe
```

After that we need to register `nrpe` as a system service—which can be done using the following command on Ubuntu:

```
# update-rc.d nrpe
```

And for CentOS, RHEL, and many other distributions the command is:

```
# chkconfig --level 345 nrpe on
```

In order for the script to work properly, we need to create a configuration file for NRPE.

The NRPE configuration file is similar to the main Nagios configuration file—all parameters are written in the form of <name>=<value>. If you have compiled NRPE from the source, then a default configuration can be found in the `sample-config/nrpe.cfg` file.

A sample NRPE configuration script that will work for both standalone installations as well as under `inetd` is as follows:

```
log_facility=daemon
pid_file=/var/run/nrpe.pid
server_port=5666
nrpe_user=nagios
nrpe_group=nagios
allowed_hosts=192.168.0.1
command_timeout=60
connection_timeout=300
debug=0
```

The first series of parameters includes information related to logging. NRPE uses standard Unix logging mechanisms. The `log_facility` parameter specifies the `syslog` facility name to be used for logging. The default value is `daemon`, but it can be set to any of the predefined syslog facility names.

A standalone NRPE daemon also allows the setting up of the IP address and the port to listen to as well as the user and group names to be used. In order to specify that NRPE should listen only on a specific IP address, you need to use the `server_address` parameter. If this parameter is omitted, then the NRPE will listen on all the network interfaces. The `server_port` parameter is used to specify the port number on which NRPE should listen.

If NRPE should accept connections only from a predefined list of machines, you need to specify the `allowed_hosts` parameter, which will contain a list of all the IP addresses of these machines, separated by commas. This should be set to the IP address of Nagios instance(s) that will be performing checks on this machine.

NRPE usually runs as a separate user for security reasons. The options to specify the user and group names that should be used by NRPE are `nrpe_user` and `nrpe_group` respectively.

We can also specify the file to which NRPE should write the PID of the daemon process; this can be useful in startup scripts or service monitoring tools that can read this file to determine if NRPE is running. The option name is `pid_file`.

We can also tell NRPE how long a command can run. The first option is `command_timeout`, and it tells NRPE how many seconds a command can run before it should be stopped. If a command is running for more than the specified number of seconds, it is terminated and a `CRITICAL` status is sent back to the NRPE client.

The `connection_timeout` option specifies the time in seconds after which a connection should be closed if no data has been received. This does not change the way the command times out, but it only specifies how much time NRPE should wait for a command to be sent.

NRPE also offers a `debug` option that can specify whether it should record a large amount of information in the system log. A value of 1 enables verbose logging and 0 disables it. This should be disabled in production, but can be useful during initial runs in case you run into a problem.

Registering NRPE check commands

We also need to configure the commands that can be run by the allowed machines.

The NRPE commands define aliases for the actual commands that will be executed. All commands have a unique name and the actual command line to be run. Usually command names are the plugin names or the plugin names with some description appended.

For example, the `check_disk` command that checks the `/home` directory could be called `check_disk_home`.

The commands are also defined in the `nrpe.cfg` file and each check is defined as `command[<command_name>]=<command_to_execute>`. The `command_name` has to be unique. The same set of commands can be run by all hosts specified in the `allowed_hosts` parameter.

An example command definition to use `check_disk` and to verify the space on the root partition is as follows:

```
command[check_disk_sys]=/opt/nagios/plugins/check_disk -w 20% -c 10%
-p /
```

It is also worth noting that there is no possibility of defining which hosts can run which commands, for example it is not possible to only allow certain hosts to run certain checks. All defined commands can be run by any host that is allowed to run commands on this instance.

It would be a good idea to create a template configuration that will contain the typical checks and the hosts that should be allowed to run the checks. These can be modified later for individual hosts, but using a template makes it easier to deploy the checks for a large number of boxes. A typical set of commands would be as follows:

```
command[check_rootdisk]=/opt/nagios/plugins/check_disk -w 20%
                        -c 10% -p /
command[check_swap]=/opt/nagios/plugins/check_swap -w 40% -c 20%
command[check_sensors]=/opt/nagios/plugins/check_sensors
command[check_users]=/opt/nagios/plugins/check_users -w 10 -c 20
command[check_load]=/opt/nagios/plugins/check_load
                    -w 10,8,5 -c 20,18,15
command[check_zombies]=/opt/nagios/plugins/check_procs -w 5 -c 10
                        -s Z
command[check_all_procs]=/opt/nagios/plugins/check_procs -w 150
-c 200
```

The parameters for several plugins may be changed according to your preferences, but they do represent reasonable defaults.

In case you need to troubleshoot why a check is failing, it would be a good idea to set the `debug` parameter to `1` in `nrpe.cfg`. If NRPE is running in standalone mode, it will need to be restarted for the changes to take effect. An example log from a connection is as follows:

```
Apr 21 20:07:29 ubuntu2 nrpe[5569]: Handling the connection...
Apr 21 20:07:29 ubuntu2 nrpe[5569]: Host is asking for command
    'check_root_disk' to be run...
Apr 21 20:07:29 ubuntu2 nrpe[5569]: Running command:
    /opt/nagios/plugins/check_disk -w 20% -c 10% -p /
Apr 21 20:07:29 ubuntu2 nrpe[5569]: Command completed with return code
0
    and output: DISK OK - free space: / 7211 MB (90% inode=96%);|
    /=759MB;6717;7557;0;8397
Apr 21 20:07:29 ubuntu2 nrpe[5569]: Return Code: 0, Output: DISK OK -
free space: / 7211 MB (90% inode=96%);| /=759MB;6717;7557;0;8397
```

Another requirement for using NRPE is that the commands need to be specified using the full path to the plugin, and no macro substitution can take place. Not being able to use any macro definitions requires more attention when writing macros. It also requires that any change to the command is edited in the NRPE configuration on the remote machine, and not in the Nagios configurations on the central server. This introduces a very strict security model, but makes NRPE a bit harder to maintain.

In some cases, it is better to be able to pass arguments to NRPE from the Nagios server and have NRPE put these into the command definition. Even though this functionality is disabled for security reasons, it is possible to enable it. How NRPE can be set up to accept parameters from the Nagios server is described in the *Using command arguments with NRPE* section in this chapter.

Configuring Nagios for NRPE

The next step is to set up Nagios to use NRPE for performing checks via a remote machine. Using NRPE to perform checks requires the creation of one or more commands that will use the `check_nrpe` plugin to send actual check requests to a remote machine.

The syntax of the plugin is as follows:

```
check_nrpe -H <host> [-n] [-u] [-p <port>] [-t <timeout>]
           [-c <command>] [-a <arglist...>]
```

The following table describes all of the options accepted by the plugin. The items required are marked in bold:

Option	Description
-H, --host	This provides the hostname or IP address of the machine to connect; this option must be specified
-c, --command	This is the name of the command that should be executed; the command needs to be defined in the `nrpe.cfg` file on the remote machine
-n, --no-ssl	This disables SSL for communication
-p, --port	This connects to the specified port; defaults to 5666
-t, --timeout	This is the number of seconds after which a connection will be terminated; defaults to 10
-u, --unknown-timeout	If a timeout occurs, this will return an UNKNOWN state; if not specified, then a CRITICAL status is returned in case of a timeout

The only two required attributes are -H and -c, which specify the host and the command alias to run on that machine, respectively.

The next thing we should do is make sure that the NRPE server on the remote machine is working correctly. Assuming that check_swap is a valid command defined in NRPE on a remote machine, we can now try to connect from the Nagios server. The first thing that's worth checking is whether calling check_nrpe directly, works:

```
$ /opt/nagios/plugins/check_nrpe -H 192.168.2.52 -c check_swap
SWAP OK - 100% free (431 MB out of 431 MB) |swap=431MB;86;43;0;431
```

In our example, 192.168.2.52 is the IP address of the remote computer. As the connection was successful, NRPE passed the actual plugin output to the standard output. After a successful check, we can now define a command in the Nagios configuration that will perform a check over NRPE:

```
define command
{
  command_name    check_swap_nrpe
  command_line    $USER1$/check_nrpe -H "$HOSTADDRESS$"
                  -c "check_swap"
}
```

We can then use the check_swap_nrpe command in a service definition. NRPE has a much lower overhead as compared to SSH. So, in some cases, it would be a good idea to use NRPE even for performing local checks.

In case we are defining a service for a group of hosts, we can use the same trick as those for checks over SSH to perform checks on a local machine by using the plugins directly and checking all of the remaining machines using NRPE. This will reduce the overhead related to monitoring the local machine and remove the need to install NRPE on the local host.

The following is a sample configuration that defines a check for swap usage locally for the computer on which it is defined, and over NRPE for all the remaining machines:

```
define service
{
  use                 generic-service
  host_name           localhost
  service_description SWAP
  check_command       check_swap
  normal_check_interval 15
}
define service
{
  use                 generic-service
  host_name           !localhost
  hostgroup_name      linux-servers
  service_description SWAP
```

```
check_command          check_swap_nrpe
normal_check_interval 30
}
```

Using command arguments with NRPE

By default, NRPE is configured to run only the predefined commands and it is not possible to pass any arguments to the commands that will be run. In some cases, this is hard to manage as changes to the command configurations need to be done at the remote machine level and not at the central Nagios server level—for example, with a large number of partitions mounted on various servers.

In such cases it might be worth investigating an option included in NRPE to pass arguments to commands. This option is disabled by default as it is considered to be a large security concern. This is because it is possible to send malicious arguments to a check command and make it perform actions other than the ones it should be doing.

If you trust all requests to NRPE to be coming from your Nagios instance it is possible to enable this functionality within the NRPE daemon. This allows easier management of NRPE and the Nagios configuration.

The first thing that needs to be done is the rebuilding of the NRPE daemon with this option enabled. To do this, run the `configure` script again with the `--enable-command-args` flag added.

For example, the configure script invocation could be as follows:

```
sh configure \
    --sysconfdir=/etc/nagios \
    --libexecdir=/opt/nagios/plugins \
    --prefix=/opt/nagios \
    --localstatedir=/var/nagios \
    --with-nrpe-user=nagios \
    --with-nrpe-group=nagios \
    --with-nagios-user=nagios \
    --with-n agios-group=nagios \
    --enable-command-args \
    --enable-ssl
```

Please note that if the `--with-ssl-lib` option had to be specified to build NRPE, it also has to be added to the example invocation above.

It is also necessary to rebuild the NRPE daemon and reinstall the binary by using the following commands:

```
make all
make install-plugin
make install-daemon
```

If you are running NRPE as a standalone daemon, then you need to restart the daemon after overwriting the binary. Only the daemon on the remote machine needs to be reconfigured and recompiled. It is not necessary to rebuild the NRPE client as it always supports the passing of arguments to the NRPE daemon.

The next step is to add the `dont_blame_nrpe` option to the `nrpe.cfg` file and set it to `1`. This option, despite its strange name, enables the functionality to use arguments in the command definitions. When NRPE is compiled with this option and the option is enabled in the NRPE configuration, passing arguments to commands is possible.

Now it is possible to use the `$ARGn$` macros in the NRPE configuration, similar to how they are defined in Nagios. This works in the same way as Nagios, where `$ARG1$` indicates the first argument, `$ARG2$` the second one, and so on for up to 16 arguments. For example, a `check` command that checks the disk space on any partition looks like the following:

```
command[check_disk]=/opt/nagios/plugins/check_disk -w $ARG1$ -c $ARG2$
-p $ARG3$
```

This requires that the warning and critical levels are passed during the check. The actual path to the mount point, which is specified as a third parameter, is essential. Arguments are passed to `check_nrpe` by specifying the `-a` flag and passing all required arguments after it, with each argument as a separate parameter. An example invocation of the `check` command as a standalone command would be as follows:

```
$ /opt/nagios/plugins/check_nrpe -H 10.0.0.1 -c check_disk -a 10% 5%
/usr
    DISK OK - free space: /usr 7209 MB (90% inode=96%)
```

After making sure that the check works, we can now define a command and the corresponding service definition. The command will pass the arguments specified in the actual service definition:

```
define command
{
  command_name      check_disk_nrpe
  command_line      $USER1$/check_disk -H "$HOSTADDRESS$"
                    -c "check_disk" -a $ARG1$ $ARG2$ $ARG3$
}
```

And, the actual service definition is as follows:

```
define service
{
    use                    generic-service
    host_name              !localhost
    hostgroup_name         linux-servers
    service_description    Disk space on /usr
    check_command          check_disk_nrpe!10%!5%!/usr
}
```

This way you can define multiple partition checks without any modifications of the configuration file on the remote machines. Of course arguments can also be used for various plugins – for example, to be able to configure the load, user, and process thresholds directly in Nagios configuration rather than in each machine's NRPE settings.

Passing arguments to NRPE is a very useful feature. However, it comes at the price of a lower security level. When enabling it, you should keep in mind that malicious users are able to send parameters to NRPE, and so they may be able to inject shell commands and run arbitrary commands under the `nagios` account.

When using the functionality, it is recommended you have a strict source IP address policy in both the firewalls and the remote machine to limit the security issues related to the passing of arguments down to the actual check commands.

Troubleshooting NRPE

Our NRPE configuration should now be complete and working as expected. In case NRPE-based checks are not working properly, there are some steps that you can take to determine the root cause of the problem.

The first thing that should be checked is whether the Nagios server can connect to the NRPE process on the remote machine. We can check if NRPE accepts connections by using `check_tcp` from the Nagios plugins.

By default, NRPE uses port 5666. Assuming that we want to test connectivity of NRPE on `192.168.2.1`, the following example shows how to check it:

```
$ /opt/nagios/plugins/check_tcp -H 192.168.2.1 -p 5666
TCP OK - 0.009 second response time on port
5666|time=0.008794s;;;0.000000;10.000000
```

If NRPE is not set up on the remote host, the plugin will return `Connection refused`. If the connection could not be established, the result will be `No route to host`. In these cases, you need to make sure that the NRPE server is working and the traffic that the TCP port NRPE is listening on is not blocked by the firewalls.

If the plugin did report a connection could be established, the next step is to try to run an invalid command. We can then check the output from the plugin and see what NRPE has reported.

The following is an example that assumes that `dummycommand` is not defined in the NRPE configuration on the remote machine:

```
$ /opt/nagios/plugins/check_nrpe -H 192.168.2.1 -c dummycommand
NRPE: Command 'dummycommand' not defined
```

If you received a `CHECK_NRPE: Error - Could not complete SSL handshake` error or something similar, it means that NRPE is not configured to accept connections from your machine—either via the `allowed_hosts` option in the NRPE configuration or in the `inetd` configuration. In order to check this, search the system logs on the machine where NRPE is running for `nrpe` text.

For example, on most systems, to check if the NRPE is configured we need to execute the following command:

```
# grep nrpe /var/log/syslog /var/log/messages
(...)
ubuntu1 nrpe[3023]: Host 192.168.2.13 is not allowed to talk to us!
```

This indicates that your Nagios server is not added to the list of allowed hosts in the NRPE configuration. Add it in the `allowed_hosts` option and restart the NRPE process.

Another error message that could be returned by the `check_nrpe` command is `CHECK_NRPE: Received 0 bytes from daemon.` `Check the remote server logs for error messages`. This message usually means that you have passed arguments or invalid characters in the command name and the NRPE server refused the request because of these.

Looking at the remote server's logs will usually provide more detailed information:

```
# grep nrpe /var/log/syslog /var/log/messages
(...)
ubuntu1 nrpe[3023]: Error: Request contained command arguments!
ubuntu1 nrpe[3023]: Client request was invalid, bailing out...
```

In this situation, you need to make sure that you enable arguments or change the Nagios configuration to not to use arguments over NRPE.

Another possibility is that the check returns `CHECK_NRPE: Socket timeout after 10 seconds` or a similar message. In this case, the check command has not been completed within the configured time. You may need to increase `command_timeout` in the NRPE configuration.

Comparing NRPE and SSH

Both SSH and NRPE are used to perform checks on remote machines. They can be set up to perform the same tasks. There are some differences and each solution is better in certain conditions.

SSH-based checks are easier to set up from a network and administrative perspective. All that is needed is to put a set of plugins on the machine, create a public key-based authentication, and you are all set to go! The main advantage of this method is that it uses the existing network protocol, which is usually running and enabled on all Unix-based machines. This way there's usually no changes in firewall configurations to pass traffic related to the Nagios checks if the server that Nagios is running on can already connect to other hosts using the SSH protocol.

Security and performance are the trade-offs. As SSH is a generic protocol, Nagios server can run any command on any of the machines that it can access. One way of limiting this problem is to set up a restricted shell for the user that performs the checks or configure `authorized_keys` file to only allow running specific commands.

Another problem with this approach is that SSH is a complex protocol, and the overheads related to connecting to a remote machine and running a plugin are high. The main problem occurs where one central Nagios server performs a large volume of tests over SSH. The problem will not be significant on remote computers, but the central server will require more processing power to handle all of the checks in a timely manner.

NRPE is an alternative to SSH. It is a daemon that is installed on remote computers that allow the running of checks. The main advantage of this approach is that it offers much better security and granularity out of the box. The administrator of the remote computer can configure NRPE to accept connections only from certain IP addresses and to allow the execution of only predefined commands, without taking any arguments into account. So, there is very little chance of a security issue because of NRPE-based checks. Another advantage is that the NRPE protocol requires much less overhead and frequent checks do not affect the central Nagios server as much as the SSH protocol.

There are some downsides to NRPE. The first one is that it needs to be set up on all of the machines that will be monitored in a remote manner. In addition to this, all configurations for the checks are kept on the remote machines. It may make it much harder for system administrators to maintain changes in the configuration when monitoring a large number of machines.

Usually it is quite obvious which solution should be used in which case. There may be cases where it's easier to use the existing SSH daemons. In other cases, security or performance is more of an issue and NRPE is a better choice. In some other cases, a custom solution will work best. How you should proceed is a matter of knowing the best tool for a particular case. In all cases, doing checks from the remote computers is not as easy as doing it locally. But, it is also not very difficult if you are using the right tools.

Alternatives to SSH and NRPE

This chapter focuses mainly on using SSH and NRPE for performing the remote checks. This is because Nagios is widely used to perform checks on the remote machines. There are also various alternate approaches that people take to invoke checks remotely.

One alternative approach is to use an agent that is running on each remote machine and use it to perform tests. A common solution for performing Nagios monitoring remotely this is **Nagios Cross-Platform Agent (NCPA)**, which is available from `https://exchange.nagios.org/directory/Addons/Monitoring-Agents/NCPA/details`. It is an open source agent written in Python that can be installed on Windows, Mac OS X and Linux machines. NCPA also provides a command for performing checks from the Nagios server.

In many cases remote monitoring involves checking the status of web-based applications. In this case it's common to use `check_http` and send requests for monitoring status to the application. This way, you can invoke a specific URL that will perform a status check of your application components or perform additional tests on the machine and provide the results over the HTTP protocol.

In such a case, an application can have a URL that is accessible only from specific IP addresses and returns diagnostic information about the website. This can mean performing a test SQL query to the database and checking the file permissions and available disk space. The application can also perform a sanity check of critical data either in the files or in a database.

The web page can return a predefined string if all of the tests are passed correctly and will return an error message otherwise. In this case, it is possible to perform the check with the `check_http` plugin.

A typical scenario is when a check is done for both the string preset in the answer and a page size range. For example, a check for the OK string combined with a page size ranging from two to eight will check whether the result contains information about the correct test and will also detect any additional messages preset in the output.

Another option is to use a generic framework for running commands remotely and simply adapt it to run Nagios checks. One such framework is the **Software Testing Automation Framework (STAF)** available at http://staf.sourceforge.net/.

This is a peer-to-peer-based framework that allows you to write code that performs specific jobs on remote machines. As the system is not centralized, there is no critical resource that can make your entire system malfunction if it is down.

One of the benefits of STAF is that is stable, actively maintained and has support for a large variety of languages—such as Java, Perl, Python, Tcl and Ant. This means that logic for performing checks can be done in languages that best fit a specific scenario.

Summary

Nagios can leverage multiple solutions to monitor resources on remote machines—such as disk usage, swap, or other metrics.

In this chapter, we have learned the following items:

- Using SSH for running checks on remote machines
- Running multiple checks at once over SSH
- Troubleshooting the SSH-based checks
- Using NRPE for performing remote checks
- Setting up NRPE server and client as well as NRPE-based checks in Nagios
- Troubleshooting SSH and NRPE connections
- How SSH and NRPE differ from each other and when to use each of them

The next chapter talks about **Simple Network Management Protocol (SNMP)**, which is a protocol for monitoring and managing various types of devices connected to a network. The protocol supports both querying the device as well as receiving information from the devices regarding the failure. The SNMP protocol is used by a large variety of devices, from network switches and routers to mainframe servers.

11
Monitoring Using SNMP

The previous chapter talked about different approaches to verifying remote computers and the services they offer. This chapter covers another way of monitoring remote machines and devices.

Simple Network Management Protocol (SNMP) is a protocol that is designed to monitor and manage various devices connected to a network. Its main purpose is to create a standardized way of getting and setting parameters regardless of the underlying hardware. The protocol allows the retrieval of information from a device, setting options, and also covers the means for a device to notify other machines about a failure.

In this chapter, we will learn the following:

- Introducing SNMP
- Working with SNMP and MIB
- Setting up an SNMP agent
- Using SNMP from Nagios

Introducing SNMP

SNMP is an industry standard and all major hardware and software vendors support it. All commonly-used operating systems can provide information using SNMP. Microsoft offers SNMP for their Windows platform; all Unix systems have SNMP daemons that receive requests from the other machines.

SNMP also offers a standardized, hierarchical way to group and access information, called **Management Information Base** (**MIB**). This defines which attributes can be accessed, and what data types are associated with them. This allows the creation of attributes that all devices should use for providing information on standard parameters such as network configuration, usage, and potential threats. It also allows custom parameters to be created so that they will not interfere with other devices' data.

Most operating systems come with various utilities that allow communication with other devices over SNMP. These utilities can be used to verify which attributes are available on specific devices and what their values are at the moment.

SNMP is designed to be easy to implement and to provide a uniform way to access information on various machines.

It is designed so that the footprint of the SNMP services is minimal. This allows devices with a very limited size of storage and operating memory to still use the protocol. SNMP uses the **User Datagram Protocol (UDP)** protocol (see `http://https://www.techopedia.com/definition/13460/user-datagram-protocol-udp`), which requires much less resources than TCP. It also uses one packet for sending a single request or response operation, so the protocol itself is stateless.

Each machine that is managed by SNMP has an application that responds to requests from this and other computers. Such an application is called an **agent**. For Unix systems, it is usually a daemon working in the background. Many devices with embedded systems have SNMP support included in the system core. In all of these cases, a device needs to listen for SNMP requests and respond accordingly.

All agents are usually managed by one or more machines called the SNMP **manager**. This is a computer that queries agents for data; it might also set their attributes. Usually, this is an application running in the background that communicates over SNMP and stores the information in some data storage.

By default, SNMP uses UDP port 161 to communicate with the agent and port 162 for sending information from the agent to the manager. In order to use SNMP, these ports need to be passed correctly by all network routers, and should not be filtered by the firewalls.

There are two types of communication that are done by SNMP; the first one is when a manager sends requests to an agent. These can be **get** requests, where the manager wants to retrieve information from an agent. If the information needs to be modified, a **set** request is sent out.

Another type of communication is where an agent wants to notify a manager about a problem. In such cases, an SNMP **trap** is sent out. An agent needs to know the IP address of the manager to send the information out to. A manager needs to be listening for SNMP traps, and should react on the issue.

The following is an illustration of possible SNMP communication types:

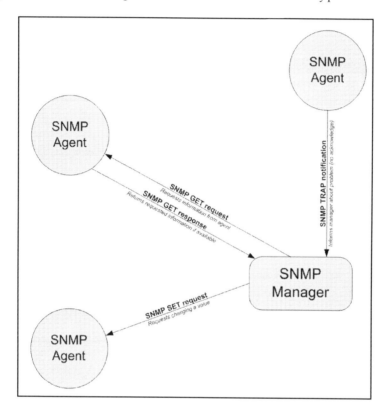

SNMP has several versions that an agent can communicate over. **SNMPv1** was the first version of the protocol. This featured get, set, and trap operations. The standard defined scalar data objects as well as tabular objects. It also featured the getnext operation, which allows iterating over the tables of data objects.

The security model related to SNMPv1 is relatively unsophisticated. A get, set, or getnext request is authenticated based on the IP address of the manager and the community string that it uses. All SNMP devices communicating over SNMPv1 use the community string for verifying that the request—whether none, only get, or both get and set operations—can be performed. By default, the `private` community string allows both reading and writing information and the `public` community string only allows reading them.

SNMP version 2 introduced improvements in terms of both performance and security. Instead of using get and getnext, it had a getbulk operation, which allows the retrieval of all entries in a table in a single operation. It also introduces an inform packet—this is a trap that requires acknowledgement from the manager. This avoids the problem where a single UDP packet gets lost, preventing a trap from being received by the manager. This version also introduced a party-based security model, which did not gain wide acceptance due to its complexity.

The most common version 2 implementation is **Community-Based Simple Network Management protocol 2 (SNMPv2c)**. It uses the features of version 2 without implementing the new security model, but using the community string mechanism that was introduced in SNMPv1.

User-Based Network Management Protocol version 2 (SNMPv2u) is another variant of SNMP version 2. This includes greater security than SNMPv2c, but does not include all security features originally developed for SNMPv2.

SNMP version 3 introduces an improved security model, including authentication, privacy, and access control. This version introduced more security than was available in SNMPv2, and one of the security frameworks uses the functionality from SNMPv2u. This standard is now gaining more attention than SNMPv2, mostly because it offers better security without the high level of complexity that SNMPv2 introduced.

Most SNMP server implementations that come integrated with operating systems support SNMPv1, SNMPv2c, and SNMPv3. Some devices only support SNMPv1 while others also offer SNMPv2. Packets from different SNMP versions are incompatible, so a device using only SNMPv1 will not recognize an SNMPv2c packet.

In many cases, devices that are used across your network will offer a different subset of versions that they support. There are two ways to work in such an environment.

The first approach is to use a proxy agent. Some SNMP management software uses SNMPv3, and devices that do not support this version will need to have the packets translated. In such cases, all requests from the manager are received by the proxy agent; this translates and passes them to the actual agent, and sends the results back to the manager. The proxy agent receives traps from the actual agent. It then passes them to the manager as a trap or translates the packet using a newer SNMP version. A proxy agent is usually an application on a computer or a physical device.

Often, SNMP managers allow the configuration of which SNMP version should be used for specific devices.

Understanding data objects

SNMP uses **Object Identifiers** (**OID**s; see `http://en.wikipedia.org/wiki/Object_ident ifier` to identify the data objects that it refers to). OIDs define a unique object for a specified SNMP agent. They are identified using a hierarchical definition, similar to how domains work on the Internet.

Object identifiers are a series of numbers separated by periods. Each number represents a part of the tree. Often, the first number in the series is also preceded by a period to indicate that this is an OID—this is not necessary, though. An example of an OID is `.1.3.6.1.2.1.1.5.0`, which maps to the system name of a machine.

As it is very hard to memorize, read, and compare OIDs written as a series of numbers, there is a standard for naming and describing the MIB tree.

The standard is called **Management Information Base (MIB)** see `http://en.wikipedia.or g/wiki/Management_Information_Base`), and it defines how various parameters are defined—how they are named, as well as what types of values these objects might return. Each MIB definition is a text file written in a subset of ASN.1 notation (see `http://www.itu .int/en/ITU-T/asn1/Pages/introduction.aspx` for more details). A file can describe a small or large subset of the MIB trees.

Currently, the standard is MIB SMIv2, and it defines all commonly-used attributes along with additional information that can be used by visualization applications.

MIB files describe fields that can be used in SNMP. They define parent nodes in the hierarchy, the numeric identifier, and the type of data that this field is associated with. SNMP uses the following basic data types:

- **String**: A string, written as bytes, that can have 0 to 65535 bytes
- **Integer and Integer32**: A signed 32 bit integer value
- **Counters32, Counter64**: Non-negative integers that increase, and are reset to 0 after they reach maximum value
- **Gauges**: Non-negative integers that can increase and decrease within a defined minimum-maximum range
- **Time tick**: Defines a time span, where the value of 100 represents one second
- **IP address**: Represents an address from the IP protocol family; SNMPv1 only supports IPv4, version 2 and 3 support both IPv4 and IPv6

In many cases, an enumeration field is returned as an integer. This means that some predefined numbers represent several predefined values. A good example is the `ifType` field when defining network interfaces—it specifies the type of network interface. Some examples are 23 for a **Point-to-Point Protocol (PPP)**; see `http://www.oreilly.com/openbook/linag2/book/ch8.html`) connection or 6 for Ethernet interfaces.

An example OID is `.1.3.6.1.2.1.1.5.0`. The following is a table describing each element, both as string and as corresponding numbers:

Identifier	Description
1	**iso**: iso standard tree
3	**org**: Organizations; this node is a placeholder for all national and international organizations
6	**dod**: Department of Defense; this is the node for the U.S. Department of Defense
1	**internet**: Subnode for the Internet; since originally the Internet was a project for U.S. military defense, its placeholder is under the **dod** subtree
2	**mgmt**: Systems management node
1	**mib-2**: Management Information Base, version 2 root node
1	**system**: Operating system information
5	**sysName**: Name of this machine; usually a fully qualified domain name
0	Index of the elements; in this case it is always 0

The string representation of this OID is
`iso.org.dod.internet.mgmt.mib-2.system.sysName.0`. Often, it is also referred to as
`SNMPv2-MIB::sysName.0`.

The `.1.3.6.1.2.1` part of the OID defines the root elements for all MIB-2 standardized
parameters. All of the standard SNMP parameters that various devices use are under this
OID node or its descendants. This node is also called the, `SNMPv2-MIB` namespace; hence,
the `SNMPv2-MIB::sysName.0` OID also maps to the same object.

The MIB tree has a few major nodes that are the base for many other subtrees that might be
significant to you under various circumstances, which are as follows:

- `.1.3.6.1.2.1` stands for `iso.org.dod.internet.mgmt.mib-2`. This is the
  base for all of the attributes that are available on the majority of SNMP-aware
  devices.
- `.1.3.6.1.4.1` stands for `iso.org.dod.internet.private.enterprise`.
  This is a root node for all corporations and companies that use private objects;
  this is used by companies such as Microsoft, Motorola, and many other hardware
  and software vendors.

The most important node is `.1.3.6.1.2.1`, which is used by all SNMP-aware devices to
report information. This part of the MIB tree is the root node for the majority of standard
objects. It is also mandatory for all SNMP-enabled devices to provide at least the basic part
of information in this subtree. For example, information such as contact information,
location, system name, and the type should be provided by all SNMP-aware devices.

SNMP can be used to retrieve different kinds of information. This information is usually
grouped into various categories. All categories also have corresponding aliases they are
usually referenced with, to avoid putting the entire structure in every OID definition or MIB
name. All applications that offer communication over SNMP allow the specification of
attributes using both OID and MIB names. Let's go over a few of the most important
sections of the MIB tree.

Information in `IF-MIB`, `IP-MIB`, `IPv6-MIB`, `RFC1213-MIB`, `IP-FORWARD-MIB`, `TCP-MIB`,
and `UDP-MIB` describe network connectivity—interfaces, IP configuration, routing,
forwarding, and the TCP and UDP protocols. They allow the querying of the current
configuration as well as currently active and listening sockets.

Data contained in `SNMPv2-MIB` and `HOST-RESOURCES-MIB` describes system information
and current parameters. This can include information on disk storage, current processes,
installed applications, and the hardware that the computer is running on.

Working with SNMP and MIB

Different operating systems can come with different SNMP applications. Many hardware vendors also offer additional software that manages multiple machines using SNMP—for example, HP OpenView or Sun Management Center. For this section and the following ones, the Net-SNMP package (see http://net-snmp.sourceforge.net/) will be used. This package is included in all Linux distributions and works with almost all Unix operating systems.

In order to install this package on Ubuntu Linux, we need to run the following command:

```
apt-get install snmp
```

For yum-based Linux distributions, the package is called net-snmp and the command to install it is as follows:

```
yum install net-snmp
```

The Net-SNMP project homepage also offers binaries for several platforms, including HP-UX and Fedora Linux. Fedora packages should also work on Red Hat Enterprise Linux systems.

It is also possible to build everything from the source for various Unix operating systems such as AIX, HP-UX, and Solaris. Exact instructions are provided on the project page (http://net-snmp.sourceforge.net/).

It is also recommended to install additional library containing MIB files, that will help using text OIDs:

```
apt-get install snmp-mibs-downloader
```

After a successful installation, we should be able to run any SNMP-related command, such as snmpget, and check the Net-SNMP version by doing the following:

```
root@ubuntu:~# snmpget -V
NET-SNMP version: 5.7.2
```

Assuming we do have a host with the SNMP agent set up, and it is accepting the SNMP protocol version 1, we can now try to communicate with it and query a few parameters:

```
root@ubuntu:~# snmpget -v 1 -c public 192.168.2.2 \
    iso.org.dod.internet.mgmt.mib-2.system.sysName.0
SNMPv2-MIB::sysName.0 = STRING: WAG354G
```

As you can see, the device returned that the system name is WAG354G. This is actually a Linksys/Cisco router and the only way to access its information is over the web interface or SNMP.

The Net-SNMP package comes with a couple of very useful commands that can be used to check current values, as well as perform a dump of a part or the whole MIB tree. These vary from simple tools for querying a single attribute to very complex ones that print out a df-like report of partitions on a remote system. There are also commands for displaying tables and for setting parameters remotely.

Throughout this section and the next ones, we'll mainly use SNMP version 1, as this is supported by almost all SNMP-enabled devices. When using SNMP in production, it's better to check which devices accept the SNMP versions, and use the most recent one a device handles correctly.

The first command that's worth getting familiar with is snmpget. This allows the querying of single or multiple attributes over SNMP.

The syntax of the command is as follows:

```
snmpget [options] IP-address OID [OID] ...
```

All of the Net-SNMP commands accept a huge number of parameters. The following parameters are the ones we will be using throughout this chapter, and they are worth knowing:

Option	Description
-h	Provides help
-V	Prints the Net-SNMP version
-c	Specifies the community name to use
-v	Specifies the SNMP version to be used; should be one of 1, 2c or 3
-r	Specifies the number of retries
-t	Timeout in seconds
-O	Output options; should be one or more of the following: n : Print OIDs as numerical values without expanding them from MIB e : Print enum and OID fields as numbers instead of string values v : Print values only instead of name = value format f : Print full OID names; disallows shortcuts such as SNMPv2-MIB

The -O option allows the retrieval of values without having to apply MIB shortcuts; hence, being able to see the entire branch. It also allows output to be changed so that only values along with data types are printed out, instead of the object names themselves.

An example of this command is as follows:

```
# snmpget -O ef -v 1 -c public rtr SNMPv2-MIB::sysObjectID.0
.iso.org.dod.internet.mgmt.mib-2.system.sysObjectID.0 =
OID: .iso.org.dod.internet.private.enterprises.ucdavis. ucdSnmpAgent.linux
```

All of the options above can also be used with other Net-SNMP commands.

Net-SNMP also offers a command to iterate through the entire MIB tree, or only a part of it. The snmpwalk command accepts the same options as shown earlier. Most versions of Net-SNMP's snmpwalk command do not require the passing of any OID to work. For older versions, in order to list the entire tree, .1 can be specified as the OID.

The following command will list the entire MIB tree of an SNMPv1 agent:

```
root@ubuntu:~# snmpwalk -v 1 -c public 192.168.2.2
```

Depending on the underlying operating system and the SNMP agent itself, the actual data may be different. Please note that if the device is not on a local network, then this operation might take a very long time to complete.

In order to retrieve only a part of the MIB tree, simply pass the prefix of the tree you are interested in. For example:

```
root@ubuntu:~# snmpwalk -v 1 -c public 192.168.2.2 1.3.6.1.2.1.1
```

The command above will limit the query to iso.org.dod.internet.mgmt.mib-2.system node and its children. It will also complete much faster than querying the entire tree.

Walking over a part of a tree is mainly useful when trying to check the objects that are available on a remote device that does not respond quickly to SNMP requests—either because of network lag or because of the computations required for some objects. It is also commonly used to find out which values are available in a specified part of the MIB tree.

Another useful utility is the snmptable command. It allows the listing of various SNMP tables, and shows them in a human readable form. The syntax is as follows:

```
snmptable [options] IP-address OIDprefix
```

For example, to list all TCP/IP connections, the following command can be used:

```
root@:~# snmptable -v 1 -c public 192.168.2.2 tcpConnTable
SNMP table: TCP-MIB::tcpConnTable

connState connLocalAddress connLocalPort connRemAddress connRemPort
   listen        0.0.0.0             23        0.0.0.0            0
   listen        0.0.0.0             80        0.0.0.0            0
   listen        0.0.0.0            199        0.0.0.0            0
```

Net-SNMP also allows the setting of new object values that can be used to reconfigure various devices. The `snmpset` command can be used to perform this. The syntax is as follows:

```
snmpset [options] IP-address OID type value [OID type value] ...
```

This command accepts all of the same standard options as the `snmpget` command. A single command invocation can be used to set more than one parameter, by specifying more than one set of OIDs to be set. Each set operation needs to specify the new value along with the data type it should be set to.

The value type can be one of the following:

Type	Description
i	Integer
u	Unsigned integer
s	String
x	Hex string: Each letter is specified as 2 hex digits
d	Decimal string: Each letter is specified as a 1-2 digit
n	NULL object
o	OID: For objects that accept an object
t	Timeticks
a	IP address
B	Series of bits

The most common types are String, Integer, and OID. The first two require the passing of either a number or a text that the object's value should be set to. Setting an OID type of object requires either providing a full OID identifier or any string that can be matched by the MIB definitions.

An example to set a system's contact name and hostname is as follows:

```
root@ubuntu:~# snmpset -v 2c -c private 192.168.2.2 \
    SNMPv2-MIB::sysContact.0 s admin@net.home \    SNMPv2-MIB::sysName.0 s
RTR
SNMPv2-MIB::sysContact.0 = STRING: admin@net.home
SNMPv2-MIB::sysName.0 = STRING: RTR
```

Some attributes cannot be set via SNMP. For example, it is not possible to modify objects that are used for the monitoring system. These attributes usually include the IP address configuration, counters, or diagnostic information, for example, TCP/UDP connection tables, process lists, installed applications, and performance counters. Many devices tend to support command line administration over SNMP, and in this case, the parameters might be read-only.

MIB definitions specify which attributes are explicitly read-only. Using a graphical tool to find out which attributes can be modified will ease automatic device configuration over the SNMP protocol.

Using graphical tools

Using SNMP and the MIB tree is not a simple task. Many people, not very familiar with command-line tools and the large amounts of information returned, might feel a bit overwhelmed by it. This is where graphical tools come in handy. And there are lots of freely-available tools that can visualize SNMP. We will discuss only a few of them.

The first tool is called mbrowse (see https://sourceforge.net/projects/mbrowse/). It is a graphical tool for browsing the MIB tree, querying attributes, and running a complete or partial walkthrough the MIB tree. This tool uses the SNMPv1 and the SNMPv2c protocols. It uses the Net-SNMP libraries and shares the same MIB definitions.

The following is a screenshot of the tool with a result from a walkthrough and an expanded TCP tree:

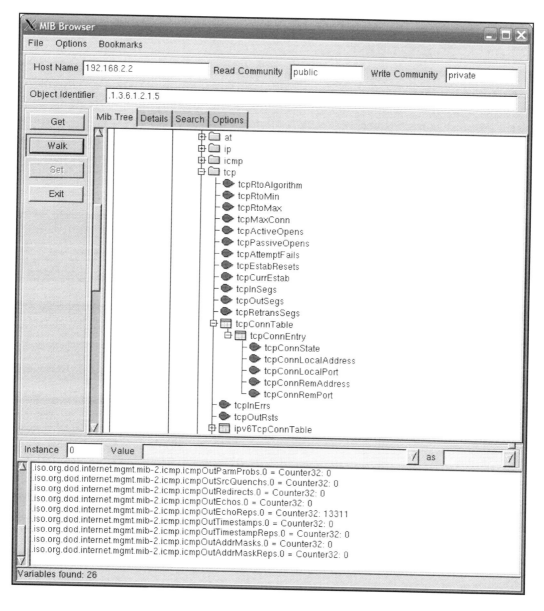

Another interesting tool is **Tcl/tK based Interactive Network Editor** (**TkIned**) from the Scotty package (`https://sourceforge.net/projects/tkined-scotty/`). This is a graphical tool that uses Tk for the graphical interface and Scotty for the SNMP protocol. It allows browsing of the MIB tree, the monitoring of hosts over SNMP, and the visualization of your network by clicking on the layout.

This tool also has another very interesting feature. Based on one or more IP network addresses, it can automatically detect your networks and try to find hosts that respond to SNMP requests. It uses the default `public/private` community pair, and communicates over the SNMPv1 and SNMPv2c protocols. This allows the detection of various operating systems and devices that are configured to respond to these communities, which are still the default ones in many cases.

The tool can be configured to monitor various parameters such as disk usage or system load over SNMP. The results are graphed and updated in real time. This can serve as a backup system to verify up to date values for various attributes. Once the SNMP or ICMP checks are set up, they will be done periodically until they are removed from the map.

The following is a screenshot of the tool after an IP-discover option has been run, where the tool has been configured to monitor the disk and memory usage of a Windows machine:

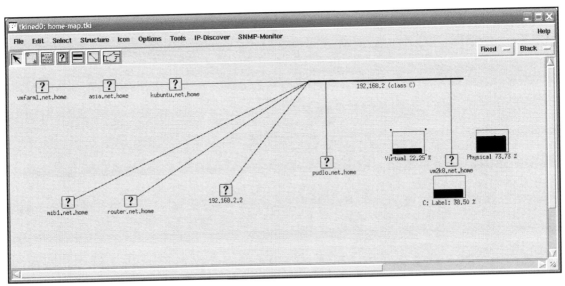

The layout of the machines on the chart can be freely edited. There is also a wide set of icons that can be associated with particular hosts.

One more tool is `SnmpB` (`http://sourceforge.net/projects/snmpb`). The tool offers the ability to use various MIB files, query SNMP agents, supports agent discovery, trap events, and many more, all of it with decent GUI.

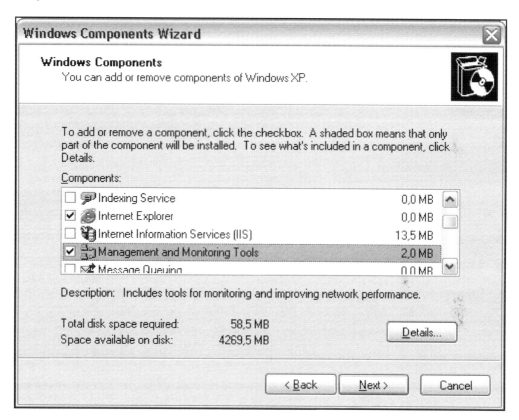

Setting up an SNMP agent

The previous section talked about how to communicate with SNMP agents. If you have a network device such as a router or Wi-Fi, WiMax, or DSL gateway, most probably it will also come with a built-in SNMP agent.

The next step is to set up the SNMP agent on one or more computers so that we can use SNMP to monitor servers or workstations. In this way, a majority of the networked equipment will allow monitoring from a single machine using the SNMP protocol.

Let's start with various Unix boxes. The SNMP agent is a part of Net-SNMP, and several distributions come with command line tools, libraries, and the SNMP agent, usually as optional packages.

In our case, we will install the SNMP agent on Ubuntu Linux. We will run the following command:

```
apt-get install snmpd
```

This will cause the SNMP daemon which is a part of Net-SNMP, to be installed. By default, the Ubuntu Linux SNMP agent only accepts connections on 127.0.0.1. This is for security reasons—in many cases, an SNMP agent is used mainly by tools such as MRTG to gather usage statistics.

To change it, we will need to either specify the IP address that SNMP agent should listen on in the /etc/default/snmpd file, SNMPDOPTS variable, or remove it completely—it should be the last argument in the SNMPDOPTS variable.

If the SNMP agent should listen on all available IP addresses, then the line should look similar to the following example:

```
SNMPDOPTS='-Lsd -Lf /dev/null -u snmp -I -smux -p /var/run/snmpd.pid'
```

The options above are standard snmpd options and may differ depending on Linux distribution and version.

Changing this option requires restarting the SNMP agent by invoking the /etc/init.d/snmpd restart command.

After a successful installation, the SNMP agent should be up and running and making a walk over the entire tree should produce some output.

To verify that the SNMP agent we have just set up is working properly, we can simply launch the following command on the same machine to see if it will return information retrieved from localhost:

```
snmpwalk -v 1 -c public 127.0.0.1
```

The agent that we have just installed supports the SNMPv1, SNMPv2c, and SNMPv3 protocol versions. It also features an extensive security model that you can configure to provide a more secure setup.

Net-SNMP agent allows you to define one or more OIDs along with all subnodes that can be retrieved, by specific security groups. These groups can be mapped to specific communities that originate from all or specific IP addresses. Security groups are also mapped using SNMP versions used by the remote machine.

A sample configuration that allows read-only access from all of the hosts is as follows:

```
com2sec readonly default public
group readonlyGroup v1   readonly
group readonlyGroup v2c readonly
group readonlyGroup usm readonly
view all     included  .1                          80
access readonlyGroup "" any noauth    exact  all   none   none
syslocation Home
syscontact Administrator <admin@yourcompany.com>
```

The first line defines a mapping between the community and a security group `readonly`. The next three lines assign `readonlyGroup` access rights to this group. The next two lines grant read-only access to all objects from the `.1` OID node and its children, which is the main OID node. The last two lines specify the system administrator and the location where the machines are stored.

For the SNMPv3 model, it is also required to specify one or more users by calling the snmpusm command (`http://linux.die.net/man/1/snmpusm`). It allows real-time configuration of the user list for local or remote SNMPv3 agents.

SNMP can also be set up on all modern Microsoft Windows operating systems. Similar to Unix systems, it is necessary to install an SNMP agent. In order to do this on Windows XP and Windows 2003 Server, we first need to go to the **Control Panel**. Next, we need to select the **Add or Remove Programs** applet and select the **Add/Remove Windows Components** option. The following window will be displayed:

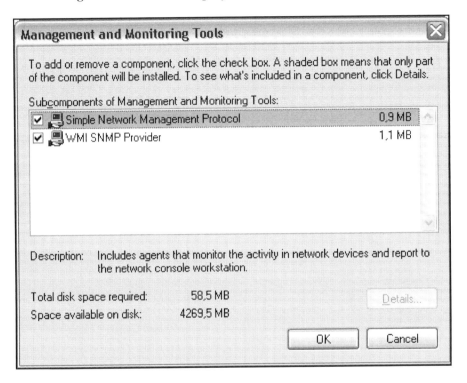

Then select both SNMP and WMI SNMP Provider from the next window to proceed with the installation of SNMP management and monitoring tools:

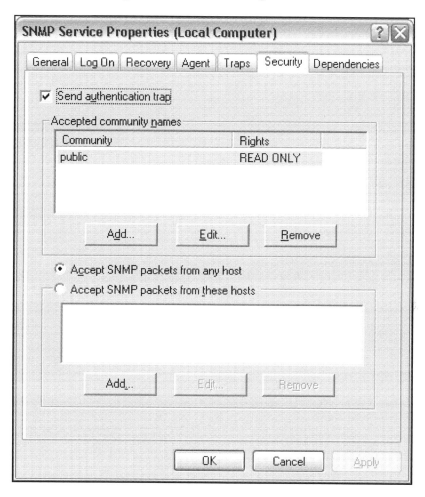

Next, we need to select **Management and Monitoring Tools**, as shown in the screenshot above. We can also select the **Details** button and choose **Simple Network Management Protocol**. The **WMI SNMP Provider** allows the retrieval of the SNMP parameters over WMI and can be left unchecked if you do not need it.

Windows SNMP agent exports information about the system in the same way as on other platforms. You can use it to query the underlying hardware, the operating system version, and the network configuration along with the currently-active connections. It is also possible to list active processes and monitor the systems load. The Windows SNMP agent also exports details of all of the installed applications along with security patches from Microsoft. This mechanism can be used to monitor whether all critical system patches are installed. It can also be used to track software license monitor compliance by checking installed and/or running software and keeping count of which machines have license-restricted software applied.

After a successful installation, we can go to the `Administrative Tools` folder and run the **Services** applet. When selecting **SNMP Service** and choosing **Properties**, the following **Service Properties** window, along with the SNMP configuration, is displayed:

The window has three additional tabs—**Agent**, **Traps**, and **Security**. The **Agent** tab allows you to configure which parts are exported over SNMP, and offers the setting up of contact and location information.

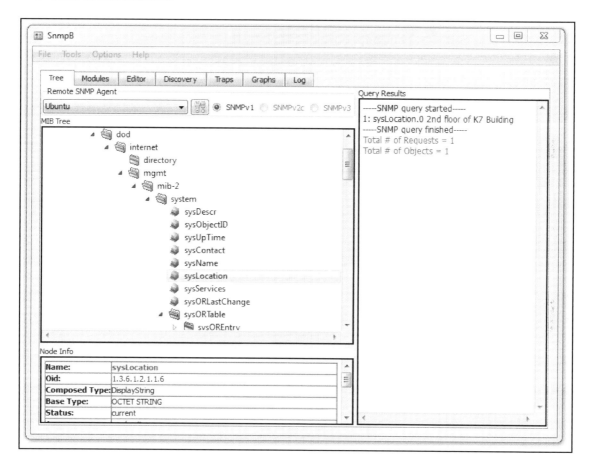

The **Security** tab allows you to configure how SNMP information from this host can be accessed. The Windows SNMP agent offers support for SNMPv1 and SNMPv2c, so the security model is based on a community string and IP addresses for authentication.

The agent can either accept SNMP queries from all hosts or only from the specific hosts listed in the bottom part of the tab. There is also the possibility of specifying one or more readable and writable communities. By default, only queries on the `public` community string are accepted and allowed read-only access.

The **Traps** tab allows configuration of Windows to send or forward traps to specific IP addresses, and indicate which SNMP community is to be used for communication.

Using SNMP from Nagios

Now that we are able to query information from Windows and Unix boxes, it would be good to know how to integrate SNMP checks with Nagios. The Nagios plugins package comes with a plugin called `check_snmp` for checking SNMP parameters and validating their value. The plugin uses the `snmpget` and `snmpgetnext` commands from Net-SNMP, and it does not work without these commands.

The following is the syntax of the command:

```
check_snmp -H <ip_address> -o <OID> [-w warn_range] [-c crit_range]
           [-C community] [-s string] [-r regex] [-R regexi]
           [-l label] [-u units] [-d delimiter]  [-D output-delimiter]
           [-t timeout] [-e retries] [-p port-number]
           [-m miblist] [-P snmp version] [-L seclevel] [-U secname]
           [-a authproto] [-A authpasswd] [-X privpasswd]
```

The following table describes the commonly-used options accepted by the plugin. Options that are required are marked in bold:

Option	Description
-H, --hostname	Host name or IP address of the machine to connect to; this option must be specified
-o, --oid	OID to get from the remote machine; can be specified either as dot-separated numbers or as a name; multiple elements can be specified and need to be separated with commas or spaces
-w	Specifies the `min:max` range of values outside of which a warning state should be returned; for integer results only
-c	Specifies the `min:max` range of values outside of which a critical state should be returned; for integer results only
-P, --protocol	Specifies the SNMP protocol version; accepted values are 1, 2c, or 3
-C, --community	Specifies the community string to be used; for SNMPv1 and SNMPv2c this defaults to `public`

`-s, --string`	Returns a critical state unless the result is an exact match of the value specified in this parameter
`-r, --regex`	Returns a critical state if the result does not match the specified regular expression; is case sensitive
`-R, --eregi`	Returns a critical state if the result does not match the specified regular expression; is case insensitive
`-t, --timeout`	Specifies the period in seconds after which it is assumed that no response has been received and the operation times out
`-e, --retries`	Specifies the number of retries that should be performed if no answer is received
`-n, --next`	Uses the `getnext` request instead of `get` to retrieve the next attribute after the specified one
`-d, --delimiter`	Specifies the deli<ie>m</ie>iter which should be used to match values in the output from the Net-SNMP commands; defaults to an equals sign: `=`
`-D, --output-delimiter`	Specifies the character used to separate output if multiple OIDs are provided

Depending on which exact flags are passed, the plugin behavior is different. In all cases, the plugin will return `critical` if the SNMP agent could not be contacted, or if the specified OID does not exist. If none of the flags `-s`, `-r`/`-R`, `-w`, and `-c` are specified, the plugin will return `OK` as long as the OID is not retrieved. Specifying `-s` will cause the check to fail if the value returned by the SNMP `get` request is different from the value supplied to this option. It is worth noting that this option uses an exact match, not a substring.

An example would be to make sure that the exact location is specified in an SNMP agent. This can be checked by the following command:

```
root@ubuntu:~# /opt/nagios/plugins/check_snmp -H 10.0.0.1 -P 2c \
    -o SNMPv2-MIB::sysLocation.0 -s "Miami Branch"
SNMP OK - VMware | SNMPv2-MIB::sysLocation.0=Miami Branch
```

Matching a part of text can be done with the `-r` or `-R` option. The first one is a case-sensitive match. The latter option ignores the case while matching the resulting value. Similarly, when making sure that the contact information field contains e-mail information, the following command can be used:

```
root@ubuntu:~# /opt/nagios/plugins/check_snmp -H 10.0.0.1 -P 2c \
    -o SNMPv2-MIB::sysContact.0 -r "@"
SNMP OK - root@company.com | SNMPv2-MIB::sysContact.0=root@company.com
```

It is also possible to match the specific value range for integer results, in which case the values indicate acceptable ranges for specific values. If the result is outside of a specified range, a WARNING or CRITICAL state is returned. It is possible to specify separate ranges for critical and warning checks.

Typical usage can be to monitor system load or the number of processes running on a specific host.

The following is an example of how to check if the number of system processes is less than 20:

```
root@ubuntu:~# /opt/nagios/plugins/check_snmp -H 10.0.0.1 -P 2c \
    -o HOST-RESOURCES-MIB::hrSystemProcesses.0 -w 0:20 -c 0:30
SNMP CRITICAL - *33* | HOST-RESOURCES-MIB::hrSystemProcesses.0=33
```

The check will return CRITICAL status if the number of processes is 30 or more. A WARNING status will be returned if the number of processes is 20 or more. If the number is less than 20, an OK status will be returned.

In all cases, it is advised that you first use the snmpwalk command and check which objects can be retrieved from a specific agent.

Nagios also comes with SNMP plugins written in Perl that allow the checking of network interfaces and their statuses. These plugins require the installation of the Perl Net::SNMP package. For Ubuntu Linux, the package name is libnet-snmp-perl.

The syntax of the plugins is as follows:

```
check_ifstatus -H hostname [-v version] [-C community]
check_ifoperstatus -H hostname [-v version] [-C community]
                    [-k index] [-d name]
```

The following table describes the options accepted by the plugins. Required options are marked in bold:

Option	Description
-H, --hostname	The host name or the IP address of the machine to connect to; this option must be specified
-v, --snmp_version	Specifies the SNMP protocol version to be used; acceptable values are 1 and 2c
-C, --community	Specifies the SNMP community string to be used

`-k, --key`	Specifies the index of the network interface to be checked (`ifIndex` field)
`-d, --descr`	Specifies the regular expression to match the interface description (`ifDescr` field) against

The `check_ifstatus` plugin simply checks if the status of all of the interfaces is up, or if they are administratively down. If at least one interface is set down, even if all other interfaces are set up properly, a critical status is reported.

The `check_ifoperstatus` plugin allows you to check the status of a specific network interface. It is possible to specify either the index of the interface or an expression to match the device name against. An example to check the `eth1` interface is as follows:

```
root@ubuntu:~# /opt/nagios/plugins/check_ifoperstatus -H 10.0.0.1 \        -d
eth1
OK: Interface eth1 (index 3) is up.
```

As we also checked the index that `eth1` is associated with, we can now use the `-k` option to check the interface status:

```
root@ubuntu:~# /opt/nagios/plugins/check_ifoperstatus -H 10.0.0.1 -k 3
OK: Interface eth1 (index 3) is up.
```

The main difference is that by using the `-d` flag, you make sure that changes to the indexes of the network interfaces shifting your configuration are not affected. On the other hand, using the `-k` flag is faster. If you are sure that your interfaces will not change, it's better to use `-k`; otherwise `-d` should be used.

The next step is to configure the Nagios commands and services for the SNMP usage. We will define a command and a corresponding service. We will also show how custom variables can be used to standardize command definitions.

The following is a generic command used to query SNMP:

```
define command
{
  command_name check_snmp
  command_line $USER1$/check_snmp -P 1 -H $HOSTADDRESS$
               -o $ARG1$ $ARG2$
}
```

Using the Nagios 3 functionality, we can also define the _SNMPVERSION and _SNMPCOMMUNITY parameters in the host object for all of the devices that are SNMP-aware, and use them in the following command:

```
define host
{
  use                      generic-host
  host_name                linuxbox01
  address                  10.0.2.1
  _SNMPVERSION             2c
  _SNMPCOMMUNITY           public
}
define command   {
  command_name check_snmp
  command_line $USER1$/check_snmp -H $HOSTADDRESS$ -o $ARG1$
            -P $_HOSTSNMPVERSION$ -C $_HOSTSNMPCOMMUNITY$ $ARG2$
}
```

Next, we should define one or more services that will communicate over SNMP.

Let's check for a number of processes and add some constraints that we want to be monitored:

```
define service
{
  use                generic-service
  hostgroup_name     snmp-aware
  service_description  Processes
  check_command       check_snmp!HOST-RESOURCES-
MIB::hrSystemProcesses.0!-w 0:250 -c 0:500
}
```

Please note that the check_command statement above needs to be specified on a single line. The above check will monitor the number of processes running on a system.

It's worth mentioning that for Microsoft Windows systems the number of processes that should trigger a warning and critical state should be much lower than shown in the above example.

Receiving traps

SNMP traps work in opposite ways to get and set requests. That is, the agent sends a message, as a UDP packet, to the SNMP manager when a problem occurs. For example, a link down or system crash message can be sent out to the manager so that administrators are alerted instantly. Traps differ across versions of the SNMP protocols. For SNMPv1, they are called *traps*, and are messages that do not require any confirmation by the manager. For SNMPv2, they are called *informs* and require the manager to acknowledge that it has received the *inform* message.

In order to receive traps or informs, the SNMP software needs to accept incoming connections on UDP port 162, which is the standard port for sending and receiving SNMP trap/inform packets. In some SNMP management software, trap notifications are handled within separate applications, while in others, they are integrated into an entire SNMP manager backend.

For a Net-SNMP trap, the daemon is a part of the SNMP daemons, but is a separate binary, called `snmptrapd`, which, by default, is not started. To change this, we will need to modify the `/etc/default/snmpd` file and change the `TRAPDRUN` variable to *yes*, as shown here:

```
TRAPDRUN=yes
```

Changing this option requires restarting the SNMP agent by invoking the `service snmpd restart` command.

On Ubuntu Linux, the trap listening daemon keeps its configuration file in `/etc/snmp/snmptrapd.conf`. For other systems, it may be in a different location.

The daemon can log specified SNMP traps/informs. It can be configured to run predefined applications or to forward all or specific packets to other managers.

A sample configuration that logs all incoming traps but only if they originate from the SNMPv1 and SNMPv2c `private` community would look like this:

```
authCommunity log,execute,net private
```

This option enables the logging of traps from the private community originating from any address. It also allows the execution of handler scripts and forwarding traps to other hosts. But this requires additional configuration directives.

Each change in the `snmptrapd.conf` file requires a restart of the `snmpd` service.

Usually, traps will be received from a device such as a network router or another computer from which we want to receive traps. We will need two machines with Net-SNMP installed—one for sending the trap and another that will process it. We can use any machine for sending the traps. However, the one processing it should be the one where Nagios is installed, so we can pass it on later. For the purpose of this section, we will use another computer and define a test MIB definition.

We need to create an MIB file called `NAGIOS-TRAP-TEST-MIB.txt` that will define the types of traps and their OIDs. On Ubuntu, the file should be put in `/usr/share/snmp/mibs`; for other platforms, it should be in the same location as the `SNMPv2-SMI.txt` file.

The contents of the file should be as follows:

```
NAGIOS-TRAP-TEST-MIB DEFINITIONS ::= BEGIN
        IMPORTS enterprises FROM SNMPv2-SMI;

 nagiostests OBJECT IDENTIFIER ::= { enterprises 0 }
 nagiostraps OBJECT IDENTIFIER ::= { nagiostests 1 }
 nagiosnotifs OBJECT IDENTIFIER ::= { nagiostests 2 }

 nagiosTrap TRAP-TYPE
        ENTERPRISE nagiostraps
        VARIABLES { sysLocation }
        DESCRIPTION "SNMPv1 notification"
        ::= 1

 nagiosNotif NOTIFICATION-TYPE
        OBJECTS { sysLocation }
        STATUS current
        DESCRIPTION "SNMPv2c notification"
        ::= { nagiosnotifs 2 }
 END
```

This contains definitions for both the SNMPv1 trap called `nagiosTrap` and the inform packet for SNMPv2c called `nagiosNotif`. The file should be copied to all of machines that will either send or receive these trap/inform packets. In this example, we are using a sub-tree of the enterprises branch in SNMPv2-MIB, but this should not be used in any production environment as this is a reserved part of the MIB tree.

In order to send such a trap as an SNMPv1 packet, we need to invoke the following command on the machine that will send the traps, replacing the IP address with the actual address of the machine that is running the `snmptrapd` process.

```
root@ubuntu2:~# snmptrap -v 1 -c private 192.168.2.51 \
    NAGIOS-TRAP-TEST-MIB::nagiostraps "" 6 nagiosTrap "" \
    SNMPv2-MIB::sysLocation.0 s "Server Room"
```

Sending an SNMPv2c notification will look like this:

```
root@ubuntu2:~# snmptrap -v 2c -c private 192.168.2.51 "" \
    NAGIOS-TRAP-TEST-MIB::nagiosNotif \
    SNMPv2-MIB::sysLocation.0 s "Server Room"
```

Please note that, in both cases, there is no confirmation that the packet was received. In order to determine this, we need to check the system logs—usually the `/var/log/syslog` or `/var/log/messages` files. The following command should return log entries related to traps:

```
root@ubuntu:~# grep TRAP /var/log/syslog /var/log/messages
```

Now that we know how to send traps, we should take care so that we handle them properly. The first thing that needs to be done is to add scripts as event handlers for the traps that we previously defined. We need to add these handlers on the machine that has the Nagios daemon running.

To do this, add the following lines to `snmptrapd.conf`, and restart the `snmpd` service:

```
traphandle NAGIOS-TRAP-TEST-MIB::nagiostraps /opt/nagios/bin/passMessage
traphandle NAGIOS-TRAP-TEST-MIB::nagiosnotifs /opt/nagios/bin/passMessage
```

We now need to create the actual `/opt/nagios/bin/passMessage` script that will forward information about the traps to Nagios:

```
#!/bin/sh

CMD=/var/nagios/rw/nagios.cmd

read ORIGHOSTNAME
read ORIGIP
# parse IP address
IPADDR=`echo "$ORIGIP" | sed 's,^...: \[,,;s,\]:.*$,,'`
HOST=""

# map IP address of the trap to host and service for which
# the check result should be sent as
case $IPADDR in
```

```
  192.168.2.52)
    HOST=ubuntu2
    SVC=TrapTest
    ;;
  esac

if [ "x$HOST" = "x" ] ; then
  exit 1
fi

# send check result to Nagios
CLK=`date +%s`
echo "[$CLK] PROCESS_SERVICE_CHECK_RESULT;$HOST;$SVC;2;Trap received"

exit 0
```

When used for a volatile service, this offers a convenient way to track SNMP traps and notifications in Nagios. A volatile service is similar to normal Nagios services, except that every time a service is in a hard non-OK state (such as WARNING, CRITICAL,or UNKNOWN) and the check (either active or passive) returns a non-OK state, contacts are immediately notified and its state is logged.

A service is configured to be volatile by enabling the is_volatile directive. It is also common to set max_check_attempts for the volatile service to 1—so that each non-OK check result will cause it to be in a hard state. For example:

```
define service
{
  hostgroup_name          snmp-trap-receivers
  service_description     TrapTest
  is_volatile             1
  max_check_attempts      1
  active_checks_enabled   0
  passive_checks_enabled  1
}
```

The directive also disables performing active checks and ensures passive checks are enabled for the service.

Using Nagios to track SNMP traps also allows you to merge it with powerful event handling mechanisms inside Nagios. This can cause Nagios to perform other checks, or try to recover from the error, when a trap is received.

Using additional plugins

NagiosExchange hosts a large number of third-party plugins under the **Check Plugins**, **Software**, SNMP category. These allow the monitoring of the system load over SNMP, the monitoring of processes, and storage space, and the performance of many other types of checks. You can also find checks that are dedicated to specific hardware, such as Cisco or Nortel routers. There are also plugins for monitoring bandwidth usage.

There are also dedicated SNMP-based check plugins that allow the monitoring of many aspects of Microsoft Windows, without installing dedicated Nagios agents on these machines. This includes checks for IIS web server, checking whether WINS and DHCP processes are running, and so on.

The Manubulon site (`http://nagios.manubulon.com/`) also offers a very wide variety of SNMP plugins. These offer checks for specific processes that are running, monitoring the system load, CPU usage and network interfaces, and options specific to routers.

Another interesting SNMP use is to monitor the network bandwidth usage. In this case, Nagios can be integrated with the **Multi Router Traffic Grapher** (**MRTG**) package (see `http://www.mrtg.org/`). This is a utility that allows the creation of graphs of bandwidth usage on various network interfaces that also use SNMP to gather information on traffic. Nagios offers a check_mrtg plugin (see `http://nagios-plugins.org/doc/man/check_mrtg.html`) that can be used to retrieve bandwidth usage information from the MRTG log files.

Most companies that need bandwidth monitoring already use MRTG, as it is the most popular solution for this task. That is why it is a good idea to integrate Nagios if you already have MRTG set up. Otherwise, it is better to use a dedicated bandwidth monitoring system.

Summary

SNMP can be used by Nagios in various ways. As the protocol is widely supported by operating systems and network devices, it is a great choice for monitoring a wide variety of machines. SNMP features a standardized way to describe typical parameters that describe a device-hardware, network connectivity, applications and services, and much more. This makes accessing this information from Nagios very easy. SNMP is enabled by default on many operating systems and most network devices, which makes it very easy to monitor such devices in Nagios.

In this chapter, we have learned the following:

- What is SNMP, how versions SNMPv1, SNMPv2c, and SNMPv3 differ
- What are OIDs as well as MIB
- Visualizing SNMP data using GUI tools
- Querying SNMP information within Nagios
- Receiving SNMP traps from other devices on the network
- Additional Nagios plugins that can be used to query data over SNMP

The next chapter will talk about monitoring Microsoft Windows machines using NSClient++. It will also describe setting up multiple Nagios instances and distributed monitoring.

12
Advanced Monitoring

This chapter describes advanced items related to monitoring. It talks about monitoring a Microsoft Windows host and its services by installing and configuring a dedicated agent in the operating system. It shows how to communicate from the Nagios server to Windows machines, as well as the other way round.

This chapter also talks about how Nagios can be configured so that it notifies other Nagios instances about the current status of all hosts and services. These techniques can be used to create a central Nagios server that receives notifications from other machines.

In addition, this chapter covers the basics of setting up Nagios so that it handles problems when receiving information from other Nagios instances. If one of your Nagios monitoring systems is down or unreachable, you will want another Nagios instance to detect this and report it to you.

In this chapter, we will cover the following topics:

- Setting up NSClient++, an agent for Microsoft Windows machines that allows them to be monitored from Nagios
- Running tests using the `check_nt` plugin and using the NRPE protocol
- Performing checks using WMI queries over the NRPE protocol
- Writing custom scripts to perform checks on Windows
- Setting up multiple Nagios instances for monitoring
- Sending notifications about host and/or service status changes from one Nagios instance to another
- Using templates to ease the process of configuring multiple Nagios instances

Monitoring Windows machines

NSClient++ (**NSCP**) is an open source project that is based on and extends the NSClient concept. The original concept was to create an agent for Windows that, once installed, allows the querying of system information. NSClient has created a de facto standard protocol that offers the ability to query variables with parameters. NSClient++ uses the same protocol, but also offers the ability to perform more complex checks using the NRPE protocol. NSClient++ has to be installed on all Windows machines that will be monitored.

Installing NSClient++

NSClient++ can be downloaded from `http://www.nsclient.org/`, and it provides client for both 32 bit and 64 bit Windows versions. At the time of writing, the latest stable version of NSClient++ is 0.4.3. It is recommended that you download the version matching your Windows. After downloading it, simply run the installer on one or more machines to be able to monitor them.

The first question shown by the installer is regarding the installation type:

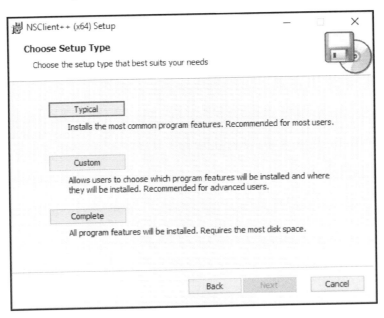

If unsure, it is recommended that you perform a complete installation, but advanced users may wish to choose which features to install. The installer will also ask for the location to install itself. Unless you need to install NSClient++ in a specific location, it is best to use the default path of `C:\Program Files\NSClient++`.

After installation, the installer will show basic options for its configuration, as follows:

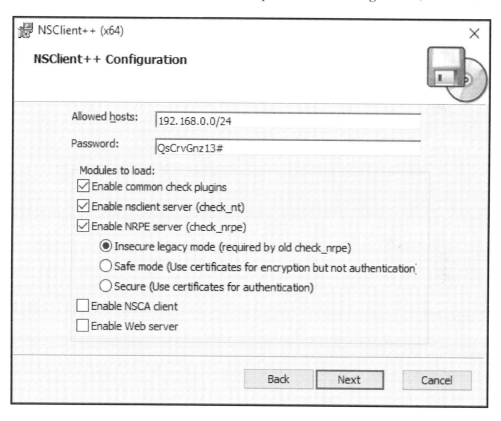

The **Allowed hosts** should be set to the IP address and/or IP address ranges of machines that will be performing the checks, such as 192.168.0.0/24, if that is the IP address range of your local network.

It is recommended that you enable the following options:

- **Enable common check plugins**: This option will enable common plugins for performing checks and set up the default configuration
- **Enable nsclient server**: This option will allow using the check_nt Nagios plugin to perform basic tests
- **Enable NRPE server**: This option will allow sending checks to the NSClient++ using the check_nrpe plugin

It is also recommended to set up the NRPE server to run in **Insecure legacy mode** as we are going to be using the check_nrpe plugin, which does not currently support the newer security features of NSClient++.

The shown password will be used to communicate with NSClient++. It will also put in the configuration file, so it is not needed to write it down at this point.

After a successful installation, NSClient++ registers itself as a Windows service and starts automatically.

Configuring NSClient++

NSClient++ is a very powerful agent and has a modular design. It consists of many modules that can be enabled or disabled.

There are multiple modules providing network protocol servers, such as NSClientServer that exposes protocol supported by the check_nt Nagios plugin or NRPEServer that allows making checks over the NRPE protocol. At installation time, the second and third checkboxes were to enable the said modules.

The check_nt (handled by the NSClientServer module) and check_nrpe (handled by the NRPEServer module) plugins both listen on connections from the Nagios server and run checks that are sent via the protocol. They each use different protocols—check_nt connects to TCP port 12489 and uses a dedicated protocol, while check_nrpe uses a more generic NRPE protocol that is described in more details in Chapter 10, *Monitoring Remote Hosts*, and is listening on TCP port 5666.

There are also many modules that provide commands—these usually do certain checks on the system. The commands can be called over NRPE or other protocols. The modules include many checks specific to Windows as well as helper checks, such as check_negate that helps validating if a condition is not met. Many of the modules were enabled by enabling the first checkbox at the end of the installation.

NSClient++ has exhaustive documentation on all of the modules available from its reference manual available at http://docs.nsclient.org/reference/index.html#window s—modules. The list includes both network protocol modules as well as those providing various types of checks.

All this is configured by editing the configuration file called nsclient.ini that is present in the installation directory. The file uses a standard ini file syntax—sections are put inside square brackets, values are put in the name = value form and comments begin with a semicolon, as follows:

```
[/modules]
; NSClientServer - A server that listens for incoming check_nt connection
and processes incoming requests.
NSClientServer = enabled

; NRPEServer - A server that listens for incoming NRPE connection and
processes incoming requests.
NRPEServer = enabled

; CheckWMI - Check status via WMI
CheckWMI = enabled
; CheckSystem - Various system related checks, such as CPU load, process
state, service state memory usage and PDH counters.
CheckSystem = enabled

; CheckExternalScripts - Execute external scripts
CheckExternalScripts = enabled

; CheckEventLog - Check for errors and warnings in the event log.
CheckEventLog = enabled

; CheckLogFile - File for checking log files and various other forms of
```

```
updating text files
CheckLogFile = enabled

; CheckDisk - CheckDisk can check various file and disk related things.
CheckDisk = enabled
```

The `/modules` section defines modules to load into NSClient++.

Global configuration is put in the `/settings/default` section:

```
[/settings/default]
password = QsCrvGnz13#
allowed hosts = 192.168.0.0/24
```

Modules may either use default configuration options or define their options in the respective section such as the NRPEServer module configuration that is placed inside the `/settings/NRPEServer` section.

Each module has all of its options mentioned in the reference manual for NSClient++ modules.

Changes in the NSClient++ configuration are mainly related to advanced features, such as enabling a specific module or configuring external scripts, which are described in more detail later in this chapter.

If you need to make any changes, they will be applied only when NSClient++ is restarted. To do this, go to the **Services** administrative panel that can be found in the start menu. Then locate the **NSClient++** service and choose the **Restart** option, as follows:

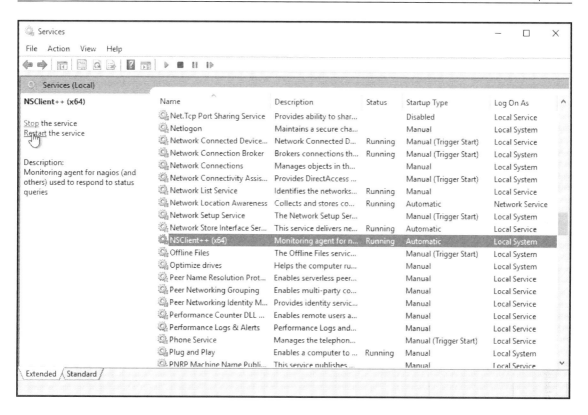

Monitoring Windows using check_nt

NSClient++ offers a uniform mechanism to query the system information. Basic system information can be retrieved using the `check_nt` command from a standard Nagios plugins package.

The syntax and options of the command are as follows:

```
check_nt -H <host> [-p <port>] [-s <password>] [-w level]
        [-c level] -v <variable> -l <arguments> -s <password>
```

Option	Description
-H , --hostname	This option must be specified to denote the hostname or IP address of the machine to connect to.

`-p` , `--port`	This specifies the TCP port number to connect to. For NSClient++, it should be set to `1248`, which is the default port.
`-s` , `--secret`	This specifies the password to use for authentication. This is optional and is needed only if a password is set up on the Windows agent.
`-v` , `--variable`	This is the variable to query. The possible variables are described further in this section.
`-l` , `--arguments`	This is for the arguments to be passed to the variable and is optional.
`-w` , `--warning`	This specifies the return values above which a warning state should be returned.
`-c` , `--critical`	This specifies the return values above which a critical state should be returned.

When using the `check_nt` plugin with NSClient++, we need to specify the port `12489`, as NSClient++ uses a different port by default. We also need to specify the password set at installation time (or manually configured in the configuration file). So the flags used for all checks will be `-H 192.168.0.210 -p 12489 -s 'QsCrvGnz13#'` assuming the IP address for the Windows machine is `192.168.0.210` and the password set at installation time is `QsCrvGnz13#`.

The variables specified with the `-v` option are predefined. Most checks return both the string representation and an integer value. If an integer value is present, then the `-w` and `-c` flags can be used to specify the values that will indicate a problem.

The first variable is `CPULOAD` which allows the querying of processor usage over a specified period of time. The parameters are one or more series of the `<time>`, `<warning>`, and `<critical>` levels, where `time` is denoted in minutes and the `warning`/`critical` values specify, in percentage, the CPU usage that can trigger a problem, as seen in the following example:

```
# check_nt -H 192.168.0.210 -p 12489 -s 'QsCrvGnz13#' \
  -v CPULOAD -l 1,80,90
CPU Load 2% (1 min average) |    '1 min avg Load'=2%;80;90;0;100
```

In order to set up a check in Nagios, it is recommended that you use a custom variable in the host to specify the `check_nt` password, as follows:

```
define host{
    host_name                   windows210
    hostgroups                  windowsservers
    alias                       Windows 2 10
    address                     192.168.0.210
    check_command               check-host-alive
    (...)
    _CHECKNTPASSWORD            QsCrvGnz13#
    }
```

Then the check command would be as follows:

```
define command{
    command_name    check_nt
    command_line    $USER1$/check_nt -H $HOSTADDRESS$
                    -p 12489 -s "$_HOSTCHECKNTPASSWORD"
                    -v $ARG1$ $ARG2$
    }
```

And finally, a service would be defined as:

```
define service{
    host_name           windows210
    service_description CPU Load
    check_command       check_nt!CPULOAD!-l 1,80,90
    }
```

The `USEDDISKSPACE` variable can be used to monitor space usage. The argument should be a partition letter. The `-w` and `-c` options are used to specify the percentage of used disk space that can trigger a problem, as shown in the following example:

```
# check_nt -H 192.168.0.210 -p 12489 -s 'QsCrvGnz13#' \
  -v USEDDISKSPACE -l C -w 80 -c 90
C:\ - total: 24.41 Gb - used: 17.96 Gb (74%) - free 6.45 Gb (26%)    | 'C:\
Used Space'=17.96Gb;0.00;0.00;0.00;24.41
```

Same as the preceding one, a Nagios service definition for this would be very similar—only changing the arguments to use a different variable and conditions:

```
define service{
    host_name           windows210
    service_description Disk usage - C:
    check_command       check_nt!USEDDISKSPACE!-l C -w 80 -c 90
    }
```

System services can also be monitored using the SERVICESTATE variable. The arguments must specify one or more internal service names, separated by commas. Internal service names can be checked in the Services management console, as shown in the following example:

```
# check_nt -H 192.168.0.210 -p 12489 -s 'QsCrvGnz13#' \
  -v SERVICESTATE -l nscp,Schedule
OK: All 2 service(s) are ok.
```

This checks that the NSClient++ service (whose internal name is nscp) and the Windows scheduler (whose internal name is Schedule) are working.

Similar to monitoring services, it is also possible to monitor processes running on a Windows machine. The PROCSTATE variable can be used to achieve this. The variable accepts a list of executable names separated by commas, as shown in the following example:

```
# check_nt -h 192.168.2.11
  -v PROCSTATE -l winword.exe
OK: All processes are ok.
```

The MEMUSE variable can be used to check memory usage. This does not require any additional arguments. The -w and -c arguments are used to specify the warning and critical limits, as seen in the following example:

```
# check_nt -H 192.168.0.210 -p 12489 -s 'QsCrvGnz13#' \
  -v MEMUSE -w 80 -c 90
Memory usage: total:5503.54 MB - used: 1317.99 MB (24%) - free: 4185.54 MB
(76%) |'Memory usage'=1317.99MB;4402.83;4953.18;0.00;5503.54
```

Another thing that can be checked is the age of a file using the FILEAGE variable. This variable allows the verification of whether a specified file has been modified within a specified time period. The -w and -c arguments are used to specify the warning and critical limits, respectively. Their values indicate the number of minutes within which a file should have been modified—a value of 240 means that a warning or critical state should be returned if a file has not been modified within the last four hours, as shown in the following example:

```
# check_nt -H 192.168.0.210 -p 12489 -s 'QsCrvGnz13#' \
  -v FILEAGE -l "C:/Program Files/NSClient++/nsclient.log" -w 120 -c 240
nsclient.log 2016-may-08 07:51:25
```

It is also possible to check the version of the agent. This makes the maintenance of upgrades and new versions much easier. The `CLIENTVERSION` variable allows the retrieval of version information, as follows:

```
# check_nt -H 192.168.0.210 -p 12489 -s 'QsCrvGnz13#' \
  -v CLIENTVERSION
NSClient++ 0.4.3.143 2015-04-29
```

Performing checks using NRPE protocol

NSClient++ allows performing a much wider set of checks using the NRPE protocol. Depending on exact modules enabled, specific checks are performed.

To perform queries using the NRPE protocol all that is needed is the `check_nrpe` plugin from the NRPE package. Installing the plugin is documented in more details in `Chapter 10`, *Monitoring Remote Hosts*. The NRPE plugin has to be compiled with the `--enable-command-args` flag so that it allows sending arguments to the checks. Monitoring machines with NSClient++ installed over NRPE does not require specifying a password.

Many of the `check_nt` tests have their equivalent options for NRPE. For example, the following is an example of querying CPU load by sending a `check_cpu` command to NSClient++:

```
# check_nrpe -H 192.168.0.210 \
  -c check_cpu -a "warn=load>80" "crit=load>90"
OK: CPU load is ok.|'total 5m'=2%;80;90 'total 1m'=5%;80;90 'total
5s'=6%;80;90
```

`warn` and `crit` define criteria for when the check result should be considered a warning or critical result, respectively. In this case, it means that the load has to be above 80% of all CPUs to consider it warning and above 90% of all CPUs to consider it a critical state.

The check and its matching criteria is documented in more detail at `http://docs.nsclient.org/reference/windows/CheckSystem.html#check-cpu`.

In order to define the commands in Nagios, we'll need to define the generic `check_nrpe` command if it was not defined already:

```
define command{
    command_name        check_nrpe
    command_line        $USER1$/check_nrpe -H $HOSTADDRESS$
                        -c $ARG1$ $ARG2$

    }
```

The service would be as follows:

```
define service{
    host_name               windows210
    service_description CPU Load
    check_command           check_nrpe!check_cpu!-a "warn=load>80"
                            "crit=load>90"

    }
```

Similarly, process and service checks can also be issued by NRPE by using `check_process` and `check_service`, as shown here:

```
# check_nrpe -H 192.168.0.210 \
  -c check_service -a service=fax crit="state='running'"
OK: All 1 service(s) are ok.|'fax'=1;0;4
```

In this case, we are checking that the service `fax` is not running.

The preceding commands are provided by the CheckSystem module and are documented in more details at `http://docs.nsclient.org/reference/windows/CheckSystem.html`. It also provides other multiple checks that can be used over NRPE.

It is also worth noting that the NRPE protocol may be more practical in most cases—as it allows more customization, more complex checks, and retrieves data such as WMI. While historically `check_nt` based monitoring is popular, using the NRPE for any new monitoring is a better idea.

Querying WMI data from Nagios

It is also possible to use `check_nrpe` to query the **Windows Management Instrumentation** (**WMI**) (`http://en.wikipedia.org/wiki/Windows_Management_Instrumentation`). It is a mechanism that allows applications to access the system management information using various programming languages.

WMI offers an extensive set of information that can be retrieved. It describes the hardware and operating system as well as the currently-installed applications and the running applications. WMI also uses a query language very similar to the **Structured Query Language (SQL)** (http://en.wikipedia.org/wiki/SQL) that makes the retrieval of specific information very easy.

The **WMI Query Language** (**WQL**) syntax is described in more details in the MSDN documentation available at https://msdn.microsoft.com/en-us/library/aa39466.aspx.

WMI allows accessing classes that provide rows of data, similar to databases, such as the Win32_Process class, which provides information about the currently running processes on Windows. Each row represents a single process and it contains multiple columns that provide specific information, such as ProcessId being the process identifier and Caption being the process name.

All available WMI classes are documented by Microsoft in MSDN at https://msdn.micros oft.com/en-us/library/aa394388.aspx.

The check_wmi command in NSClient++ can be used to perform a check using WMI.

Observe the following example:

```
# check_nrpe -H 192.168.0.210 \
  -c check_wmi -a "query=Select ProcessId FROM Win32_Process
  WHERE Caption='requiredapp.exe'" "crit=count<1"
|'count'=0;0;0
```

The preceding example checks if requiredapp.exe is the process running using WMI. It runs a query to retrieve rows where the name of the process is requiredapp.exe, which is quoted as required by the WQL syntax (which is also similar to the SQL syntax). The last argument will cause the check to return the CRITICAL status if the number of rows is smaller than 1.

In order to use the query in Nagios, all that is needed is to set up a command service in a manner similar to other NRPE examples.

```
define service{
    host_name              windows210
    service_description    requiredapp is running
    check_command          check_nrpe!check_wmi!-a
      "query=Select ProcessId FROM Win32_Process WHERE
        Caption='requiredapp.exe'" "crit=count<1"
    }
```

Note that the entire value for `check_command` has to be put in a single line.

WMI can be used for a large variety of tests as its querying syntax is quite powerful. For example, the following check can be used to ensure that there are no directories shared on the local network on Windows:

```
# check_nrpe -H 192.168.0.210 \
  -c check_wmi -a "query=Select Status FROM Win32_Share
      WHERE Type=0 AND NOT Name LIKE '%$' AND NOT Name='Users'"
      "crit=count>0"
  |'count'=0;0;0
```

This will list all shared directories exported by users. The condition to limit results to rows with TYPE=0 indicates that only directory sharing should be considered. The query also filters out built-in shared directories—those ending with a $ sign and `Users` share.

The `Win32_Share` class and fields such as `TYPE` and `NAME` are described in more details in the MSDN documentation available at `https://msdn.microsoft.com/en-us/library/aa3 94435.aspx`.

The WMI querying module is described in more details in the reference manual available at `https://docs.nsclient.org/reference/windows/CheckWMI.html`.

Implementing external scripts

Another feature available in NSClient++ is the ability to write custom scripts that will perform checks. This is provided by the CheckExternalScripts module and allows writing specific checks without implementing a dedicated module.

The script can be implemented in any language as the module provides a way to define how scripts with specific extensions should be run. The checks work similar to Nagios checks on Unix systems; the script has to return the message to be provided to Nagios to standard output and exit with one of the following exit codes:

Exit code	Status	Description
0	OK	Working correctly
1	WARNING	Working, but needs attention (for example, low resources)
2	CRITICAL	Not working correctly or requires attention
3	UNKNOWN	Plugin was unable to determine the status for the host or service

The NSClient++ installation comes with a few sample scripts, but they are not enabled by default. Each script has to be explicitly defined in the configuration file.

To add a sample `check_no_rdp.bat` script that ensures that the remote desktop is not enabled, simply add the following to the `nsclient.ini` configuration file:

```
[/settings/external scripts/scripts]
check_no_rdp_script = scripts\check_no_rdp.bat
```

`check_no_rdp_script` is the name of the command that will be made available. So this is the name to use when querying over NRPE. The name can be the same as script or a different name can be used.

We also need to restart the NSClient++ service, which was described earlier in this chapter.

After that we can perform a check using it:

```
# check_nrpe -H 192.168.0.210 -c check_no_rdp_script
RDP not listening!
```

The `/settings/external scripts/scripts` section allows specifying raw commands to run. It is also possible to specify scripts that will be wrapped into valid commands based on their extension by defining them in the `/settings/external scripts/wrapped scripts` section:

```
[/settings/external scripts/wrapped scripts]
check_updates = check_updates.vbs
```

This defines a `check_updates` command that maps to the `check_updates.vbs` script. We can now test it by running the following:

```
# check_nrpe -H 192.168.0.210 -c check_updates
OK: There is no critical updates <br />Number of software or driver updates
not installed: 1|
```

The extension determines how the command is run and the `/settings/external scripts/wrappings` configuration section specifies how to run a command with a specific extension. For example, by default it defines the following ways to run scripts:

```
[/settings/external scripts/wrappings]

; POWERSHELL WRAPPING -
ps1 = cmd /c echo scripts\\%SCRIPT% %ARGS%; exit($lastexitcode) |
powershell.exe -command -

; BATCH FILE WRAPPING -
bat = scripts\\%SCRIPT% %ARGS%

; VISUAL BASIC WRAPPING -
vbs = cscript.exe //T:30 //NoLogo scripts\\lib\\wrapper.vbs %SCRIPT% %ARGS%
```

This means the actual command in this case will be `cscript.exe //T:30 //NoLogo scripts\\lib\\wrapper.vbs check_updates.vbs`. `wrapper.vbs` provides common VBS functions for writing Nagios checks that are used by various scripts such as `check_updates.vbs`.

The default definitions provide ways to run bat, PowerShell, and VBS scripts. It is also possible to register any language. For Node.js, it would be as follows:

```
[/settings/external scripts/wrappings]
js = C:\\Program Files\\nodejs\\node.exe scripts\\%SCRIPT% %ARGS%
```

This assumes Node.js is installed in `C:\Program Files\nodejs`, which is the default installation location. Assuming that it is installed, we can now create a sample JavaScript code inside the NSClient++ directory as `scripts\check_nodejs.js`:

```
console.log("Hello from Node.js version " + process.versions.node);
process.exit(0);
```

We can now also define the script itself:

```
[/settings/external scripts/wrapped scripts]
check_nodejs = check_nodejs.js
```

After restarting NSClient++, we can now test that our script is working properly:

```
# check_nrpe -H 192.168.0.210 -c check_nodejs
Hello from Node.js 4.4.4
```

In order to run the query from Nagios all that is needed is a very simple service configuration such as the following:

```
define service{
    host_name           windows210
    service_description Node.js sample service
    check_command       check_nrpe!check_nodejs
    }
```

Understanding distributed monitoring

There are many situations in which you may want to have more than one Nagios instance monitoring your IT infrastructure. One of them can be because of firewall rules that force checks to be made within local networks. Another reason could be the need to load balance all checks across machines due to latency or the number of checks. Others may need to monitor machines in different physical locations from separate machines to check what is wrong within the local infrastructure, even if the links to the central servers are temporarily down.

Regardless of the reason you may want or need to have the execution of checks split across multiple computers. This type of setup might sound complicated and hard to configure, but it is not as hard as it seems. All that's necessary is to set up multiple Nagios instances along with the NRDP agents or daemons.

There are subtle differences in how various instances need to be configured. Usually, there are one or more Nagios instances that report information to a central Nagios instance. An instance that reports information to another Nagios machine will be referred to as a **slave**. A Nagios instance that receives reports from one or more slaves will be called a **master**.

Let's consider a simple organization that has four branch offices and a headquarters. Each branch office is connected to the main office and has a local set of computers. A typical scenario is that a local instance of Nagios monitors the computers and routers in a single branch. The results are then sent to the central Nagios server over an NRDP protocol. These are instances of slave Nagios. If a connection to one of the branches is broken, the local administrators will continue to have access to the status of the local machines. This information is not propagated to the master Nagios server. Setting up the services on the central Nagios server to use freshness checks will cause the central Nagios server to generate an alert when no results are received within a predetermined time frame. Combining this with parent configurations will allow Nagios to accurately determine the root cause of the problems.

The following diagram shows how a typical setup in a multiple branch configuration is done. It shows the network topology as: which machines are checked by which Nagios servers, and how this information is reported to the central Nagios server.

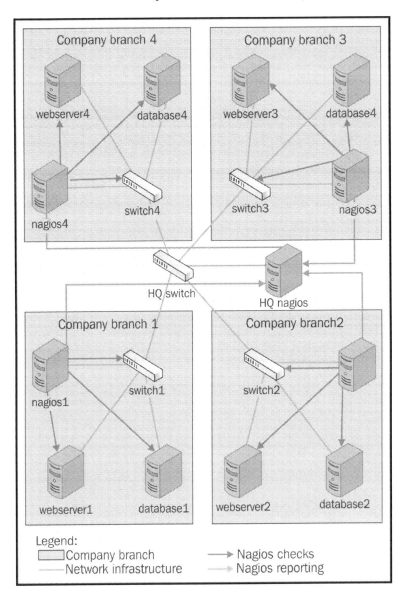

In this example, each branch has a Nagios slave server that monitors and logs information on the local computers. This information is then propagated to the master Nagios server.

Introducing obsessive notifications

Monitoring IT infrastructure using multiple Nagios instances requires a way to send information from slave servers to one or more master servers. This can be done as event handlers that are triggered when a service or a host state changes, however, this has a huge drawback; it requires the setup of an event handler for each object host and service. Another disadvantage is that the event handlers are only triggered on actual changes and not after each test is done.

Nagios offers another way to do this through **obsessive notifications**. These provide a mechanism to run commands when a host or service status is received, regardless of whether it is a passive or an active check result. This functionality is also set up across the system, which means that the object definitions do not need to be changed in any way for Nagios to send information about their status changes.

Setting up obsessive notifications requires a couple of changes in your configuration. The first one is to define a command that will be run for each notification. An example of this is shown as follows:

```
define command
{
    command_name   send-ocsp
    command_line   $USER1$/send-ocsp 192.168.0.1 $SERVICESTATE$
                   $HOSTNAME$ '$SERVICEDESC$' '$SERVICEOUTPUT$'
}
```

The code needs to be entered in a single line in your configuration file. Also, put the actual IP address of the central Nagios server instead of 192.168.0.1 in the preceding example.

We now need to write commands that simply pass the results to the other server over NRDP.

A sample script is as follows:

```
#!/bin/sh

# args: nrdp-server hostname svcname output

URL=http://$1/nrdp/
TOKEN=cu8Eiquasoomeiphahpa
```

```
# map status to exit code
STATE=3
case "$2" in
  OK)
    STATE=0
    ;;
  WARNING)
    STATE =1
    ;;
  CRITICAL)
    STATE=2
    ;;
esac

/opt/nagios/bin/send_nrdp.php \
  --url=$URL --token=$TOKEN -host="$3" --service="$4" \
  --state=$STATE --output="$5"

exit 0
```

The script passes information to send to the Nagios master instance to the send_nrdp.php script. This requires the NRDP client to be set up on the Nagios slave machine. Installing the NRDP client is described in more details in Chapter 9, *Passive Checks and NRDP*.

The TOKEN variable in the script should be set to a valid token defined in the NRDP server configuration file.

The script first converts the status from text (OK, WARNING, or CRITICAL) to exit code that is required by the send_nrdp.php script. It also passes the name of the host and service as well as output from the script.

The following are the required parameters along with the sample values that should be set in the main Nagios configuration file (nagios.cfg):

```
obsess_over_services=1
ocsp_command=send-ocsp
```

The command name should match the name in the command definition.

That's it! After reloading your Nagios configuration, the send-ocsp script will be run every time a check result comes in.

Configuring Nagios to send host status information is very similar to setting up a service status to be sent. The first thing to do is to set up the command that will be run for each notification, which is as follows:

```
define command
{
    command_name   send-ochp
    command_line   $USER1$/send-ochp 192.168.0.1
    $HOSTSTATE$ $HOSTNAME$ '$HOSTOUTPUT$'
}
```

Note that the `command_line` directive in the preceding example needs to be specified in a single line.

The script to send information will look exactly like the one for sending the host status information, except that the actual command sent over NRDP will be generated a bit differently. It also converts the status from text to exit codes and passes the hostname (without the service name), exit code, and output from the check to the `send_nrdp.php` script that sends it to Nagios by sending only the hostname to indicate that it's a host check result:

```
/opt/nagios/bin/send_nrdp.php \
  --url=$URL --token=$TOKEN -host="$3" \
  --state=$STATE --output="$4"
```

In order for Nagios to send notifications to another Nagios instance, we need to enable *obsessing* over hosts and specify the actual command to use.

Here are some sample directives in the main Nagios configuration file (`nagios.cfg`):

```
obsess_over_hosts=1
ochp_command=send-ochp
```

Restart Nagios after these changes have been made to the configurations. When it restarts, Nagios will begin sending notifications to the master server.

A good thing to do is to verify the `nagios.log` file to see if notifications are being sent out after a check has been made. By default, the file is in the `/var/nagios` directory.

If the notifications are not received, it may be a good idea to make the scripts responsible to send messages to log this information in either the system log or in a separate log file. This is very helpful when it comes to debugging instances where the notifications sent out by slave Nagios instances are lost.

Writing information to the system log can be done using the logger command (for more details, refer to `http://linux.die.net/man/1/logger`). The following example shows how to write information to the log:

```
logger --priority info --tag nagios \
   "Sending host $3 state $STATE ($4)"
```

This code will log all of the data that would also be sent using the `send_nrdp.php` script to the log, so it can be found if needed.

Configuring Nagios instances

Setting up multiple servers to monitor infrastructure using Nagios is not easy, but it is not too hard either. It only requires a slightly different approach as compared with setting up a single machine. That said, there are issues with the configuration of hosts and services. It is also necessary to set up all slave and master servers correctly and in a slightly different way.

Distributed monitoring requires a more mature change control and versioning process for Nagios configurations. This is necessary because both the central Nagios server and its branches need to have a partial or complete configuration available, and these need to be in sync across all machines.

Usually, it is recommended that you make the slave servers query both the service and the host status. It is also recommended that you disable service checks on the master Nagios server, but keep host checks enabled. The reason is that host checks are not usually scheduled and are done only when a service check returns a WARNING, CRITICAL, or UNKNOWN status. Therefore the load required to only check the hosts is much lower than the load required to perform regular service checks. In some cases, it is best to also disable host checks. Either the host checks need to be performed regularly or the security policies should disallow checks by the central server.

To maintain Nagios configurations, we recommend that you set up a versioning system such as Git (`http://git-scm.com/`), Subversion (`http://subversion.tigris.org/`), or Mercurial (`http://www.mercurial-scm.org/`). This will allow us to keep track of all the Nagios changes and make it much easier to apply configuration changes to multiple machines.

We can store and manage the configuration similar to how we had done it previously. Hosts, services, and the corresponding groups should be kept in directories and separate for each Nagios slave—for example, `hosts/branch1` and `services/branch1`. All other types of objects, such as contacts, time periods, and check commands, can be kept in global directories and reused in all branches—for example, the single `contacts`, `timeperiods`, and `commands` directories.

It's also a good idea to create a small system to deploy the configuration to all the machines, along with the ability to test new configuration before applying it in production. This can be done using a small number of shell scripts. When dealing with multiple computers, locations, and Nagios instances, doing everything manually is very difficult and can get problematic over the long term. This will cause the system to become unmanageable and can lead to errors in actual checks caused by out-of-sync configurations between the slave and master Nagios instances.

A very popular tool that is recommended for this purpose is **cfengine**(`http://www.cfengine.com/`). There are other tools that can be used for automating configuration deployment, such as **Chef** (`http://www.getchef.com/`), **Puppet** (`http://www.puppetlabs.com/`), or **Ansible** (`http://www.ansible.com/`). They can be used to automate configuration deployment and to ensure that Nagios is up to date on all the machines. It also allows for customization; for example, a set of files different from the set on the master server can be deployed on slave servers. If you are already familiar with such tools, we recommend that you use them to manage Nagios deployments. If not, try them out and choose one that best suits you.

The first step in creating a distributed environment is to set up the master Nagios server. This will require you to install Nagios from a binary distribution or build it from sources. Details related to Nagios installation are described in Chapter 2, *Installing Nagios 4*.

The main changes in a single Nagios set up for a master server are defined in the main Nagios configuration file—`nagios.cfg`. This file must contain the `cfg_dir` directives for objects related to all of the slave servers. If not, the master Nagios instance will ignore the reports related to hosts that it does not know about.

We'll also need to make sure that Nagios accepts passive check results for services and that the master Nagios instance does not independently perform active checks. To do this, set the following options in the main Nagios configuration file on the master server:

```
check_external_commands=1
accept_passive_service_checks=1
execute_service_checks=0
```

If you also want to rely on passive check results for host checks, you will also need to add the following lines to your main Nagios configuration:

```
accept_passive_host_checks=1
execute_host_checks=0
```

You will also need to set up the NRDP server on the master Nagios instance. Details of how to set this up are described in Chapter 9, *Passive Checks and NRDP*.

The next step is to set up the first slave server that will report to the master Nagios instance. This also means that you will need to set up Nagios from a binary or source distribution and configure it properly.

All of the slave Nagios instances also need to have the send_nrdp.php script from the NRDP package in order to communicate changes with the master instance. It is also a good idea to check whether the sending of dummy reports about an existing host and an existing service works is done correctly.

All of the slave instances need to be set up to send obsessive notifications to the master Nagios server. This includes setting up the OCSP and OCHP commands and enabling them in the main Nagios configuration file. (obsessive notifications have already been described earlier in the chapter, in the *Introducing obsessive notifications* section).

After setting up everything it's best to run notification commands directly from the command line to see if everything works correctly. Next, restart the slave Nagios server. After that, it is a good idea to check the Nagios logs to see if the notifications are being sent out.

It would also be a good idea to write down or automate all the steps needed to set up a Nagios slave instance. Setting up the master is done only once, but large networks may require you to set up a large number of slaves.

Performing freshness checking

We now have set up distributed monitoring and the slave Nagios instances should report the results to the master Nagios daemon. Everything should work fine and the main web interface should report up-to-date information from all of the hosts and services being monitored.

Unfortunately, this is not always the case. In some cases network connectivity can be down or, for example, the NRDP client and server on the network might fail temporarily. At that point the master Nagios instance may not even know about it.

Based on our assumption that the master Nagios instance is not responsible for monitoring the IT infrastructure, therefore it needs to rely on other systems to do it. Configuration that we have set up earlier does not take the situation where checks are not sent to master the instance into account.

Nagios offers a way to monitor whether results have come within a certain period of time. If no report comes within that period, we can specify that Nagios should treat this as a critical state and warn the administrators about it. This makes sense as obsessive notifications are sent out very frequently. So if a service is scheduled to be checked every 15 minutes and no notification has come within the previous hour, this may indicate a problem with some part of the distributed monitoring configuration.

Implementing this in the master Nagios configuration requires a slightly different approach to the one mentioned in the previous section. The approach in the previous section was to disable service checks completely. This is why all services and/or hosts needed to have their active checks reconfigured for the new approach to work correctly. In this case, it is necessary to enable service checks (and host, if needed) on a global basis in the `nagios.cfg` file.

For the reasons given earlier, all of the services and/or hosts that receive notifications from slave Nagios instances need to be defined differently in the master configuration from the definitions that are set for the Nagios slaves.

The first change is that active checks for these objects need to be enabled, but should not be scheduled, that is, the `normal_check_interval` option should not be set. In addition, the `check_freshness` and `freshness_threshold` options need to be specified. The first of these options allows monitoring whether results are up to date and the second one specifies the number of seconds after which the results should be considered outdated.

This means that Nagios will only run active checks if there has been no passive check result for a specified period of time. It is very important that the host and service definitions on both the master and slave instances have the same value specified for the check_period directive. Otherwise, the master Nagios instance will raise an alert only for services that are checked during specific time periods. An example could be the workinghours time period, which is not checked on weekends.

For example, the following service definition will accept passive checks, but will report an error if they are not present:

```
define service
{
  use                      generic-service
  host_name                linuxbox02
  service_description      SSH
  check_command            no-passive-check-results
  check_freshness          1     freshness_threshold
43200
  active_checks_enabled    1
  passive_checks_enabled   1
}
```

The freshness_threshold option specifies the number of seconds after which an active check should be performed. In this case, it is set to 12 hours.

It is also necessary to define a command that will run if no passive check results have been provided.

The following command will use the check_dummy plugin to report an error:

```
define command
{
  command_name       no-passive-check-results
  command_line       $USER1$/check_dummy 2 "No passive check
results"
}
```

It is important to make sure that all of the services and/or hosts are defined, so only dummy checks that report problems (and not actual active checks) are performed. This is different from our previous approach that made sure active checks were not performed.

The main drawback of this approach is that it makes the management of configurations on master and slave instances more difficult. We need to maintain the configuration for the master Nagios instance with the service that contains only the dummy freshness checks. However, slave configurations need to have complete check definitions in place.

Using templates for distributed monitoring

Multiple inheritances can be used to manage the configurations for distributed Nagios setups. This can help avoiding reconfiguring all of the objects and managing two sets of configurations. Multiple inheritance can be used to separate parts that are common to both master and slave Nagios instances from information that is local to each Nagios instance. We'll assume each location will have a single Nagios instance that is a slave instance to the central Nagios instance.

For each location, there will be `local` and `remote` templates. Slave instances will load the `local` template for its own location and not load the configuration for other locations. Master instance(s) will load the `remote` template for each location that will report information to this machine.

The actual hosts and services will inherit a template for a specific check such as the CPU load or the service template monitoring the HTTP server. They will also inherit a location's template— `local` or `remote` as first items in the inheritance list. This will allow the location templates to override all the configuration options set by other templates.

The `local` and `remote` templates will define whether regular checks will be done or if the passive check results should be used. Each Nagios instance will load the local or remote definition of the location template.

For the examples mentioned in previous sections, the following would be loaded in branch 1:

```
cfg_dir=global_configuration
cfg_dir=branch1
cfg_dir=branch1_local
```

This will cause Nagios to load the definition for the global configuration, which may include users, time periods, generic hosts, and service templates. It will also load the `local` templates and the definition of objects for `branch1`. All other branches' configurations will load their respective branch objects.

For master Nagios instances, the loaded configurations will be as follows:

```
cfg_dir=global_configuration
cfg_dir=branch1
cfg_dir=branch1_remote
cfg_dir=branch2
cfg_dir=branch2_remote
cfg_dir=branch3
cfg_dir=branch3_remote
cfg_dir=branch4
cfg_dir=branch4_remote
```

This will load the global configuration objects, definitions of objects for all branches, and each branch's remote templates.

Creating the host and service objects

For the examples mentioned in previous sections, a typical host definition will be in the `branch1` directory and will look as follows:

```
define host{
    use                         branch1-server
    host_name                   branch1:webserver
    hostgroups                  branch1-servers
    address                     192.168.0.1
    }
```

The `branch1-server` will be defined in both the `branch1_local` and `branch1_remote` directories. The definition in the `branch1_local` directory will be as follows:

```
define host{
    register                    0
    use                         generic-server
    name                        branch1-server
    contact_groups              branch1-admins
    obsess_over_host            1
    }
```

The definition for the remote location will be as follows:

```
define host{
    register                    0
    use                         remote-server
    name                        branch1-server
    contact_groups              branch1-admins
    }
```

The `generic-server` can be a typical host template. The `remote-server` uses this definition, but disables active checks and enables the accepting of passive check results. An example definition of `generic-server` is as follows:

```
define host{
    register                0
    use                     generic-server
    name                    remote-server
    active_checks_enabled   0
    passive_checks_enabled  1
    notifications_enabled   0
    }
```

With this definition, the host for a local branch will perform active checks if it is alive. The `obsess_over_host` will cause results to be sent to the master Nagios instance. For remote locations, it will only accept remote check results and will not send any notifications, so each host that is down is only reported from the local Nagios instance.

A typical service is defined as follows:

```
define service{
    use                  branch1-service, service-http
    host_name            branch1:webserver
    service_description  HTTP
    }
```

The `service-http` service will define a check using `check_http` and additional options for the check itself.

The local definition for `branch1-service` will be similar to the following code:

```
define service{
    register            0
    name                branch1-service
    contact_groups      branch1-admins
    obsess_over_service 1
    }
```

For the remote services, it should be as follows:

```
define service{
    register            0
    name                branch1-service
    use                 remote-service
    contact_groups      branch1-admins
    }
```

The `local` definition does not perform many changes in the service. It specifies the default contact group to use for all services and enables obsession over the service—so status updates are sent to the master Nagios instance.

The `remote` directory uses the `remote-service` definition, which will disable active checks unless no passive check result is received. For example, a `remote-service` definition can be as follows:

```
define service{
    register                0
    name                    remote-service
    active_checks_enabled   0
    check_freshness         1
    freshness_threshold     43200
    check_command           check_dummy!3!No recent passive check
result
    notification_options    u
    event_handler_enabled   0
    }
```

This makes Nagios run an active check in case no passive result is received for 12 hours. The active check will simply report an unknown status stating that no recent passive check was received.

Notifications for remote services is only enabled for an unknown status. This sends out notifications whenever no active check results are received by the master Nagios instance, but prevents sending of notifications to statuses sent by the slave server as passive check results.

The `check_dummy` command simply invokes the `check_dummy` plugin, which reports an UNKNOWN status and a message that no recent result was received. The `check_dummy` command definition is as follows:

```
define command{
    command_name        check_dummy
    command_line        $USER1$/check_dummy $ARG1$ "$ARG2$"
    }
```

This way the host and service definitions can be shared for all Nagios instances and the templates for each location determine whether the active checks should be run.

The `remote-server` and `remote-service` templates are shared across all Nagios instances, which can be helpful in managing configurations that consist of many branches.

Customizing checks with custom variables

This approach has a downside—each service check has to be defined as a template. However, Nagios custom variables can be used to allow the fine-tuning of the service check for each object. For example, for the HTTP check, it could be as follows:

```
define command{
    command_name   check_http_port
    command_line   $USER1$/check_http -H $ARG1$ -p $ARG2$
    }

define service{
    use                      generic-service
    name                     service-http
    register                 0
    check_command
check_http_port!$_SERVICEHOSTNAME$!$_SERVICEHTTPPORT$
    _HTTPPORT                80
    }
```

This allows us to override the port to use the HTTP checks by specifying _HTTPPORT in the actual service as follows:

```
define service{
    use                      branch1-service,service-http
    host_name                branch1:webserver
    service_description      HTTP on port 8080
    _HTTPPORT                8080
    }
```

Summary

Nagios offers multiple ways of monitoring the Microsoft Windows workstations and servers. These vary from monitoring computers remotely and querying SNMP, to installing dedicated agents. Another very interesting feature of Nagios is its ability to effortlessly configure multiple machines in order to perform monitoring and to have a single place where the results are easily available.

In this chapter, you learned the following items:

- Installing an NSClient++ agent that can be used to monitor Microsoft Windows based machines using Nagios
- Running checks using both the `check_nt` plugin and the NRPE protocol
- Querying information from WMI using the NRPE protocol
- Writing custom checks for NSClient++
- Setting up multiple Nagios instances and reporting all host and service status to other Nagios instances
- Managing configuration for distributed monitoring using multiple templates and custom variables

The next chapter will talk about how to write your own Nagios plugins to monitor services that require customized checks.

13
Programming Nagios

The previous chapter provided information about monitoring Microsoft Windows machines and several approaches to more advanced monitoring using Nagios.

One of the key features of Nagios is its extensibility. There are multiple ways in which Nagios can be tailored to suit your needs. This chapter focuses on extending Nagios functionality using code written by yourself. It is possible to integrate Nagios tightly with your applications and benefit from a powerful mechanism for scheduling and performing checks.

You will learn how to perform both active and passive checks, send custom notifications to users on behalf of Nagios, access Nagios status information, and manage it.

Nagios 4 provides an interface called **query handler**, which is a general purpose mechanism that allows other processes to communicate with Nagios. It allows two-way communication. So, it is possible to both send commands to Nagios, similar to external commands pipe, as well as receive information—either answers to a command that was previously sent to the query handler or asynchronous notifications such as information about host and/or service status change.

You will also find out about **Nagios Event Radio Dispatcher** (**NERD**) service, which is a part of the query handler that allows receiving notifications about host and/or service status updates—both active and passive. We will use this service in a sample application that shows real-time information about hosts and services.

In this chapter, we will cover the following items:

- Understanding the aspects of Nagios that can be customized
- Writing plugins that perform active checks
- Checking websites

- Creating commands to send custom notifications
- Managing Nagios
- Using passive checks for long running tests
- Understanding what the query handler is
- Using the NERD service to receive real-time notifications about host and service status changes

Introducing Nagios customizations

The most exciting aspect of using Nagios is the ability to combine your programming skills with the powerful engine offered by the Nagios daemon. Your own pieces of code can be plugged into the Nagios daemon, or can communicate with it in various ways.

One of the best things about Nagios is that, in most cases, it does not force you to use a specific language. Whether the language of your choice is PHP, Perl, Tcl, Python, Ruby, or Java, you can easily use it with Nagios. This is a fundamental difference between Nagios and majority of monitoring applications. Usually, an application can only be extended in the same language it is written in. Across this chapter, we will use the language that is recently gaining huge popularity—JavaScript.

Our code can cooperate with Nagios in various ways—either by implementing commands or by sending information to the Nagios daemon. The first case means that we create a script or executable that will be run by Nagios, and its output and exit code is then processed by Nagios. Running external commands is used for performing active checks, sending notifications, and triggering event handlers. Using macro substitutions and variables available in the current context (refer to `http://nagios.sourceforge.net/docs/nagioscore/4/en/macrolist.html`), we're able to pass down all of the information that's needed for the command to do its job.

The alternative method of extending Nagios is to send information to it from other applications. The first option is that external applications (such as Web or typical user interface) allow the configuration and management of the Nagios system. This is done by sending control commands over Unix sockets to Nagios. Because this involves opening and writing to a Unix socket, which works just like a file, it can be done in any programming language that handles I/O.

Yet another option is that the other applications reporting to your application or a system scheduling mechanism, such as `cron`, are responsible for running the checks. A test needs to be carried out on its own and the application itself is responsible for sending results back to Nagios. Results of those checks can be sent directly via a Unix socket.

Your software can also get information related to Nagios easily. All that's needed is to monitor Nagios' `status.dat` file for changes, and read it as if it contains all object definitions along with the current soft and hard states. The format of the file is quite simple, and the task of writing a parser for it is quite trivial. The file format and how to parse its contents is described later in this chapter.

There are ready to use Nagios status file parsers for multiple languages such as **nagios-status-parser** for JavaScript (available at `https://github.com/bahamas1/node-nagios-status-parse`), **Pynag** for Python (available at `http://pynag.org/`), **nagios_analyzed** for Ruby (available at `https://github.com/jbbarth/nagios_analyzer`) and there are multiple ready to use PHP solutions for parsing statuses such as **Naupy** (available at `http://sourceforge.net/projects/naupy/`).

Assuming that you need to write a piece of code on your own, the first thing you should start with is choosing the programming language. If you already know a language that would fit this task, stick to it.

Over the course of this chapter we will use the JavaScript programming language (`https://en.wikipedia.org/wiki/JavaScript`). Even though many people may not know all the intricacies of that language, the code will only use the basic functionality so that it is understandable to nontechnical users.

JavaScript is a very popular object-oriented scripting language that has large variety of uses. It started as a marginalized addition to web browsers, but over the years gained popularity, and it was only a matter of time when more advanced applications would be possible. As any function inside the code is treated as the object, it allows the functional programming style to be used.

To run JavaScript code, you will need a runtime environment that is able to parse and execute it. In our examples, we use **node.js** (`https://nodejs.org`) that comes with its own, very popular packages distribution system **Node Package Manager** (**npm**, `https://www.npmjs.com`). Among these packages are libraries that will ease up most of tasks. Consult documentation on installing node.js and npm on your system. Every node.js application should come with the special file `package.json`, which specifies (in **dependencies** section) a list of libraries the application depends on, along with their versions. Observe the following example:

```
{
  "name": "mysql_check",
  "version": "0.0.1",
  "dependencies": {
    "mysql": "^2.11.1",
    "yargs": "^4.8.0"
```

```
    }
  }
```

The contents of this file are rather straightforward: they define the name and version of our plugin, and state all dependencies—in our case, two libraries along with their minimal required versions.

Thanks to npm, there is no need to care about libraries on your own. Once the dependencies list is done, simply run the `npm i` (or npm install) command to get them automatically downloaded and ready to use (an Internet connection will be required). Then the only step is to actually run your code with the node `<file_name.js>`.

Even though we'll focus only on one language, keep in mind that almost any technology can be used. Nagios mainly uses basic functionality for interaction—exit codes, reading the program's output, and passing commands via a pipe. Also, all of its interaction is in text mode and both the active check output and command pipe use a very basic format.

Creating custom active checks

One of the most common areas where Nagios can be suited to fit your needs is that of active checks. These are the checks that are scheduled and run by the Nagios daemon. This functionality is described in more detail in `Chapter 2`, *Installing Nagios 4*.

Nagios has a project that ships the commonly-used plugins and comes with a large variety of checks that can be performed. Before thinking of writing anything on your own, it is best to check for standard plugins (described in detail in `Chapter 6`, *Using the Nagios Plugins*).

 The NagiosExchange (`http://exchange.nagios.org`) website contains multiple ready to use plugins for performing active checks. It is recommended that you check whether somebody has already written a similar plugin for your needs.

The reason for this is that even though active checks are quite easy to implement, sometimes a complete implementation that handles errors and command-line options parsing is not very easy to create. Typically, proper error handling can take a lot of time to implement. Another thing is that plugins that have already existed for some time have often been thoroughly tested by others. Typical errors will have already been identified and fixed; sometimes the plugins will have been tested in a larger environment, under a wider variety of conditions. Writing check plugins on your own should be preceded by an investigation to find out whether anybody has encountered and solved a similar problem.

Active check commands are very simple to implement. They simply require a plugin to return one or more lines of check output to the standard output stream and return one of the predefined exit codes—OK (code 0), WARNING (code 1), CRITICAL (code 2), or UNKNOWN (code 3). How active check plugins work is described in more detail at the beginning of Chapter 6, *Using the Nagios Plugins*.

Testing MySQL database correctness

Let's start with a simple plugin that performs a simple active check. It connects to a MySQL database and verifies if the specified tables are structurally correct. It will accept the connection information from command line as a series of arguments.

From a technical point of view, the check is quite simple—all that's needed is to connect to a server, choose the database, and run the CHECK TABLE (http://dev.mysql.com/doc/mysql/en/CHECK_TABLE.html) command over SQL.

The plugin uses the mysql driver for Node.js (https://github.com/mysqljs/mysql). The driver is available via npm, therefore, the first thing to do is to define the package.json file as follows:

```
{
  "dependencies": {
    "mysql": "^2.11.1"
  }
}
```

The contents of this file are rather straightforward: they state all dependencies—in our case, it is the driver mentioned earlier. In order for npm to download the libraries, once package.json is created, run the following command:

```
# npm i
```

We will also need a working MySQL database that we can connect to for testing purposes. It is a good idea to install MySQL server on your local machine and set up a dummy database with tables for testing.

In order to set up a MySQL database server on Ubuntu Linux, install the mysql-server package as follows:

```
# apt-get install mysql-server
```

In Red Hat and Fedora Linux, the package is called `mysql-server` and the command to install is:

```
# yum install mysql-server
```

After that, you will be able to connect to the database locally as root, either without a password or with the password supplied during the database installation.

If you do not have any other databases to run the script against, you can use `mysql` as the database name as this is a database that all instances of MySQL have.

The following is a sample script that performs the test. It should be saved as the `index.js` file, and needs to be run with the hostname, username, password, database name, and the list of tables to be checked as arguments. The table names should be separated by a comma:

```
var mysql       = require('mysql');
var args = process.argv.slice(2);
var connection = mysql.createConnection({
  host      : args[0],
  user      : args[1],
  password  : args[2],
  database  : args[3]
});

var tables = args[4];
var errors = [];
var count = 0;

connection.connect();

tables = tables.split(',').map(function (string) {return string.trim();});
var queriesLeft = tables.length;

var onResult = function (table, msg) {
  if (msg === 'OK') {
    count++;
  } else {
   errors.push(table.trim());
  }
  if (--queriesLeft === 0) {
    connection.end();
    if (errors.length === 0) {
      console.log('check_mysql_table: OK', count, 'table(s) checked');
      process.exit(0);
    } else {
      console.log('check_mysql_table: CRITICAL: erorrs in', errors.join(',
 '));
```

```
        process.exit(2);
      }
    }
  };

  tables.forEach(function (table) {
    connection.query('CHECK TABLE ' + table.trim(), function(err, rows,
  fields) {
      if (!err) {
        onResult(table, rows[0].Msg_text);
      } else {
        console.log('Error while performing Query.', err);
      }
    });
  });
```

The code consists of four parts—initializing, argument parsing, connecting, and checking each table. The first part loads the mysql driver. In the second part, the arguments passed by the user are mapped to the various variables, and a connection to the database is made. If the connection succeeds, for each table specified when running the command, a CHECK TABLE command (http://dev.mysql.com/doc/refman/5./en/check-table.html) is run. This makes MySQL verify that the table structure is correct.

To use it, let's run it by specifying the connection information, and tables tbl1, tbl2, and tbl3.

```
root@ubuntu:~# node index.js \
    127.0.0.1 mysqluser secret1 databasename tbl1,tbl2,tbl3
check_mysql_table: OK 3 table(s) checked
```

As you can see, the script seems quite easy and it is usable.

Monitoring local time against a time server

The next task is to create a check plugin that compares the local time with the time on a remote machine and issues a warning or critical state if the difference exceeds a specified number.

We'll use npm's `ntp-client package` (`https://github.com/moonpyk/node-ntp-clien t`) to communicate with remote machines. See contents of the `package.json` file using the following:

```
{
  "dependencies": {
    "ntp-client": "^0.5.3"
  }
}
```

The script will accept the host name and the warning and critical thresholds in a number of seconds. The script will use these to decide on the exit status. It will also output the difference as the number of seconds for informational purposes.

The following is a script to perform a check of the time on a remote machine:

```
var ntpClient = require('ntp-client');

var args = process.argv.slice(2);
var host = args[0];
var warnDiff = args[1];
var critDiff = args[2];

ntpClient.getNetworkTime(host, 123, function(err, date) {
    if(err) {
        console.error(err);
        return;
    }
    var states = ['OK', 'WARNING', 'CRITICAL'];
    var diff = Math.abs((new Date().getTime()) - date.getTime());
    var i = diff < warnDiff ? 0 : (diff < critDiff ? 1 : 2);
    console.log('check_time', states[i] + ':', diff, 'seconds difference');
    process.exit(i);
});
```

This command is split into three parts: initializing, parsing arguments, and checking status. The first part loads the `ntp-client` module and the second maps the arguments to variables. After that, a connection to the remote host is made, the time on the remote machine is received, and this remote time is compared with the local time. Based on what the difference is, the command returns either a `CRITICAL`, `WARNING`, or `OK` status.

And now let's run it against a sample machine:

```
root@ubuntu:~# node index.js \
    ntp2a.mcc.ac.uk 60 120
check_time WARNING: 76 seconds difference
```

As shown, the script works properly and returns a WARNING state as the difference is higher than 60 but lower than 120.

Writing plugins the right way

We have already created a few sample scripts, and they're working. So it is possible to use them from Nagios. But these checks are very far from being complete. They lack error control, parsing, and argument verification.

It is recommended that you write all the commands in a more user-friendly way. The reason is that, in most cases, after some time, someone else will take over using and/or maintaining your custom check commands. You might also come back to your own code after a year of working on completely different things. In such cases, having a check command that is user friendly, has proper comments in the code, and allows debugging will save a lot of time. The standard Nagios plugins guidelines (available at `https://nagio s-plugins.org/doc/guidelines.html`) documents good practices for standard Nagios plugins package developers. While some parts may be specific to C language, it is worth reading when developing in other languages as well.

The first thing that should be done is to provide the proper handling of arguments—this means using a functionality such as the **node-getopt** or **yargs** node.js library (`https://github.com/yargs/yargs`, `https://github.com/jiangmiao/node-getopt`), the getopt package for Python (`http://www.python.org/doc/2.5/lib/module-getopt.html`), or the cmdline package for Tcl (`http://tcllib.sourceforge.net/doc/cmdline.html`) to parse the arguments. This way, a functionality such as the `--help` parameter will work properly and in a more user-friendly way. The majority of programming languages provide such libraries and it is always recommended that you use them.

Another thing worth considering is proper error handling. If connectivity to a remote machine is not possible, the check command should exit with a critical or unknown status. In addition, all other pieces of the code should be wrapped to catch errors depending on whether an error suggests a failure in the service being checked, or is due to a problem outside a checked service.

Using the example of the first check plugin, we can redesign the beginning of the script to parse the arguments correctly. The reworked plugin defines all the required parameters, so, whenever any of them is missing, the usage information will be printed.

The following code extract shows the rewritten `index.js` script that uses `yargs` to parse arguments:

```
var mysql = require('mysql');
var argv = require('yargs')
  .demand(['h', 'u', 'p', 'd', 't'])
  .alias('h', 'hostname')
  .alias('u', 'username')
  .alias('p', 'password')
  .alias('d', 'dbname')
  .alias('t', 'tables')
  .array('t')
  .argv;

var connection = mysql.createConnection({
  host     : argv.hostname,
  user     : argv.username,
  password : argv.password,
  database : argv.dbname
});

var errors = [];
var count = 0;

connection.connect();
var queriesLeft = argv.tables.length;

var onResult = function (table, msg) {
  if (msg === 'OK') {
    count++;
  } else {
   errors.push(table.trim());
  }
  if (--queriesLeft === 0) {
    connection.end();
    if (errors.length === 0) {
      console.log('check_mysql_table: OK', count, 'table(s) checked');
      process.exit(0);
    } else {
      console.log('check_mysql_table: CRITICAL: erorrs in', errors.join(',
'));
      process.exit(2);
    }
  }
};

argv.tables.forEach(function (table) {
  connection.query('CHECK TABLE ' + table, function(err, rows, fields) {
```

```
    if (!err) {
      onResult(table, rows[0].Msg_text);
    } else {
      console.log('Error while performing Query.', err);
    }
  });
});
```

The dependencies must now include the `yargs` library:

```
{
  "dependencies": {
    "mysql": "^2.11.1",
    "yargs": "^4.8.0"
  }
}
```

In case we run our code without arguments, it will automatically print out usage information.

```
root@ubuntu:~# node index.js
Options:
  -h, --hostname                              [required]
  -u, --username                              [required]
  -p, --password                              [required]
  -d, --dbname                                [required]
  -t, --tables                      [array] [required]
Missing required arguments: h, u, p, d, t
```

As another example, we can update our time checking code as follows:

```
var ntpClient = require('ntp-client');

var argv = require('yargs')
  .help('H')
  .alias('H', 'help')
  .options({
    h: {
      alias: 'hostname',
      describe: 'NTP server',
      default: 'ntp2a.mcc.ac.uk',
      nargs: 1
    },
    w: {
      alias: 'warning',
      describe: 'positive number of seconds',
      default: '300',
      type: 'number',
```

```
      nargs: 1
    },
    c: {
      alias: 'critical',
      describe: 'positive number of seconds',
      default: '600',
      type: 'number',
      nargs: 1
    }
  })
  .argv;

['warning', 'critical'].forEach(function (param) {
  if (argv[param] <= 0) {
    console.log('Invalid', param, 'time specified');
    process.exit(3);
  }
});

ntpClient.getNetworkTime(argv.hostname, 123, function(err, date) {
    if(err) {
        console.error(err);
        return;
    }
    var states = ['OK', 'WARNING', 'CRITICAL'];
    var diff = Math.abs((new Date().getTime()) - date.getTime());
    var i = diff < argv.warning ? 0 : (diff < argv.critical ? 1 : 2);
    console.log('check_time', states[i] + ':', diff, 'seconds difference');
    process.exit(i);
});
```

In this case, we use `yargs` more deeply, not only to define arguments but also to specify their default values along with the types for numeric values. As a result, we not only have better value checking but the help information is much more descriptive.

```
root@ubuntu:~# node index.js -H
Options:
   -H, --help       Show help
[boolean]
   -h, --hostname   NTP server                        [default: "ntp2a.mcc.ac.uk"]
   -w, --warning    positive number of seconds     [number] [default:
"300"]
   -c, --critical   positive number of seconds      [number] [default:
"600"]
```

The code also verifies that the passed numbers are positive and prints out the relevant message if any of them is no:

```
root@ubuntu:~# node index.js -w -10
Invalid warning time specified
```

Of course, the changes mentioned here are just small examples of how plugins should be written. It's not possible to cover all the possible aspects of what plugins should take into account. It's your responsibility as the command's author to make sure that all scenarios are covered in your plugin.

Typically, this means correct error handling—usually related to catching all of the exceptions that the underlying functions might throw. There are also additional things to take into account. For example, if you are writing a networked plugin, the remote server can return error messages that also need to be handled properly.

An important thing worth considering is handling timeouts properly.

Usually, a plugin tries to connect in the background, and if it fails within a specified period of time, the plugin will exit the check and report an error status. This is usually done through the use of child threads or child processes. In languages that are event driven, this can be done by scheduling an event that exits with a timeout message after a specified time interval.

Checking websites

Nagios ships with a very powerful `check_http` plugin that allows you to monitor websites in quite a simple way. This plugin should be enough for a large variety of tasks. However, there are often situations where only using this plugin is not enough.

If you are running a website that is critical to your business, only checking that the main page is showing up correctly may not be enough. In many cases, you might actually want to be sure that the users are able to log in, orders can be sent out, and reports can be generated correctly.

In such cases, it is not sufficient just to check if a couple of pages work correctly. It might be necessary to write a more complex check that will log you into the website, fill out an order form, send it, and verify that it shows up in the order history. You may also want to check that specified text is present on specific pages.

This task is very common when performing automated tests during the development of a site. Not many people perform such tests regularly when the site is in production. A downside of this is that if the version control of your website is not very strict, then small bug fixes can break things in a different part of the website and those might go on unnoticed for a long time.

One might argue whether this is a task for system monitoring or for the testing phase of the development and maintenance cycles. For a number of reasons, this task should be common to both development and maintenance, but it should also be a part of system monitoring. The first reason is that such tests make sure that the overall functionality of the site is working as expected. It can also be used to detect defacing or other unauthorized modification of the page. It can also be used to monitor response time. Monitoring the web page's functionality should normally be performed rarely, but checks of the web server and the main page should be done more often.

There are a couple of approaches to this problem, depending on what you actually want to monitor. The first one is using the `http` or `https` protocol directly using various libraries such as `requests` for Python (`https://github.com/kennethreitz/requests`), `http` (`http://www.tcl.tk/man/tcl8.4/TclCmd/http.htm`) for Tcl/Tk, and `LWP` (`http://search.cpan.org/~gaas/libwww-perl/lib/LWP.pm`) for Perl. By deciding on the appropriate approach, you will need to hardcode your URLs along with the queries to send and, in some cases, also implement cookie handling on your own.

Another approach is to use automated test frameworks. This includes `mechanize` (`http://wwwsearch.sourceforge.net/mechanize/`) for Python, `webautotest` (`http://sourceforge.net/projects/dqsoftware/`) for Tcl, and `WWW::Mechanize` (`http://search.cpan.org/dist/WWW-Mechanize/`) for Perl. There are also multiple Java frameworks for this, such as `HttpUnit` (`http://httpunit.sourceforge.net/`) and `HtmlUnit` (`http://htmlunit.sourceforge.net/`). These packages offer the automated parsing of HTML, reading of the DOM tree, and operating similar to how a browser would work. This allows scripts to be written at a higher level without having to care about low-level things such as reading and passing values from all fields. A typical script would consist of going to an URL, locating forms, setting values, and sending these values.

The last approach is to use packages that take advantage of Internet Explorer over **Component Object Model (COM**; `http://www.microsoft.com/com/`). This approach uses an entire browser and, therefore, is the most accurate method of testing the website's correctness. It also requires a much larger setup to accomplish the same task—tests need to be performed on a Microsoft Windows system and require a separate account for proper cookie management. For example, in the cases where tests need to start after all of the cookies have been removed, Perl offers the ability to automate Internet Explorer using the PAMIE package (`http://pamie.sourceforge.net/`), while for Python it is SAMIE (`http://samie.sourceforge.net/`). Tcl offers Internet Explorer automation in the `autoie` (`http://sourceforge.net/projects/dqsoftware/`) package. For Ruby, the most popular utility is called Watir (`http://wtr.rubyforge.org/`). In order to use IE and COM based automation, you should set up all the checks on a Microsoft Windows based machine and set it up so that the results are sent back via NSCA.

Usually, the best choice is to use automated web testing frameworks. These require much less overheads when developing the code for performing checks and tend to react nicely to small changes in the way your website works.

As an example, we will write a simple script in JavaScript that communicates with a website using the `phantomjs` headless browser (`http://phantomjs.org`). To use it, PhantomJS must be installed appropriately for the operating system you are using.

The plugin logs into the backend of a WordPress content management system (`http://wordpress.org`) and makes sure that it works correctly.

The following is the source code of the plugin (let's name it `test.js`):

```
var page = require('webpage').create();
var system = require('system');

var url = system.args[1];
var user = system.args[2];
var password = system.args[3];

page.open(url, function (status) {
  if (status !== 'success') {
    console.log('WORDPRESS CRITICAL: Could not open page.');
    phantom.exit(2);
  }
  page.onLoadFinished = function () {
    var loggedIn = page.evaluate(function () {
      var logoutElement = document.getElementById('wpcontent');
      return !!logoutElement;
    });
    if (loggedIn) {
```

```
          console.log('WORDPRESS OK: Administrative panel loaded correctly.');
          phantom.exit(0);
        } else {
          console.log('WORDPRESS CRITICAL: Administrative panel does not
  work.');
          phantom.exit(2);
        }
      };

    var err = page.evaluate(function (user, password) {
      try {
        document.getElementById('user_login').value=user;
        document.getElementById('user_pass').value=password;
        document.getElementById('loginform').submit();
      } catch (err) {
        return err;
      }
    }, user, password);
    if (err) {
      console.log('WORDPRESS CRITICAL: Administrative panel DOM incorrect.');
      phantom.exit(2);
    }
});
```

To check the plugin, simply run the following command:

```
root@ubuntu:~# phantomjs test.js http://192.168.137.51/admin \
              admin adminpassword
WORDPRESS OK: Administrative panel loaded correctly.
```

Writing commands to send notifications

Another part of Nagios that can be extended to fit your needs are notifications. These are messages that Nagios sends out whenever a problem occurs, or is resolved.

One way in which the Nagios notification system can be expanded is to create template-based e-mail sending. This will send notifications as both plain text and HTML messages. The template of the e-mail will be kept in separate files.

We will use two **npm** libraries: handlebars (http://handlebarsjs.com) for template processing and emailjs (https://github.com/eleith/emailjs) for the e-mail sending functionality.

E-mails that contain content in multiple formats need to be wrapped in the multipart/alternative MIME type. This type will contain two sub-parts—first the plain text version, and following this is the HTML version. This order makes e-mail clients choose HTML over plain text if both the types are supported. For the sake of example, we will ignore plain text.

In the same way as how macro substitution works in Nagios commands, templates will replace certain strings such as {{hoststate}} within the template. For example, the following can be used in an HTML template:

```
<tr><td>Notification type</td>
<td><b>{{hoststate}}</b></td></tr>
```

Similar macros can be used in plain text templates and will be substituted as well.

The following is a script that allows users to be notified in HTML format, through the use of templates:

```
var handlebars = require('handlebars')
var email = require('emailjs');
var fs = require('fs');

var map = {}
var args = process.argv.slice(2);
['template', 'email', 'type', 'hostname', 'hoststate',
'hostoutput'].forEach(function (key, index) {
  map[key] = args[index];
});


var template = fs.readFileSync(map.template, 'utf8');
var html = handlebars.compile(template)(map);

var server = email.server.connect({
    user:     process.env.SMTP_USER,
  password:process.env.SMTP_PASSWORD,
  host:     process.env.SMTP_HOST,
  ssl:      true
});

var message = {
  from:    'Nagios <nagios@yourcompany.com>',
  to:      map.email,
  subject: 'Notification from Nagios',
  attachment:
  [
    {
```

```
        data: html,
        alternative: true
      }
  ]
};

server.send(message, function(error, message) {
  console.log(error, message);
});
```

To test it, simply run the following:

```
root@ubuntu:# node index.js template1.html \
    jdoe@yourcompany.com RECOVERY myhost1 OK "OK: host is alive"
```

This should cause an e-mail to be sent to jdoe@yourcompany.com. Note that, in our case the script reads credentials for SMTP e-mail server from environment variables, so they must be set correctly, or another way of passing them should be applied.

We can now define a command that will send a notification for the host, as shown here:

```
define command{
    command_name        notify-host-by-email-html
    command_line        $USER5$/notify-email-html
                        template1 '$CONTACTEMAIL$'
                        '$NOTIFICATIONTYPE$' '$HOSTNAME$'
                        '$HOSTSTATE$' '$HOSTOUTPUT$'

    }
```

It will pass the appropriate arguments for the user's e-mail address, notification type, host's name, state, and output from the host check. The command can then be used for one or more contacts by setting the host_notification_commands option:

```
define contact{
    name                            jdoe
    host_notification_period        24x7
    host_notification_options       d,u,r,f,s
    host_notification_commands      notify-host-by-email-html
    (...)
    }
```

Managing Nagios

Your application might also want to have some control over Nagios. You might want to expose an interface for users to take control of your monitoring system, for example, a web interface or a client-server system. You might also want to handle custom authorization and access the control list. This is something that is beyond the functionality offered by the web interface that Nagios comes with.

In such cases, it is best to create your own system for reading the current status as well as for sending commands directly over the external command pipe. In both cases, this is very easy to do from any programming language.

The first thing that we can do is to show Nagios' current status. This requires reading the `status.dat` file, parsing it to any data format, and then manipulating it. The format of the file is relatively simple—each object is enclosed in a section. Each section contains one or more `name=value` directives. For example, the following is a definition of information about the `status.dat` file:

```
info {
    created=1388002190
    version=4.0.1
}
```

All hosts, services, and other objects are defined in the same way as the preceding definition. There can be multiple instances of a specified object type; for example, each `hoststatus` object definition specifies a single host along with its current status.

Sending commands to Nagios also seems trivial. The details of the most commonly used commands were given in Chapter 8, *Notifications and Events*. Sending commands simply involves opening a pipe for writing, sending commands, and closing the pipe again.

Controlling Nagios from an external application written in JavaScript is easy. Thanks to the existing **nagios-status-parser** library (https://github.com/bahamas10/node-nagios-status-parser) that is capable of parsing the Nagios `status.dat` file into a JavaScript object. Consider the following sample usage:

```
var fs = require('fs');
var parse = require('nagios-status-parser');
var status = parse(fs.readFileSync('/path/to/status.dat', 'utf8'));

console.log(status.info);
```

The output is as follows:

```
root@ubuntu:# node parse.js
[ { created: 1468269833,
    version: '4.1.1',
    last_update_check: 1468261385,
    update_available: 0,
    last_version: '4.1.1',
    new_version: '4.1.1' } ]
```

Having such a powerful tool, it's also relatively easy to write a function that allows you to search for objects by their type so that they match the specified criteria, for example, all the services associated with a host. A sample code to do this is as follows:

```
var fs = require('fs');
var parse = require('nagios-status-parser');

var status = parse(fs.readFileSync('/path/to/status.dat', 'utf8'));

var findObject = function (status, type, filter) {
  var array = status[type];
  if (array) {
    return array.filter(function(entry) {
    return Object.keys(filter).every(function(key) {
      return filter[key] === entry[key];
    });
    });
  }
};

var type = 'servicestatus';
var filter = {
  last_hard_state: 2,
  host_name: 'localhost'
};
findObject(status, type, filter).forEach(function (object) {
  console.log(object.service_description, '-> Last state change:',
    new Date(object.last_state_change * 1000)
    .toLocaleDateString("en-US"));
});
```

The `findObject` function takes all objects of the said type and checks if all of the fields and expected values are matched to specified filtering criteria. In this case, we find all of the services on the `localhost` machine that have critical statuses, and display their descriptions along with the last state change date:

```
root@ubuntu:# node find_status.js
HTTP -> Last state change: Monday, July 04, 2016
Total Processes -> Last state change: Monday, July 04, 2016
```

This approach can be used to perform complex searches and show the status depending on many configuration options.

Sending commands to Nagios from JavaScript is also a very simple thing to do. The following is a class that offers internal functions for sending commands, as well as two sample commands that cause Nagios to schedule the next host or service check on the specified date. If the date is omitted, then the check is run immediately:

```
var fs = require('fs');
var os = require('os');

var Nagios = function () {
  var pipeFileName = '/var/nagios/rw/nagios.cmd';
  var writeCommand = function (command, callback) {
    fs.appendFile(pipeFileName, command + os.EOL, callback);
  };
  this.scheduleHostCheck = function (host, when, callback) {
    if (when === undefined) {
      when = Math.round(Date.now() / 1000);
    }
    writeCommand('SCHEDULE_FORCED_HOST_CHECK;' + host + ';' + when,
callback);
  };
  this.scheduleServiceCheck = function (host, svc, when, callback) {
    if (when === undefined) {
      when = Math.round(Date.now() / 1000);
    }
    writeCommand('SCHEDULE_FORCED_SVC_CHECK;' + host + ';' + svc + ';' +
when, callback);
  };
};
```

A small section of code to test the functionality is as follows:

```
var nagios = new Nagios();
nagios.scheduleHostCheck('linux1');
var when = new Date();
when.setDate(when.getDate() + 1); // tomorrow
nagios.scheduleServiceCheck('localhost', 'APT', Math.round(when.getTime() /
1000));
```

This initializes an instance of the Nagios class, and then schedules a host check for the linux1 machine immediately. Next, it schedules the APT service check on the localhost machine to occur one day from now.

Implementing additional commands should be as simple as specifying new functions that send commands (http://www.nagios.org/developerinfo/externalcommands) to Nagios over the external command pipe. Usually, the functionality base grows as a project grows, hence, we should not define unused functions on a just-in-case basis.

Using passive checks

Nagios offers a very powerful mechanism for scheduling tests. However, there are many situations where you might want to perform tests on your own and just tell Nagios what the result is. One of the typical scenarios for using passive tests can be when performing the actual test takes very little time but the startup overhead is large. Refer to Chapter 9, *Passive Checks and NRDP* for details.

The next code print contains an example of an application that periodically performs tests and sends their results to Nagios over the external command pipe. This code consists of a method to supply information to Nagios, and a main loop that performs tests every five minutes. It does not contain the actual test that should be performed as this might vary depending on your needs:

```
var fs = require('fs');
var os = require('os');

var Nagios = function () {
  var pipeFileName = '/var/nagios/rw/nagios.cmd';
  var writeCommand = function (command, callback) {
    fs.appendFile(pipeFileName, command + os.EOL, callback);
  };

  this.writeStatus = function (host, svc, code, output, callback) {
    var time = Math.round(Date.now() / 1000);
    writeCommand('[' + time + '] PROCESS_SERVICE_CHECK_RESULT;' + host +
```

```
';' + svc + ';' + code + ';' + output, callback);
  };
};

var nagios = new Nagios();

var performTest = function () {
  //to be implemented
  return {
    code: 0,
    output: 'check_service: OK'
  }
};

setInterval(function () {
  var result = performTest();
  nagios.writeStatus('hostname', 'service', result.code, result.output,
function (err) {
    console.log(err);
  });
}, 300 * 1000); //every 5 minutes
```

Note that the actual implementation of the `performTest` method should perform real tests.

Very often, you will need to create or extend applications to perform checks on remote machines. In this case, NRDP is used to send the check results to the Nagios server.

The following is a JavaScript code for sending service check results over NRDP. It uses the `request` and `xmlbuilder` libraries (http://github.com/request/request and http://github.com/oozcitak/xmlbuilder-js) for building an XML payload and sending it to Nagios.

```
var request = require('request');
var builder = require('xmlbuilder');

var token = 'cu8Eiquasoomeiphahpa';
var url = 'http://your.nagios.server/nrdp/';


var xml = builder.create('root').ele('checkresults').ele('checkresult',
{'type': 'service'});
xml.ele('hostname', 'localhost');
xml.ele('servicename', 'HTTP');
xml.ele('state', '1');
xml.ele('output', 'check result output here');

xml = xml.end({ pretty: true});
```

```
request.post(
    url,
    {
      form: {
        cmd: 'submitcheck',
        token: token,
        XMLDATA: xml
      }
    },
    function (error, response, body) {
      console.log(response.statusCode);
      console.log(body);
    }
);
```

In order to test it, first we need to define `package.json`, as follows:

```
{
  "name": "nrdp_post",
  "version": "0.0.1",
  "dependencies": {
    "request": "^2.73.0",
    "xmlbuilder": "^8.2.2"
  }
}
```

Next, install the dependencies with `npm i`, and finally run it:

```
root@ubuntu:# node index.js
200
<?xml version="1.0" encoding="utf-8"?>
<result>
  <status>0</status>
  <message>OK</message>
  <meta>
    <output>1 checks processed.</output>
  </meta>
</result>
```

This will prepare the XML representation of an HTTP service check notification on the `localhost` machine, submit it to the NRDP endpoint, and then print out the response.

Introducing the query handler

The query handler allows two-way communication with Nagios internal processes and external applications. It is designed to be extensible, and future versions of Nagios may provide more functionality using the query handlers.

The query handler communicates using Unix domain sockets (refer to `http://en.wikipedia.org/wiki/Unix_domain_socket` for more details). These are meant for communication between processes on the same machine. Unix domain sockets use filesystem as names for remote addresses. The location (address) of the Nagios query handler is similar to the Nagios external command pipe—it is called `nagios.qh` and by default resides in the same directory as the external commands pipe. For example, `/var/nagios/rw/nagios.qh` is the path to query handler's Unix domain socket for an installation performed according to the steps given in `Chapter 2`, *Installing Nagios 4*. Filesystem permissions are used to determine if a process can connect to the other side or not. So, it is possible to limit access to the query handler only to specific operating system users or groups.

Unix domain sockets are very similar to named pipes (such as the Nagios external commands pipe), however, it is not possible to use named pipes for two-way communication with more than one client. Another difference is that it is not possible to open it as a file and/or send commands to the socket using shell commands such as `echo`—which is possible for named pipes such as the Nagios external command pipe.

Nagios provides its functionality through the query handler using services. There are several built-in services and the ones that are public are described throughout this chapter. Future versions of Nagios (or third-party software) may provide additional services. Each command sent to Nagios is prefixed with the service name, so each service may use any names for its sub-commands.

Nagios uses the query handler internally to distribute jobs to worker processes. Child processes connect to the query handler and receive tasks that should be performed. This is one of the reasons the query handler was originally created—to be able to control the worker processes. The worker processes use the `wproc` service, which is an internal service and should only be used by Nagios processes.

Nagios also provides services that can be used by external applications. The first and most basic one is `echo`, which simply responds with the data that was sent to it. It is mainly a useful tool for learning to communicate with Nagios.

The `core` service allows information about Nagios processes and scheduled jobs queue. The `nerd` service allows subscribing to events and can be used to receive real-time updates about Nagios host and/or service status changes.

Communicating with the query handler

Let's start understanding the query handler by communicating with it from the shell. There are multiple commands that allow connecting to Unix domain sockets such as `netcat` (refer to `http://netcat.sourceforge.net/` for more detail) and `socat` (refer to `http://www.dest-unreach.org/socat/` for more details). Both can be used to send commands to the Nagios query handler and to install the tools; simply run the following command on Ubuntu:

```
root@ubuntu:# apt-get install socat netcat
```

For Red Hat Enterprise Linux, CentOS, and Fedora Core you can run the following command:

```
# yum install socat nc
```

For Red Hat Enterprise Linux / CentOS 7 and later, both packages are available by default. For earlier versions, the `socat` package is available as part of EPEL (refer to `https://fedoraproject.org/wiki/EPEL` for more detail) and is not available unless EPEL is installed.

This will install both of the tools, which will be used later to check communication with the query handler.

The communication protocol for the query handler is simple. There is no initial message, so after connecting we can simply send commands to the query handler.

All commands that are sent to the query handler are prefixed with the name of the handler and are sent in the following way:

```
@service command\0
```

Where, `@service` is the name of the service prefixed with the @ character, `command` is the command (and parameters) to send and `\0` is a character with the ASCII code of 0 that indicates end of command. Nagios may also send information—either responses to commands or notifications. The format of the response varies on the service that implements it.

Many commands return an answer or start sending notifications after the command is invoked. However, some commands, such as modifying settings, will return an exit code. The code is modeled after HTTP status codes (refer to `http://en.wikipedia.org/wiki/List_of_HTTP_status_codes`) where codes from 200 indicate success and codes from 400 indicate an error.

Nagios provides the @echo service that can be used to test connectivity to the query handler. It will return the same message that was sent to it. To test connectivity, we can simply run the following command:

```
root@ubuntu:# echo -e '@echo Query handler is working!\0' | \
    socat - UNIX-CONNECT:/var/nagios/rw/nagios.qh
```

The first line generates a command to send to the @core service. The -e option passed to the echo command enables interpretation of backslash escapes, which changes \0 to the ASCII character 0.

Next, the output from the echo command is sent to the socat command, which sends its output to the query handler and prints out the result to standard output. The socat command takes two arguments-the channels to relay data for. The - indicates using standard input/output and UNIX-CONNECT:/var/nagios/rw/nagios.qh indicates Unix domain socket to the Nagios query handler.

If the command succeeds, its output should be Query handler is working properly! as the output.

If the current user does not have access to connect to the socket, the output will indicate an error as follows:

```
socat E connect(3, AF=1 "/var/nagios/rw/nagios.qh", 26): Permission denied
```

For netcat, the command is similar:

```
root@ubuntu:#  echo -e '@echo Query handler is working!\0' | \
    nc -U /var/nagios/rw/nagios.qh
```

The first line of the command is identical to the previous example. The -U option for the netcat command causes it to connect to the Unix domain socket with the address specified from the command line.

It is also perfectly possible to communicate with the query handler from the code, as will be shown in the next section.

A single connection to Nagios can be used to send multiple commands and/or receive multiple types of information, however, as the formats of the responses may vary, it is best to use a single connection only for single service, that is, use one connection for managing the Nagios load and another connection for getting notifications about host and/or service check results.

Using the query handler programmatically

Now that we know how to communicate with the Nagios query handler, we can do so programmatically. Almost all languages provide a mechanism to communicate using Unix domain sockets.

For example, to send a test message using JavaScript, we can use the node.js built-in `net` module to communicate with the query handler:

```
var net = require('net');

var msg = 'Query handler is working properly!'

var client = net.connect({
  path: '/var/nagios/rw/nagios.qh'
}, function () {
  client.write('@echo ' + msg + '\0');
});

client.on('data', function (data) {
  if(data.toString() === msg) {
    console.log('Return message matches sent message');
    client.end();
    process.exit(0);
  } else {
    console.log('Return message does not match');
    client.end();
    process.exit(1);
  }
})

client.on('error', function (err) {
    console.log(err);
})
```

The preceding code sends a test message to the `@echo` query handler service and retrieves the result.

For other programming languages, the support for Unix domain sockets may be built-in or require additional modules or packages, but as the technology is quite common, commonly used languages should provide support for it.

Using the core service

The Nagios query handler provides the @core service, which can be used to get information about Nagios processes and set some of the information.

For all commands handled by the @core service, the result is a text ending with the \0 character. To read a response, all that is needed is to read until we receive \0, which indicates an end of response.

It allows querying information about the queue of scheduled jobs such as the next active checks or the background operations to be performed. The command name is squeuestats. The following is the full command to send:

```
@core squeuestats\0
```

The result is a string with multiple statistics information in the form of name=value, separated by semicolon.

```
name1=value1;name2=value2;....
```

For example, to print all information we can simply prepare core.squeuestats.js with the following contents:

```
var net = require('net');

var client = net.connect({
  path: '/var/nagios/rw/nagios.qh'
}, function () {
  client.write('@core squeuestats\0');
});

client.on('data', function (data) {
  data.toString().split(';').forEach(function (line) {
    console.log(line);
  });
  client.end();
})

client.on('error', function (err) {
    console.log(err);
})
```

The code connects to the Nagios socket, sends the `@core squeuestats` command, and then reads the response. Then the result is split by a semicolon, next, it is sorted, and finally it is printed as text:

```
root@ubuntu:# nodejs core.squeuestats.js
CHECK_PROGRAM_UPDATE=1
CHECK_REAPER=1
COMMAND_CHECK=0
EXPIRE_COMMENT=0
EXPIRE_DOWNTIME=0
HFRESHNESS_CHECK=0
HOST_CHECK=4
LOG_ROTATION=1
ORPHAN_CHECK=1
PROGRAM_RESTART=0
PROGRAM_SHUTDOWN=0
RESCHEDULE_CHECKS=0
RETENTION_SAVE=1
SCHEDULED_DOWNTIME=0
SERVICE_CHECK=18
SFRESHNESS_CHECK=1
SLEEP=0
SQUEUE_ENTRIES=29
STATUS_SAVE=1
USER_FUNCTION=0
```

Another command the `@core` service provides is `loadctl`, which can be used to get values for all available load control settings or change one of their values. The syntax for the command is as follows:

```
@core loadctl
@core loadctl setting=value
@core loadctl setting1=value1;setting2=value2;...
```

Let's send the first one.

```
var net = require('net');

var client = net.connect({
  path: '/var/nagios/rw/nagios.qh'
}, function () {
  client.write('@core loadctl\0');
});

client.on('data', function (data) {
  data.toString().split(';').forEach(function (line) {
    console.log(line);
  });
  client.end();
})
```

It returns a list of all load control settings in the form of the `setting=value` option, separated by semicolon, as shown here:

```
jobs_max=3896
jobs_min=20
jobs_running=0
jobs_limit=9999
load=0.00
backoff_limit=2.50
backoff_change=4855
rampup_limit=0.80
rampup_change=1213
nproc_limit=47150
nofile_limit=4096
options=0
changes=0
```

If the `loadctl` command has any settings specified, they are changed and the command returns whether it succeeded or failed.

For example, we can change the `jobs_max` setting by executing the following:

```
client.write('@core loadctl jobs_max=9999\0');
```

The Nagios query handler will return the `200: OK` message in case of success. A response with the `400` code indicates that the setting was not found or not modified.

 The load control settings are Nagios internal settings, it is not recommended that you modify them unless needed. The preceding example simply illustrates how this can be done if needed.

Introducing the Nagios event radio dispatcher

The query handler also includes a NERD service, which allows subscribing to service or host check results. The service name is `@nerd` and it accepts the following commands:

```
@nerd list\0
@nerd subscribe <channel>\0
@nerd unsubscribe <channel>\0
```

The `list` command returns a list of channels separated by newlines, where channel name is the first word of a line followed by channel description. The `subscribe` and `unsubscribe` commands can be used to start and stop getting notifications for a specified channel.

For example, to list all available channels we can simply do the following from the shell:

```
# echo -e '@nerd list\0' | \
    socat - UNIX-CONNECT:/var/nagios/rw/nagios.qh
```

The output should be as follows:

```
hostchecks      Host check results
servicechecks   Service check results
opathchecks     Host and service checks in gource's log format
```

The `opathchecks` channel for notifications can be used together with the **Gource** visualization tool to show the animated host and service check updates. This functionality is described later in this chapter.

The `hostchecks` and `servicechecks` channels can be used to receive updates regarding host and/or service status changes. The format for the respective channels is as follows:

```
<hostname> from <old_code> -> <new_code>: <description>
<hostname>;<servicename> from <old_code> -> <new_code>: <description>
```

Where `<old_code>` and `<new_code>` correspond to the exit codes for check results.

For host checks, the codes map is as follows:

Exit code	Description
0	UP
1	DOWN
2	UNREACHABLE

For service checks, the values are as follows:

Exit code	Description
0	OK
1	WARNING
2	CRITICAL
3	UNKNOWN

Once a socket is subscribed to a channel, updates regarding hosts and/or services are sent separated by a newline character. Reading status updates for hosts or services can be done by simply subscribing to one or more channels and reading from the socket line by line.

For example, the following code subscribes for both host and service updates and prints out the results accordingly:

```
var net = require('net');

var client = net.connect({
  path: '/var/nagios/rw/nagios.qh'
}, function () {
  client.write('@nerd subscribe hostchecks\0');
  client.write('@nerd subscribe servicechecks\0');
});

var statuses = {
  host: ['UP', 'DOWN', 'UNREACHABLE'],
  service: ['OK', 'WARNING', 'CRITICAL', 'UNKNOWN']
};
```

```
var serviceRegExp = /(.*?);(.*?) from ([0-9]+) -> ([0-9]+): (.*)$/;
var hostRegExp = /(.*?) from ([0-9]+) -> ([0-9]+): (.*)$/;
client.on('data', function (data) {
  var msg = data.toString().trim();
  if (serviceRegExp.test(msg)) {
    var tokens = serviceRegExp.exec(msg);
    var status = Math.max(0, Math.min(tokens[4], 3));
    console.log('Service', tokens[2], 'on', tokens[1], 'is',
statuses.service[status], ':', tokens[5]);
  } else if (hostRegExp.test(msg)) {
    var tokens = hostRegExp.exec(msg);
    var status = Math.max(0, Math.min(tokens[3], 2));
    console.log('Host', tokens[1], 'is', statuses.host[status], ':',
tokens[4]);
  }
})

client.on('error', function (err) {
    console.log(err);
})
```

The code uses regular expressions to parse the lines and first tries to parse the result as service status updates and then checks if it matches the host status expression.

Note that the code is mainly meant for demonstration and is far from being a complete example. A final application that uses NERD to receive notifications should handle the case when the socket is closed and retry connecting back to Nagios to handle cases such as Nagios is restarted.

Summary

Nagios has many places where it can be extended with external scripts or applications. Although we used JavaScript in code samples, Nagios is not bound to any specific language and its real power comes from the fact that you can choose the language you'll use to program your code. Of course, this chapter does not cover all of the aspects in which Nagios can be customized.

In this chapter you learned the following:

- Which aspects of Nagios can be customized
- How to write plugins that perform active checks
- Sending custom notifications
- Managing Nagios and reading its status information
- Working with passive checks for long running tests
- What the query handler is, what services it offers, and how to communicate with them
- How to use the NERD service to receive real-time notifications

This chapter concludes the book. You are encouraged to run the examples that were shown throughout the book as well as experiment on your own with Nagios. We hope that the book will be the beginning of your journey into IT monitoring and Nagios in particular.

Index

Made in the USA
Middletown, DE
04 October 2018